MOVEMENT, ACTION, IMAGE, MONTAGE

University of
Minnesota Press
Minneapolis
London

Movement, Action, Image, Montage

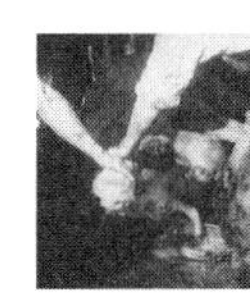

SERGEI EISENSTEIN AND THE CINEMA IN CRISIS

Luka Arsenjuk

Portions of chapter 3 were previously published in "The *Notes for a General History of Cinema* and the Dialectic of the Eisensteinian Image," in *Sergei M. Eisenstein: Notes for a General History of Cinema,* edited by Naum Kleiman and Antonio Somaini (Amsterdam: Amsterdam University Press, 2016), 289–98.

Published by the University of Minnesota Press
111 Third Avenue South, Suite 290
Minneapolis, MN 55401-2520
http://www.upress.umn.edu

Printed in the United States of America on acid-free paper

24 23 22 21 20 19 18 10 9 8 7 6 5 4 3 2 1

Library of Congress Cataloging-in-Publication Data
Names: Arsenjuk, Luka, author.
Title: Movement, action, image, montage : Sergei Eisenstein and the cinema in crisis / Luka Arsenjuk.
Description: Minneapolis : University of Minnesota Press, 2018. | Includes bibliographical references and index.
Identifiers: LCCN 2017022053 (print) | ISBN 978-1-5179-0319-0 (hc) | ISBN 978-1-5179-0320-6 (pb)
Subjects: LCSH: Eisenstein, Sergei, 1898-1948—Criticism and interpretation.
Classification: LCC PN1998.3.E34 A88 2017 (print) | DDC 791.4302/33092—dc23
LC record available at https://lccn.loc.gov/2017022053

For Lindsey

CONTENTS

Introduction

A DIALECTIC OF DIVISION

> I no longer remember when and where it was that I read the funny notion that creation (one's work) was first and foremost a division of oneself, a separation.
>
> This was entertainingly demonstrated by the Lord God's activity in the first week of restless existence, when he created the universe from chaos.
>
> Indeed: he divided light from dark.
>
> Land from sea.
>
> And finally Eve from Adam (Eve was made from Adam).
>
> Chaos began to assume a sort of constant appearance.
>
> ■ Sergei Eisenstein, *Beyond the Stars: The Memoirs of Sergei Eisenstein*

The Many Shadows of a Figure

Sergei Eisenstein stands in the history of cinema a central, unavoidable figure, projecting a shadow as imposing as the one thrown by his Ivan the Terrible on the cavernous walls of the Kremlin. In his film work, Eisenstein developed the first major film poetics. By formalizing it in his writings, he laid the foundations of the discipline of film theory. Eisenstein's texts served, according to François Jost, as the Archimedean point that enabled a setting into movement of the entire world of "cinematic reasons that would make it possible to understand what a film does to us."[1] Indeed, what path would the project of making cinema intelligible have taken had there been no Eisenstein? He is in some sense as canonical as it gets, the one indispensable figure in the empire of cinema. Appropriately, his is also the fate that accompanies most canonical figures: most people revere them without encountering them, refer to them without assuming the need to read them closely. They are often so much part of the background of common sense that their singularity dissolves and soon becomes invisible.

Yet Eisenstein is also proof that canonicity might simply be another name for controversy and that centrality does not necessarily refer to a fixedness of place. His is, namely, a figure whose historical sense has been constructed primarily through a series of disagreements and displacements—not so much a figure and its projected shadows as a series of shadows that, projected in a constant conflictual play, produce the plastic appearance of a figure. Eisenstein himself, of course, became *Eisenstein* only through the element of polemical engagement, which he cultivated and relished. But the work of polemical elaboration has been continued and intensified by the subsequent generations and periods that have shaped the interpretation of his work, whose heterogeneous and multiple character we inherit today. In the already quoted essay, Jost follows his remark on the foundational importance of Eisenstein for film theory by observing that he is "not an author one cites, he is an author one summons, not so much for the purposes of debate as for the sake of struggle."[2] There is a certain idea of conflict, of instability and tension, that is essentially linked to Eisenstein.

Eisenstein has, for instance, played a crucial role in the antagonistic positioning of the debate over cinema's modernity. He has been considered the "exemplary modernist,"[3] a fellow traveler of the formalist and structuralist revolutions: the first to truly free cinematic form from the question of naive referentiality and grasp it in terms of a differential system of signs—the first, then, to have grasped cinema as something like a language, thereby placing it on the plane of semiological analysis, whose denaturalization of meaning could be mobilized toward a critique of other artistic forms and the totality of culture as such.[4] The remarkable plasticity of the figure of Eisenstein, however, begins to reveal itself if we consider how he appeared as crucial also for the poststructuralist project of cinematic *écriture*—the intramodernist reversal of structuralist semiology that set its aim at undoing the primacy of the linguistic metaphor. In this variation, Eisenstein is not someone who identifies cinema with language. Rather, his theory of montage "inscribes this language in writing [*l'écriture*]"[5] and shows the extent to which any fixity of the (linguistic) concept of the sign is undone by the primacy of the graphic trace and the work of figural displacement and condensation anterior to the question of meaning. By placing writing and form's figural play before meaning, Eisenstein was among the first to open cinema as a genuinely experimental domain, to say nothing of the position he has occupied in the discussion of cinema as a critical and politically revolutionary art. Eisenstein has in these ways played the role of the very *type* of the modern filmmaker or artist, without whom the idea of cinema as modern art would have been virtually unthinkable.

Almost simultaneously, however, Eisenstein managed to fulfill an opposite role—not as the harbinger of modern cinema but as a figure negated by modern cinema's emergence. This is most obvious in the case of André Bazin, whose interdiction of montage, the crucial gesture of his neorealist project, treated Eisenstein as its main target and enemy. In Gilles Deleuze's *Cinema* books, Eisenstein's "dialectical method" of constructing movement is discussed as the exemplary, most exhaustive, and most self-reflexively aware incarnation of the prewar cinema of the movement-image. And yet this moment of remarkable praise is precisely what allows Deleuze to leave Eisenstein behind as he turns to the great break of World War II and the Copernican revolution of postwar cinema—a cinema that, according to Deleuze, was no longer a classical cinema of movement (not even of dialectical movement) but rather a cinema of the direct presentation of time.[6] Here Eisenstein is not seen as someone who any longer contributes to cinema's modernity but rather as a great figure whose idea of cinema had to run the historical course of its exhaustion before a different existence of cinema, a truly modern one, could be actualized. Analogously, Eisenstein can no longer be considered someone who holds open the door for the arrival of cinema's experimental possibilities. And what to some appeared to be the pioneering work of a modern revolutionary artist might now be considered a didactic manipulation of a militant preacher who stunk up the place selling nothing but smoke to his audience.[7]

If we ask a slightly different question, one not posed as often as that of his modernism—namely, the question of Eisenstein's relationship to postmodernity—we encounter a similar situation. In the eyes of the postmodern judgment, which privileges the plural and the multiple, Eisenstein appears too totalizing, too systematic a thinker. His is a thought seeking unity and integration. It represses difference, which returns in the form of an excess this thought is itself unable to grasp:

> In the process of synthesis, which occupied Eisenstein throughout his career, the structure of difference is replaced by a dissolving of all differences into a utopian unified whole, a totality that is merely an attempt to restore the original state and that is not achieved by means of transformation; a false totality in the dialectical sense, and certainly a false dialectic. By subsuming the dialectics and the very structure of difference into a romanticized whole, Eisenstein tends to the opposite of his quest: instead of "going out of one's self" in ex-stasis, he in fact ends up

> solipsistically projecting himself onto the rest of the world, eradicating "the other." The stronger this tendency in his writing, the more excessive and baroque his images become.[8]

One can imagine the list of postmodern accusations extended further: Eisenstein's vision of history is too heroic and teleological for a period distinguished by the collapse of all great narratives; his resolute pursuit of the problem of form and synthesis is much too severe for the dispersive passion for the informal; his insistence on the inseparability of affect from reason, body from signification, the particular from the general, all embarrassingly idealist and outmoded.

Recently, however, Eisenstein has begun to emerge also as a thinker who in his work crucially prefigured the "postcontemporary" situation of cinema in which we find ourselves today. "Postcontemporary" designates a situation in which neither the heteronomy of the classical genre system nor the autonomy of the modernist gesture—nor, for that matter, the dialectic between the two—any longer guarantees cinema's contemporaneity with its own time. The "postcontemporary" situation is characterized by a constitutive heterogeneity of cinema's conditions. These new conditions force both artists and researchers to approach images through the lens of a discipline increasingly composed of little more than an eclectic combination of advances—anthropological, art-historical, media-theoretical, and so on—that try to grasp images within a set of discontinuous and differentially overlaid *dispositifs* or dispensations.[9] As archival discoveries make more and more of his fragmented writing projects publicly available, Eisenstein has begun to appear as someone whose work seems to have always navigated a terrain of precisely this sort. His case can be reinterpreted as one of continuous struggle against any homogenous set of conditions for the production of cinematic images. He appears as a figure for whom cinema meant not only engaging and arranging images and sounds but more fundamentally experimenting with and transforming the very *dispositifs* that determine the limits of such work. This dimension of Eisenstein's idea of cinema is most visible in his resistance to Hollywood's progressive consolidation of cinema's classical disposition (the overcoming of Griffith; the insistence on sound as a category of montage; the screen as a dynamic and transformable square), but it also plays a crucial part in his desire to treat the entire history of art and human culture as forming a kind of proto-cinematic patchwork, a "prehistory" of cinema that cinema can disentangle and entangle anew as it develops its own expressive capacities.[10]

Even a cursory glance presents, then, not one but several images of Eisenstein: the modernist Eisenstein *and* Eisenstein the not-yet-modern; Eisenstein the antithesis of postmodernism *and* Eisenstein the postmodernist avant la lettre. How to grasp this multiplicity? Not only, Why has Eisenstein been reread and reinterpreted so frequently? Why has his figure projected so many different shadows? but also, How is Eisenstein to be figured today, having already occupied so many incongruous and mutually exclusive positions? How to once more perceive a figure from the incongruous series of its past projections? It must first be said that the multiplicity of interpretations, the many "Eisensteins," cannot be explained simply by referring to the diversity of those who have followed and appropriated his work in accord with the demands and needs of their respective projects and historical situations. A purely perspectival and relativist explanation of this sort ("There is no figure, only shadows"), even if historically informed, must necessarily give up on the consistency of Eisenstein's thought. On the other hand, it would also be wrong to assume that the existence of such diverse and conflicting interpretations in no way essentially affects the unity of Eisenstein's thought, that his figure can be seen as standing somehow unperturbed behind (or beyond) them.

The only satisfying solution, it seems, lies in seeing the shape-shifting plasticity of Eisenstein's thought (the many shadows) as indicative of something at work in this thought itself (a sort of crack or a fissure in the figure). The multiplicity of external perspectives on Eisenstein's work should be reflexively perceived as a mark of a division that dynamizes this work already from inside. It is, in other words, the internal division of Eisenstein's thought that opens up the possibility of its multiple appropriations. What creates the effect of tension between the unity of the figure and its many shadows is the internal split of the figure, the fact that the figure is in its unity already something divided, at odds with itself. The generative and often incongruous role Eisenstein has played in the many projections of the idea of cinema in the twentieth century has to do with the fact that he managed to articulate an idea of cinema that is somehow consistent and *as such* struck through by tensions and contradictions. That Eisenstein's thought has been summoned so often is the effect of its ability to present itself one cohesive enough to exert a tremendous force, yet also one not simply given but instead inhering in conflict and division—a *problematic* unity whose achievement is impossible to separate from its undoing.

"Attainment of Unity" and the Dialectic of Division

It is Eisenstein himself who offers us a model with which to think of the existence of such a problematic, self-divided unity. According to his own statements, the question of unity occupied a crucial position in his work. In his autobiography, for instance, Eisenstein retrospectively characterizes the intention of his entire project as "the realization of the ultimate goal—the attainment of unity."[11] There is no doubt that Eisenstein strove to make cinema into a place for thinking the new possibilities of unity and to turn cinema itself into an agent of synthesis. The unity to be furnished by his idea of cinema meant, for Eisenstein, the possibility of a new unified place for the plurality of arts. In its capacity for *artistic unity,* cinema could function as the historical horizon of a new synthesis of expressive forms and the practice of the total work of art.[12] At the same time, Eisenstein related the question of synthesis to the sense of *anthropological unity.* Cinema could become the testing ground for the human being observed in the act of configuring a new relation between thought and sensuousness, consciousness and drive, thus arriving at a new ground from which the multiplicity of expressive forms in art and culture could be grasped as manifestations of a unified human subjectivity. Finally—but then, the questions of artistic and anthropological unity already imply this—cinema was intended by Eisenstein as a place for thinking the *historical unity* of humanity engaged in the process of overcoming its alienated existence.

Eisenstein's idea of cinema is that of a grand synthesizing machine capable of securing a new relation to the unities of art, subjectivity, and collective or historical humanity. At face value, this hardly gives us the impression of a problematic unity. On the contrary, one might gather from this the sense of a unity that is realized fully, or at least imagined as fully realizable—a *positive* unity that also gives itself as such. What is less commonly observed, however, is how it is precisely this metaphysical horizon of Unity that causes the entire Eisensteinian machinery to constantly engage in the language of contradiction, conflict, splitting, doubling, recoil, negation—the Eisenstein who, late in life, spoke of his "unity craze"[13] and proclaimed the attainment of unity the ultimate intention of his work is the same Eisenstein who describes the experience of his pursuit in the following way:

> Is it not also the case that, through the process of its realization, the *unity* of any *intention* at all turns into the *binomial* of the "negation of negation"? Something that could plastically be drawn as a shift from a two-point into a *three-point* schema.
>
> 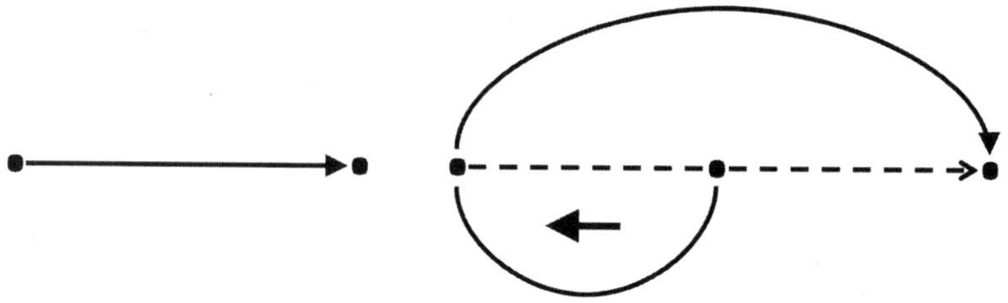
>
> And precisely not into a "logical" pair:
> the point of departure and the point of the aim;
> but rather into a dynamic triad: the point of intention, the point of its negation, and the sublation of the latter by a new negation on the path towards realization?[14]

Eisenstein here explains that any unity of intention—but it is also possible to say any intention of unity—necessarily relates to the moment of its own splitting. Movement toward an object can be realized only after it finds its orientation in a moment of recoil. It is only in the abandonment of the aimed-at object that this object can appear as the aim of movement. Which is to say that the concretely realized outcome of the process needs to be grasped not simply as a positive result but through the instance of a self-relating negativity (negation of negation), which provides the process with its dynamism. All these figures of division—the split, movement-in-recoil, negativity turning upon itself—are for Eisenstein not simply opposed to unity but in a more radical way function precisely as the forms of unity's attainment. They are what unity must assume if it is to be realized as something concrete.

It is enough to read literally what the text says—there is no unity, *concretely*, without its self-division—to see that the passage presents not an affirmation but a subversion of a certain positive figure of unity, stripping the latter of its privileged position in the schema of thought. Take the example of intention used by Eisenstein in the quoted passage. That intention is compelled to turn away from its trajectory if it is to reach its aim shows that it must carry the moment of division in itself from the very beginning. We know this from experience: our intentions, while not without some kind of unity, are always accompanied by an element that clouds them, an element we find impossible to reconcile with their purity. My intentional activity brings into existence a dimension that seems to undermine it almost immediately: I stumble upon some "external" obstacles and blockages that prevent me from realizing what I want, or there emerge some "unintentional" consequences of an intention "successfully" realized, among which might be the discovery that the "end" I have reached is somehow not quite (or perhaps even the exact opposite of) the one I had initially envisioned. The problem lies, of course, in the fact that as soon as I strip these seemingly extraneous, "unintentional" aspects away from my intentional activity—wishing perhaps to preserve the integrity of my intention—what dissolves is the interest and the intelligibility of my intention itself. What I perceive as the opposite of my intention (the "external," the "unintended") is also what, in its very division from it, first constitutes the intention's unity and integrity.

Any moment is always already haunted by its negation and therefore divided from itself. Unity—whether it be of intention, a work of art, or the social order—for this reason never gains traction as an autonomous or primary element in its own right. Alone, it does not have the capacity to organize the movement of its own realization. Which is to say that we must think unity as something that exists, but always as lost and divided in its very beginning—lost and divided originally, as its own cause. No matter how imposing and all-encompassing the unity one envisions, it is never able to act fully as the cause of its self-realization; nor is it really ever able to assume and take upon itself the fact that it can only become concrete due to the lack of its fullness.

Though he often recites some version of the dialectical *doxa,* according to which unity and synthesis should be thought as something positive and substantial, we tend to miss something essential about Eisenstein—not so much *what* he says but *how* he says it—if we fail to see that his thought puts division first and, even more important, treats the sense of unity itself as possible only from the primary perspective of (self-)division.[15] Yuri Tsivian has described this dimension of Eisenstein's thought by way of a remarkable formula. No matter how far down one digs to arrive at the most basic elements of Eisenstein's thinking, he says, "the smallest indivisible unit always consists of two things, not one. . . . Not only Eisenstein's vision of things, but also his image of himself, were predicated on the paradox of *indivisible duality.*"[16] What is striking about Tsivian's formulation—which says something like the minimal unit is disunity, the only indivisible thing is the self-division of the thing itself—is that it does not simply discard the question of unity or render it obsolete but instead performs something considerably more challenging. It recasts unity itself as nothing but another, perhaps the crucial, figure of division. Strictly speaking, unity in Eisenstein is *and* is not. As such, it is certainly nothing conciliatory. In place of the stereotypical image of the dialectical *doxa* (overcoming of division in unity, triumph of synthesis over moments of nonsynthesis), one finds in Eisenstein the contours of another, more critical dialectic, which we may call the *dialectic of division.* The dialectic of division considers division (or self-division) the primary and irreducible moment of thought, whose movement must for this reason be seen as simultaneously destructive and constructive of unity.[17]

Immanent Antagonism (Marx)

For an example of the logic of division that constitutes/destitutes a unity by way of its immanent traversal, we may approach Eisenstein's essay "Dickens, Griffith, and Ourselves" (1942), the *locus classicus* of film analysis. In this essay, Eisenstein charts the ideological dispute between his and D. W. Griffith's conceptions of montage. He takes Griffith as the inventor of Hollywood cinema and thus the paradigmatic figure of a dominant and rival model of filmmaking. Stating famously that "montage thought is inseparable from the common ideological grounds of thought as a whole,"[18] Eisenstein identifies in Griffith's masterful invention of alternating montage a formal equivalent of bourgeois ideology. As Griffith's montage sequences alternate between two distinct lines of action, so too, in the bourgeois view of society, is any division treated essentially as a parallelism. This is to say, division is treated as an external relation, one that juxtaposes phenomena "dualistically" as two separate realities whose existence or coming into being need not be explained as belonging to the same situation:

> According to [Griffith's] point of view—which we find both primitive and ridiculous—there are "the poor" and "the rich" existing as two independent parallel phenomena, which are also, incidentally . . . inexplicable!
>
> We find this formula laughable.
>
> But that is exactly how bourgeois theoreticians discuss it, and those grey-haired magnates who philosophise on "social themes" imagine it in precisely those terms! . . .
>
> And everything is done to conceal the real state of affairs, namely that "the poor" and "the rich," so far from being *two independent,* unrelated *parallel phenomena,* are actually *two sides of the same phenomenon*—a society built on exploitation.[19]

Griffith's method displaces the division between "the rich" and "the poor" into an external parallelism of two sides. This melodramatic gesture ensures that class opposition will ultimately be coded moralistically rather than politically. Whatever reality is put into the form of the Griffithian parallelism must somehow be accommodated within the binary opposition between "good" and "evil," "virtue" and "corruption." Intercutting between the two sides as parallel realities, this opposition in no way disrupts the sociability of the "good" that Griffith's cinema wishes to uphold. It is the "good" and the "virtuous" that stand for the unity of the social, while "the evil" and "the corrupt" are presented as antisocial, an external threat to unity.

From Eisenstein's perspective, which is the perspective of Marx, the question of the social is posed faultily if one construes it merely through such external opposition. Eisenstein proposes, contra Griffith, that the dynamic of a society be grasped through an antagonism that is immanent to it—an antagonism, in other words, that is itself fully social: not the unity of society (the good) and its negative, antisocial outside (the evil) that confront each other as parallel realities but rather society as a unity constituted and continuously traversed from within by conflict and negativity, a society that is, so to speak, its own antisocial "outside." (And is this not the basic experience of capitalism, namely, that it stands for a historical form of social relations produced by an activity that is essentially antisocial?) The question of social unity can thus be posed only if we first refer it to the primacy of division (the reality of exploitation, the antagonism of class struggle). The point, Eisenstein claims, is not to juxtapose "the rich" and "the poor" as parallel and distinct worlds but to grasp how the "two sides" emerge in the conflictual, self-divided unity of a single world.

In assuming division as immanent, the conception of (social) unity is thoroughly reconfigured. What emerges is a qualitatively different type of unity, one that must from now on bear the indelible mark of conflict and strife. Unity is constitutively self-divided. It is a partisan affair, inseparable from the subjectivity of struggle: a unity, to be sure, "but from our own perspective, in the light of our own orientation."[20] As we know, this militantly oriented idea of unity gives rise to a conception of montage very different from Griffith's parallelisms. Montage, says Eisenstein, will not proceed by an alternation between two parallel realities, the shot of "good" and the shot of "evil," which leaves each of them as is. On the contrary, it is necessary to start from the division of a single shot. Only from this point—which is precisely the point of unity as the immanence of a division—will montage be able to construct its associative chains that can further the thought of a conflict-ridden reality.[21]

Cinematism, or the "Synthesis of All Arts"

Eisenstein's insistence on the primacy of division in thought—the need to see any unified or synthetic achievement of thought as concretely realized only in the form of self-division—tells us something about thought itself, but it can also help us better grasp Eisenstein's understanding of cinema and its relation to art. Art is a divided object, an object whose unity appears in Eisenstein's theoretical construction only through the acknowledgment of a more basic split. In "The Dramaturgy of Film Form" from 1929, perhaps the best known of his texts, Eisenstein describes art as ontologically (that is, *"Because of its nature"*) constituted by the conflict between nature and human praxis, between the passivity of the organic and the activity of the rational, between inertia and productivity.[22] During the later part of his career, this conflict that is constitutive of art's existence persists, though it also shifts its position. From the opposition between activity of form and passivity of nature, Eisenstein begins to place the conflict into form itself. According to this later perspective, art remains divided and projects thought simultaneously in two opposite directions: the "progressive" direction of reason, rationality, and logic and the "regressive" direction of sensuousness, irrationality, and the "prelogical." Throughout the 1930s and 1940s, the work of art remains for Eisenstein determined as an internally split object, a dual unity or a "bi-unity" *(dvoedinost')*:

> The dialectic of a work of art is constructed upon a most interesting "dyad" [*dvoedinost'*]. The effect of the work of art is built upon the fact that two processes are taking place within it simultaneously. There is a determined progressive ascent towards ideas at the highest peaks of consciousness and at the same time there is a penetration through the structure of form into the deepest layer of sensuous thought. The polarity between these two tendencies creates the remarkable tension of the

unity of form and content that distinguishes genuine works. All genuine works possess it.[23]

The unity of art has no sense in itself but receives its meaning and justification from a more basic split, the fundamentally problematic tension between two types of thought whose polarity it traverses.[24]

And yet, is it not possible to find in Eisenstein's theory another approach, one that dissolves the conflictual being of art within the totalizing movement of art's historical becoming, in which division and conflict give rise to an ultimately far less problematic idea of art's unity—particularly as this unity realizes itself in cinema, the youngest of arts? Does Eisenstein not transform the *ontological* grasp of the divided object of art by placing it in a perspective of *historical* development, whose main effect lies precisely in viewing cinema as the overcoming of art's divided existence? Eisenstein indeed proposes an evolutionary view of cinema as the "synthesis of all arts," the crucial and the most advanced moment in the history of the total (perhaps it is better to say collective) work of art.[25] For him, cinema appears as the Art of arts, capable of ultimately asserting the unity of the idea of art over the conflictual and divided artistic being of the past. According to this view, cinema, which Eisenstein considers the paradigmatic art of modernity, emerges historically as the evolutionary heir of the entire history of art, growing out of and surpassing the fragmented paths traced in the development of the individual arts. More precisely, cinema finds its historical mission as a response to the disintegration of "the arts as a whole into sharply differentiated compartments." Cinema is a response to the process of differentiation and offers a challenge to the atomizing tendencies of capitalist society and its bourgeois culture, whose corrosive effects not only dismember the idea of art as a whole but repeat their destructive path also "within the various arts themselves."[26] In relation to this "decadent" splintering of art, accompanied by the collapse of coherence within each art individually, cinema presents itself as the necessary next step—a cure for what is essentially a religious crisis of art (the crisis of art as, precisely, *religio*)—capable of restoring the bond and once again performing "a full-blooded synthesis of the constituent elements of art and a synthesis of the arts themselves."[27]

This is indeed how Eisenstein's view of the historical mission of cinema has most often been interpreted. Yet it is possible to question the smoothness of this evolutionary narrative of cinema as the historical completion or unification of art(s). For cinema might historically be thought of not only as a great reconciler but also as a great divider, the agent of an irrecoverable break in the history of art. And consequently, a historical perspective of cinema's emergence might serve not only to resolve the conflictual being of art by translating it onto a different plane but also to transpose the reality of conflict and division onto the plane of history itself. Alongside considering it the evolutionary heir and unifier of other classical artistic forms, which have by the end of the nineteenth century suffered their terminal crisis, Eisenstein thinks of cinema as a radically new beginning. Cinema is thus marked not only by evolutionary continuity but also by disruption. And in this perspective of the break, which we should not too readily identify with that of the evolutionary inheritance, cinema is said by Eisenstein to "begin from level zero"[28]—a formulation suggestive of a discontinuity more radical than the one offered by the figure of the heir: the absolution of a new beginning rather than a solution in unity of the detritus left behind by the decadent downfall of (the) art(s).

There exist in Eisenstein's thought not one but two images of the historical emergence of cinema at the turn of the twentieth century, which means that the unity of cinema as a historical phenomenon can itself be seen as divided. There is the evolutionary perspective, according to which cinema discloses a new unity for the "constituent elements of art" that have found themselves in a state of disarray. Then, there is the perspective of disjunction that takes up the language of the zero degree, of a radical event, and implies the absence of the perspective from which it would be possible to recollect the "constituent elements of art" as something given or inherited. In other words, cinema finds its orientation not only in disclosure and recollection of the fragmented past but also in the void—in the discontinuous interval of a cut. Historically, cinema appears for Eisenstein as both a break or cut, which always involves a certain degree of contingency and uncertainty, and a new evolutionary recollection of an artistic past caught in the process of unrelenting disintegration. If the dimension of the break, the evental side of cinema's appearance, assumes priority between these two aspects, it is because the past can only become the object of recollection in the moment in which one has already separated from it. Only through the contingency and uncertainty of a rupture does the perspective of the historical continuity of an evolutionary process make any sense.

In its historical appearance, cinema is divided between event and evolutionary continuity. This division informs also Eisenstein's conception of cinema as the end or the *telos* of art's historical development. "All arts appear to stretch across the ages towards cinema; and conversely, cinema in many ways helps us understand their method."[29] Eisenstein presents the history of different arts as though each of them already carried within itself the principle of cinema—which is to say, the idea of montage—making cinema the place where this principle finally reaches its fulfillment and becomes fully conscious of itself: "It is well-known that, in historical terms, art first becomes acquainted with the principle of montage to its full extent at the cinema stage."[30] A statement such as this one can be read in the following way: the principle of art remains in essence the same throughout history, which makes it possible for us to maintain the idea of history as a unified process (history as the process of the unfolding and fulfillment of art's unified essence). Cinema is in this view "merely a technically more complete device"[31] for the performance of artistic operations one finds already in Homer, Leonardo da Vinci, El Greco, Shakespeare, Pushkin, and Rodin. And as such, cinema is able to bring art to a certain self-understanding, but this act of completion is essentially continuous with all of art's history and fulfills what was already there in its origin.

Eisenstein's statements, however, also suggest that he sees cinema not merely as a fulfillment of some originary principle of art, a historical coming-to-consciousness of art's transhistorical essence, but as a fundamental modification of the very essence of art, the appearance of something that is precisely not originally there. That what Eisenstein calls "montage-thought" seems as old as art—and perhaps even older—"in no way diminishes the fact that montage is at its *most specific and significant* as a method of influence in the field of cinema."[32]

The notion of cinema as the *telos* of art contains two seemingly incompatible meanings. There is first the sense of finality and completion, of a certain reflexive turning of the historical development of artistic essence upon its own original nature, which is fully realized in cinema. Yet there is also the sense of a "specific and significant" new moment in the history of art that, on the contrary, suggests an opening. The instability of cinema's teleological status in Eisenstein's imagining of the history of art(s) produces a peculiar effect. Namely, it seems that, for Eisenstein, the very imposition of the cinematic *telos* of art, far from organizing the sense of art's history into a linear, developmental, and unified sequence, in fact undoes any such figure of historical order and unity. If "all arts appear to stretch across the ages towards cinema," as Eisenstein says, then reaching this end, which we may have expected to stitch together the history of art into a meaningful whole, has precisely the opposite effect. The attainment of *telos* retroactively desutures the artistic phenomena in this history from any such holistic impression of meaningfulness or linear, developmentally sequenced totality.

Arriving at an end carries a sense of completion, but it also functions as a break. As such, it bears not only on the experience of the present but, even more importantly, on the status of the past whose sequence it supposedly brought to closure. The end is not simply a peaceful conclusion; it is also an imposture. And as an evental cut, the assumption of a *telos* that has been reached has the effect of transforming the very nature of the process that led to it. In other words, our arrival at the end never simply affirms the order of moments or actions that helped us reach it but instead discloses their series in a different light. Some moments may suddenly appear more important than others, some may reveal themselves as unnecessary and superfluous, and some may change their valence entirely. The chronological ordering of moments that led us to the end may all of a sudden appear at odds with the ordering projected retroactively by the end itself. It might, for instance, be clear that, chronologically, the sequence of moments that leads to a particular outcome is ABC. And yet it is often the case that, from the perspective of the outcome itself, a different sequence (let's say BAC) appears somehow truer, more significant, or necessary. Chronologically speaking, of course El Greco precedes painters who worked at moments closer to the appearance of cinema. Yet from the perspective of cinema, imposed violently by Eisenstein as the realized *telos* of the history of art, El Greco must clearly be considered an immediate and intimate predecessor, if not quite simply a contemporary: El Greco, the great montageur.[33] The assumption of a *telos* as something already arrived at therefore has the effect not of rigidifying time into an actual unity but of "possibilizing" the received unity of time, of loosening time's actual sedimentations and opening its repressed virtualities.[34]

It is clear that, in Eisenstein's thinking, cinema, which is affirmed as the end of art, has precisely such a "possibilizing" effect on art's history. By completing itself in cinema, the artistic past becomes available in the simultaneity of all its nonsimultaneous moments—a vast, contemporaneous space of combinatory play with the noncontemporaneous traces of history. It is wrong to assume, as simplistic critiques often do, that teleology is the same as (or that it necessarily implies) linearity and unity. On the contrary, the positing of a *telos* as something achieved or arrived at might be one of the most striking ways of freeing time and history from precisely such constraints. The assumption of an end has the capacity to open the past, and the end may in this sense be considered as, above all, an agent of disorder. It does not pacify the history that led to it but introduces into this history a sense of possibility—or better said, it introduces the sense of history *as* possibility. There is perhaps nothing more critical of history, nothing that opens history to a more radical questioning, than the feeling of the end to which it has led us.

In the case of Eisenstein, the assumption of cinema as the realized *telos*, the unifying end, of the entire history of art prepares the possibility for the retroactive discovery of unexpected connections, new passages and interactions between arts and artworks, links that remained invisible or quite improbable up to the very end, but which the end suddenly makes possible, and which have the effect of profoundly troubling any ideal of a unified history of art or culture. As Marie-Claire Ropars puts it, "Eisenstein . . . wishes to at the same time reintegrate cinema into the cultural field as a whole and to use it as an instrument for the critique of this culture." Which is to say, cinema is for Eisenstein the completion of the history of art—it integrates this history by inserting itself into it as its synthesis. But it is at the same time the moment at which there emerges within this history a crucial and critical distance from history itself. This distance, which puts the very model of history and of art's historical development into play to the point of making them almost unrecognizable, allows not exactly for the destruction of history but rather for something like its critical re-representation: "On the theoretical plane, it is less a question of breaking with literature or art as it is of producing a different representation of it."[35]

The paradoxical nature of Eisenstein's teleological vision—it orders history by disorienting and "possibilizing" its evolutionary unity—can be observed in the textual construction of the idea of cinema in his writing. In *Nonindifferent Nature,* for instance, Eisenstein attempts to present the artistic logic of pathos (ex-stasis, leaps of affect) by traversing a series that includes

Zola's *Rougon-Macquart* cycle
Walt Whitman's "The Song of the Broad Axe"
descriptions of theatrical performances of Frédérick Lemaître
the stained-glass windows of the Chartres Cathedral
El Greco's *Christ Driving the Money Changers from the Temple* and *The Resurrection*
Giovanni Battista Piranesi's *Carceri*
Picasso's *Guernica*
the "ecstatic quietism" of Chinese landscapes
the Bell X-1 rocket plane (first to exceed the speed of sound in 1948)
Gogol's writings on architecture
Dithyramb and *danse macabre*
the meditations of St. Ignatius of Loyola
a funny drawing from a 1914 issue of the *Strand Magazine*
the New Yorker drawings of Saul Steinberg
and Leonardo da Vinci's *The Virgin and Child with St. Anne*[36]

What interests Eisenstein in these cases—which he organizes into an incongruous series, combining literature, painting and graphic art, religious architecture, architectural and religious meditations, military and transportation technology, theater acting, and caricature in the popular press—is what he elsewhere calls the "'operational' problem" of pathos, the question of an "operational aesthetic": "how to do it. How to 'do' pathos clearly."[37] It is, in other words, not the question of an evolutionary-historical nature that motivates; he is after the *procedure* of pathos, of ecstatic form as it is deployed in these various artistic and nonartistic constructions. The series of examples offers fragments of a method whose elucidation must, however, constantly postpone the positing of its own systematic nature. "I am too occupied with analytically ripping open the phenomena of the form of works of art to give any thought to anything bigger."[38] Rather than an aesthetic *system* that would, for instance, guarantee the grasp of the unity of art as pathetic construction, one gets an experimental inquiry into the "*formulas* of pathos" through a collage that jumps across historical periods as much as it does between different media, and in which the "keyword of [Eisenstein's] approach," as François Albera puts it, "is the one of 'circulation,' 'passage,' 'exchange,' rather than 'specificity,' 'influence,' 'filiation.'"[39]

David Bordwell, in a passage worth quoting at length, describes this operational approach that can be found everywhere in Eisenstein's writings as a distinctive trait that separates Eisenstein from other early film theorists:

> Most generally, "film theory" refers to any reflection on the nature and functions of cinema. In the period 1920–1960 the most significant European and American theorists concentrated on defining cinema as a specific art or medium. What features set it off from literature, theatre, painting, and other arts? What is the nature of cinematic representation, and what relation does it have to the physical and perceptual world it portrays? Such questions were answered in various ways by Hugo Munsterberg, Rudolf Arnheim, André Bazin, and other theorists. Classical film theory also had a prescriptive bent: once one had isolated the differentiating figure of cinema, one could judge films according to how fully they realized the unique possibilities of the medium. . . .
>
> Throughout his career Eisenstein was no less prescriptive in his aims than his contemporaries. . . . In supporting his claims, however, he seldom tried to locate the essence of cinematic representation or to determine its sharply unique relation to physical or perceptual reality. He did not try to demarcate film sharply from other arts. His main effort was to unite his practice with a theory that would provide a wide-ranging, detailed reflection on film form, material and effect.[40]

To which it is possible to add a small but crucial caveat: it is not exactly the case, as Bordwell claims, that Eisenstein did not seek to formulate the essence of cinematic representation. What makes Eisenstein singular and rather striking within the field of film theory is that he indeed sought the essence of cinema but was only able to conceive it as something nonspecific and nonsubstantial. He was only able to locate it by way of an eccentric movement that led him out of cinema itself, a possibility Eisenstein clearly stages in his analysis of Japanese culture, which appeared to him as thoroughly cinematic, a culture imbued with "cinematism"—*except* in its films.[41] We may say that, for Eisenstein, the idea of cinema depended essentially on its ability to stand eccentrically in relation to itself, to come to itself from outside or by way of a recoil movement that necessarily had to pass through other arts, other forms of expression, and nonart.

In positing Eisenstein's lack of interest in the essence of cinema, Bordwell thus neglects to theorize something a bit more radical taking place in Eisenstein's thought, namely, a reconfiguration of the very question of essence, which has been divorced from the notions of specificity and substantial unity and has instead become linked by Eisenstein to the dynamic and constructive movements of what we may call the process of cinema's eccentric self-constitution. The essential unity of cinema, upon which depends also its role as the *telos* and the "synthesis of all arts," is unthinkable apart from such decentering, according to which cinema's essence can come into being only through a moment of self-estrangement or self-division. Cinema's identity depends essentially on what is cinematically inessential; as Bordwell himself notes: "[Eisenstein] asserts film's kinship to other arts and searches for constructive principles that transcend media. As a historical phenomenon, cinema poses problems of form, expression, and a response that are central to all arts. These problems can be illuminated by findings in other domains of research. This is the Eisenstein who is interested in 'everything . . . besides the cinema.'"[42]

As cinema comes into contact with other arts, the arts themselves do not remain unaffected. In their encounters with cinema, the individual arts reveal within themselves the presence of certain cinematic operations, the discovery of which makes them suddenly appear at odds with their own recognizable identities. Touched by the eccentric movement of cinema, the arts begin to divide and depart from themselves, returning to us profoundly estranged. Take, for instance, the case of literature, so vital in Eisenstein's construction of some of the key cinematic operations.[43] If literature allows Eisenstein to grasp something essential about the working of cinematic form, it is also the case that this essential eccentricity of cinema manages to displace literature in relation to its own self-understanding. Borrowing from literature, Eisenstein at the same time seeks "to redefine . . . the practices of language in light of cinema, which is thus endowed with a destructuring function."[44] This destructuring function of cinema is understood by Eisenstein as a sign of cinema's anticlassicism, which he opposes to both the classical refusal to allow an individual art beyond its specific limits and an emerging neoclassical desire to return the arts from their decadent dispersal back into their proper domains. Neoclassicism in painting is, for instance, characterized by "a consistent refusal to tackle problems that lie outside the scope of painting. . . . But it is precisely this ability which is the starting-point for the next art form after the qualitative leap from painting: namely, the cinema."[45] In leading arts beyond their classical limits, cinema therefore has the ability to organize their decadent disintegration differently, at a distance from the (neo)classical temptation of a return to order:

> It certainly seems that all art forms *in their extreme manifestations,* i.e. where they attempt to expand the limits of their potential and their material, invariably end up by trying to appropriate the rudiments of the art of the future: the art of cinema. And that when they attempt this, things which in those other art forms can only be done successfully by outstanding talents and geniuses, in cinema are found to be the basic principles of its methods![46]

"Cinema" might thus also be considered a name for that which renders an individual art legible only in that crucial moment in which this art divides from itself. The becoming-cinematic of an individual art form draws into its interiority the very limit that in the (neo)classical perspective separates and guards it from what stands outside it. Through this, the art form turns into a contested terrain, where its future is suddenly drawn into a confrontation with its past, the distinction between the art's proper and "extreme" manifestations collapses, and an entirely new configuration—nonclassical and nonhierarchical—emerges, in which the art's "democratic" capacities take possession of the "aristocratic" height of genius.

Eisensteinian Concepts: Movement, Action, Image, Montage

The present study pursues the dialectic of division across four main concepts with which Eisenstein sought to give shape to his idea of cinema: movement, action, image, and montage. The book is, first of all, a theoretical reconstruction of these basic Eisensteinian concepts, which in their various arrangements guarantee the presence of cinema. Yet this presence is never simply given or stable. Instead, Eisenstein presents the idea of cinema as a process of ceaseless division. *Movement, Action, Image, Montage* thus proceeds by treating these Eisensteinian concepts as unities concretized through the form of contradiction. The concept of movement is discussed in terms of the contradiction between Eisenstein's assertion of movement as both something absolute, a pure *figurability* or indeterminacy of things, and something that must necessarily take the shape of a determinate visible *figure.* Movement for Eisenstein is, in other words, divided between a nonfigurative force and a figurative appearance, which we will think together with the concept of the *figure-in-crisis* (chapter 1).

When the concept of movement is considered in relation to action, there emerges a different opposition: between the form of *theatrical* or *grotesque* action, which Eisenstein inherits from his master Vsevolod Meyerhold, and action that is *epic* or *heroic* in its form, in which one may recognize the pressure of the revolutionary situation seeking to represent itself in a manner adequate to its world-historical scope. The tension between theatrical–grotesque action and epic–heroic action constitutes the most basic formal contradiction, the *form-problem,* of all of Eisenstein's films (chapter 2).

Turning to the concept of the image *(obraz),* an analysis of Eisenstein's attempt to define what he means by this term shows that the image is ultimately thought by Eisenstein to possess two distinct and incompatible forms of agency. On one hand, the image performs the function of the Symbol. As a *symbol-image,* the image plays the role of an underlying, invisible agent that dynamizes and informs the visible fragments on the surface of perception and ties them into an affective and intelligible unity. On the other hand, there exists in Eisenstein's work a form of imagistic agency opposed to image's symbolic function, a form that, rather than endowing representation with a symbolic unity, resists the symbolic status of the image. We will name this other imagistic agency the *symptom-image* and explore how, in Eisenstein's conception, the image exhibits a fundamental contradiction between the symbolic function and its symptomatic rupture (chapter 3).

The final chapter of the book (chapter 4) engages the famous Eisensteinian concept of montage. It begins by considering the specific and privileged relationship montage maintains to other Eisensteinian concepts and shows that montage is not simply one of Eisenstein's concepts but that it has something to do with their very "conceptuality." Following this, the chapter proceeds to a discussion of montage and of what Eisenstein called "montage-thought" as it relates to the question of form. The main argument of the final chapter could be summarized by saying that montage should be understood not so much as a form but (at the risk of sounding tautological) as a *montage of forms.* Or, to put it differently, montage-thought signals the appearance of a form that is not one but consists of a confrontation or juxtaposition of two contradictory forms (concept and *Witz,* evolutionary organic whole and repetitive inorganic series).

The primacy of division is maintained throughout the tracing of Eisensteinian concepts. Each concept is treated as a dialectical "unity of opposites," a unity composed of contradictory determinations that do not make up a Whole. Such treatment of Eisenstein's concepts as a "unity of opposites" may be distinguished from at least two other ways in which the operation of his thought has been interpreted in the past:

1. In the first interpretation, the Eisensteinian concept functions as an instrument of unfettered synthesis, of a Whole that dissolves opposing determinations and leads thought to a state of reconciliation and rest. Understood in this way, the concept shelters the phenomenon it thinks

from the ravages of division and contradiction; it protects thought from negativity. Mikhail Iampolski has, for instance, defined "Eisenstein's entire theoretical adventure as a movement from an initial stage of fragmentary exposition of material (the Constructivist stage of 'quotations,' when synthesis is often still lacking) toward a later stage of all-embracing synthesis."[47] According to his interpretation, the concept could, in the endgame of Eisenstein's thought, be cast as a kind of transcendental abolisher of Difference. And Iampolski indeed proposes "a chart for Eisenstein's theorization at work: a passage from an opposition of poles, where polarity is replaced by similarity, to a total, narcissistic, empathic absorption into an all-devouring, all-absorbing instance, where it is impossible to trace any distinction."[48] Such a reading strikes us as rather tendentious and selective. It focuses too much on certain of Eisenstein's statements while neglecting others that contradict this vision of thought as immersive narcissism. Even more important, Iampolski's interpretation, despite first bringing attention to it, ultimately disregards the very form in which Eisenstein's statements are rendered (the form of quotation and the fragment). It seems necessary to insist in this regard that it is precisely the purportedly great synthetic and systematic attempts in Eisenstein's work (*Method, Nonindifferent Nature,* etc.) that remain in their form and exposition the most fragmentary and divided, thus belying the claim that Eisensteinian thought serves as the agent of some all-embracing absorption—"a certain kind of intellectual totalitarian utopia," as Iampolski calls it.[49] Should we simply disregard the fact that Eisenstein's writing lacks any formal unity—that it concretely fails to absorb the fragment and raise itself to the level of an "all-devouring, all-absorbing instance"? Obviously not. What Eisenstein's writing shows is that the moment of synthesis, in which one assumes to have reconciled opposing phenomena under a single conceptual roof, is also the very point at which the contradictory determinations turn out to have been the purpose of this synthetic operation all along. The ground of the entire edifice gives way and the building to be built begins to slide in opposing directions, as though its foundations were suddenly caught in a landslide. The momentary shelter of thought is seized by the dynamism of division.

2. The second interpretation is more open. It holds that the Eisensteinian concept should be viewed not as an all-embracing and difference-dissolving Whole but as a unity-in-multiplicity, what—in distinction from the dialectical "unity of opposites"—we may call a *pluri-unity.* The concept as a pluri-unity can be understood as a form of synthesis that contains within itself references to a multiplicity of different moments. The concept "montage," considered as a pluri-unity, refers not only to a variety of cinematic

operations (in Griffith, Pudovkin, Vertov, and Eisenstein himself) but also to a large number of cases taken from plastic arts (El Greco, Daumier, Serov), literature (Dickens, Whitman, "Pushkin-the-montageur"), and nonart (popular culture, ethnographic material, religion). It also relates to moments in the fields of physiology of perception (perception of overtones), psychology (the coexistence of prelogical and logical thought), philosophy ("contradiction"), and so on. Elaborated as a pluri-unity, the concept of montage exhibits a remarkable internal diversity as it gathers and determines a multiplicity of individual moments, containing them within its own space. We may call this the extensive and expansive function of the Eisensteinian concept. Conceived as a pluri-unity, the concept allows Eisenstein's thought to reach outward and encompass a truly remarkable and often surprising arrangement of materials. It creates the sense of a potentially infinite richness and opens the possibility of an unlimited accumulation of ever-new artistic references, experiences, and insights pillaged from an equally varied set of disciplines and fields of research. This is the side of Eisenstein's "encyclopedism," the voracious appetite for knowledge exhibited by the autodidact in building up the reservoir and consistency of his thought. Yet what is it that drives this voraciousness? What is it that pushes the concept (as a pluri-unity) to expand and strive to contain an ever-increasing plurality of references? The pluri-unity of the concept gives us insight into the operation of conceptual containment that Eisenstein's thought seeks to perform as it proliferates through the individual moments of its articulation, but it in some sense fails to explain the dynamism or the intensity of the concept itself. This is necessarily so because what ultimately drives the concept is not the multiplication of references it may expand over and contain, however pleasurable it might be for the concept to impress us with its encyclopedic reach. What forms the internal dynamo of the concept is the simple fact that, regardless of how expansive a plurality it comes to contain, it never manages to be fully congruent with itself. That is, the concept never reconciles the fact that as a synthetic vehicle of thought, it is fated to assume the form of a "unity of oppositions," a series of not only plural but contradictory determinations. One might even suggest that the "encyclopedism" of the concept as a pluri-unity, the concept's voracious appetite in Eisenstein's thought, is nothing more than a coping mechanism, a sort of desperate countermeasure meant to fascinate and distract from the realization that, in its intimacy, every concept exists only as a split or divided entity. Therefore, if one is to truly grasp the dynamic of the Eisensteinian concept, it is necessary to shift focus from its marvelous and at times overwhelming pluri-unity—the breathtaking containment of a multiplicity of moments ("How did Eisenstein know all this?!")—to the concept as a "unity of opposites," a gesture of synthesis that inheres not in the act of gathering a multiplicity of moments (and certainly not in an all-embracing moment of narcissistic immersion within a Whole) but in the concreteness of a contradiction. One has, in other words, to refuse to be taken in by the rich plurality of Eisenstein's thought and pursue instead the reflexive austerity of the divided and contradictory concept.

In what follows, the concepts of movement, action, image, and montage are thus neither treated as all-embracing, difference-dissolving monuments to synthesis nor pursued as extensive unities that contain a plurality of instances. Rather, the concepts are taken up as dialectical syntheses of opposing determinations. They can be followed as unities whose synthetic force inheres in moments of division, in the formation of contradictions and coordination of conflicting series. The idea of cinema such concepts allow us to articulate is a critical one, according to which the identity of cinema is constitutively traversed by tensions. Insofar as they make cinema's existence intelligible through an elaboration of its rationality, the dialectical concepts, split as they are, at the same time point to the nonexistence of some unitary reason of cinema. If there were a lesson to be drawn from tracing the Eisensteinian concepts of cinema, it may indeed be that no reasons can be given in the name of cinema that do not touch on cinema's unreason, that any rational idea of cinema must also disclose in its very trajectory the crisis of cinema's rationality.

■ ONE

The Figure-in-Crisis

FROM INTUITION TO THE DIALECTIC, FROM KINEMATOGRAPHY TO CINEMATIC MOVEMENT

Movement and movement.

■ Sergei Eisenstein, "Pantagruel Will Be Born"

A Fetishist of Movement?

The fundamental characteristic of Eisenstein's thought is his unconditional affirmation of movement, which has the effect of turning movement into the most elementary condition of his artistic and theoretical work. References to movement proliferate in his writing, and one feels the omnipresence of movement through his near-constant use of terms that belong to its semantic field: *becoming, dynamism, transition, transformation, process, leap, development, evolution, emergence, growth* or *outgrowth, decay, plasmaticity, metaphoricity* or *transfer,* and so on. If Eisenstein can be said to have made a decisive contribution to the cinema of the movement-image, it was certainly as its apotheosis. In his films and writings, movement is raised to its highest point, its possibilities explored and experimented with to a striking degree. It is no coincidence that, for Gilles Deleuze, Eisenstein could stand as the paradigmatic figure of the entirety of the classical, prewar cinema of movement.[1]

The reference to movement does so much work in Eisenstein's thought that one may rather quickly become suspicious and distrustful of its validity as a concept. Does saturating all phenomena with movement and turning it into a sort of universal *explanans* not constitute an ingenious strategy of imposing on movement a certain form of stability, of disciplining movement and thereby avoiding any concrete confrontation with it? "This uninterrupted, universal movement," Jacques Aumont writes in his *Montage Eisenstein,* "appears throughout all of Eisenstein's writings as literally fetishized, and his obsession is to find traces of it everywhere. . . . *Movement* is what comes to unify all the specific cases, all the levels of the problem of montage . . . , elsewhere, it will account for the predilection for a 'linear' drawing and it is what finally comes to replace, or to enlarge, the *drive,* desire itself."[2] We may add to Aumont's list the way movement comes to unify in Eisenstein's view the author and spectator, who are said to undergo the same dynamic process in relation to the work of art.[3] To describe the overuse of the term as fetishization, as Aumont does, is to suggest that the term functions as a point of arrest, a capture of movement. The fetish is what fixes and demobilizes; it introduces stability to an experience that does not want to go (look) any further. One holds on and returns to the venerated fetish precisely to avoid having to move on or confront the consequences of doing so. To say that Eisenstein's constant affirmation of movement amounts to a fetishization of movement is therefore to say that his concept of movement itself opposes movement; it is to say that the concept of movement does not move and in this sense amounts to a contradiction, because the task of any concept is to act as a vehicle of thought. In fetishizing movement, Eisenstein turns it into an imaginary terminus that may be applied to make sense of all kinds of phenomena—the sense of the universe in its totality, in fact—without itself undergoing any real movement. What irony—that movement should come to a halt precisely in the *concept* of movement!

The question of movement thus appears settled before it has even been posed; in the overextension of the term, movement becomes a nonquestion. Such has, however, always been the judgment leveled against the dialectic, namely, that despite its claims to unleash thought in its universal restlessness, it merely captures movement and erects it as a fetish. Dialectical movement is feigned, the accusation goes, because dialectical thought always knows in advance how it will proceed and where it will ultimately find itself. The dialectic, somehow always sure of the ways of movement, enacts its controlled explosion so as to be able to stem it and put it to rest. What is lacking in the dialectic—the image of which would therefore be confirmed also by Eisenstein, the most avowedly dialectical of all filmmakers—is a certain intuition or vitality of real movement. One may, for instance, be skeptical of Eisenstein's suturing of the question of movement to the universal (dialectical) model of conflict, which, precisely because its formula is supposed to encompass everything, loses its dynamic force. To quote once more from Aumont:

> For Eisenstein (in ["The Dramaturgy of Film Form"], but also more or less everywhere else), a conflict *must* be found apropos of everything—even if it means producing, as in "Dramaturgie der Film-Form," a classification which is more evocative of the famous Borgesian "catalogue" than it is of scientific explanation. He seems to believe that every conflict, every contradiction (taking those words in their most ordinary sense) participates in the dialectic, and he does not deny himself, when he sees fit, to define pairs of "antagonistic" terms. Thus, in this area of "conflict," it is most important not to let Eisenstein fill us up with empty words.[4]

Our doubt in Eisensteinian movement might grow even stronger if we begin to consider the preposterous-seeming organicism, the dialectic of organic synthesis, proposed in Eisenstein's writings from the late 1930s onward. For this "late" Eisenstein, movement seems to be placed in a vision of a uniformly evolving and self-completing whole (the organic spiral), whose carefully maintained proportionality stages outbursts of movement (leaps of pathos) at the same moment it tightens control over them. In both places, typically considered to be the two distinct stages of his thought, Eisenstein installs a fetish of a general form or Law of movement (the "early" dialectic of conflict and the "late" organic dialectic of the Whole), but not movement itself, its force, its singularity.

Our purpose here will be to unsettle somewhat this impression of movement as virtually fetishized in Eisenstein's thought. Though he seems to wish to produce its universal formula, Eisenstein never firmly settles the question of movement. Despite his best efforts—to be further complicated late in his career by an intense ideological pressure to attune the frequency of his thought to the official broadcasts of Stalinist dialectical materialism—he never succeeded in finding movement a stable or proper form. We will suggest that the problem of Eisenstein's conception of movement can be productively recast in the form of the following question: how does a certain powerful *intuition* of movement come to assume its *dialectical form* in Eisenstein's idea of cinema? What the question seeks is a new lease on the Eisensteinian dialectic. It is, namely, possible to treat dialectical movement in Eisenstein not as a case of fetishistic disavowal but as something *problematic,* that is, something for which no solution is given in advance and that thus preserves movement as a question. The dialectic does not serve Eisenstein merely as shorthand for the law of universal dynamism, asserted at the price of movement's anomalous and aberrant aspects. It is, to the contrary, the very element of thought that grants anomalous and aberrant movements a degree of intelligibility they would otherwise not possess.

"First the Movement . . ." (Intuition)

The drama of movement in Eisenstein's thought takes place within a tension between a vital intuition of movement and the famous "dialectical approach to form." Understanding Eisenstein's thinking of movement means understanding how one might pass from an intuitive experience to a dialectical grasp of movement, and how each of the two approaches, without being simply subsumed by its opposite, interferes with and modifies the other. The advantage of stating the question in this fashion is that it allows us to place Eisenstein in relation to a fundamental theoretical dispute, a philosophical quarrel that separates those thinkers for whom thought's movement follows the force and the vital method of *intuition* (Nietzsche, Bergson, Deleuze) from those who, on the contrary, assert that thought takes place in the dialectical movement of the *concept* (Hegel and others). According to the intuitionist position, movement cannot be reduced to the dialectic of concepts, because conceptual distinctions and mediations follow from the intuitive immediacy and vitality furnished by thought. For the dialecticians, any intuitive immediacy must itself be grasped as always already caught and critically displaced by the work of conceptual and formal mediation. Placing Eisenstein in the context of this philosophical dispute is useful not only because it clarifies his conception of movement but also because it gives him the status of a philosophical thinker he undoubtedly deserves. It treats him, in other words, as more than a glorified craftsman or an empirical explorer of cinematic techniques, which he has unfortunately become for much of contemporary film studies.

The Eisensteinian intuition of movement can be presented with the help of a simple formula often used in his writing. In a set of notes, written in 1947 under the title "Conspectus of Lectures on the Psychology of Art," Eisenstein jots down a parenthetical phrase containing a concise expression of the intuition of movement characteristic of his work. He writes, "First the movement, and then *what* moves."[5] This maxim at once affirms movement as separable from the object that moves and asserts the movement's primacy over the object. Movement is the primary reality; only then come the things that move. In the text of the "Conspectus," the maxim follows a series of notes that raise the question of the nature of artistic work: what makes art's expressiveness "readable"? Or, because "readable expressiveness" is another name for form, how may one explain the "mystery of form"? Or simply, what is it that we—as artists or spectators—do in a work of art? In this context, the seemingly offhand "first the movement, and then *what* moves" can be seen to carry in itself an entire artistic program. Eisenstein closely relates the intuition of the primacy of movement to the question of the intelligibility of artistic form. To be able to think what an artist does, or simply to be able to think *as* an artist, one will have to be sensitive to form as an instance in which movement asserts itself as the primary reality, irreducible to any particular *what* that moves.

The formula "first the movement . . . ," which has the merit of appearing intimately Eisensteinian, is in fact an opportunistic appropriation and condensation of a longer passage from Friedrich Engels's *Socialism: Utopian and Scientific*:

> When we consider and reflect upon nature at large, or the history of mankind, or our own intellectual activity, at first we see the picture of an endless entanglement of relations and reactions, permutations and combinations, in which nothing remains what, where, and as it was, but everything moves, changes, comes into being and passes away. We see therefore, at first the picture as a whole, with its individual parts still more or less kept in the background, rather than the things that move, combine, and are connected.[6]

Engels here describes a general intuition of movement that, he goes on to explain, belonged to the Greeks and found its expression in the philosophy of Heraclitus, who was the first to formalize its metaphysical attitude. Engels contrasts this ancient intuition of movement, the metaphysics of the Heraclitean world in flux, which he describes as a "primitive" and "naive" image of the world, against the properly scientific and dialectical comprehension of totality. The Heraclitean vision "correctly . . . expresses the general character of the picture of appearances as a whole," Engels says, but it is ultimately of limited importance to the modern dialectic, which must leave behind the generality of such a vast and direct intuitive grasp of the restless cosmos and busy itself instead with critical isolation and scientific analysis of particular phenomena to reconstitute the process of the whole in its concreteness. The Heraclitean intuition, which takes in the picture of the whole before perceiving the individual parts that compose it, is not false. The world is a totality in movement; it *is* nothing but dynamic process. But this intuition is also false, because it does not furnish the dialectical laws of the world's dynamism and neglects to think the totality in the concrete form of its movement. Only modern dialectical thought—the thought of Marx weaponized by Hegel and modern science—can properly break down the primitive Heraclitean picture of the whole and analyze it in parts, which gives a new concreteness to the dialectically articulated totality and its dynamism.[7]

What is for Engels an abstract, proto-dialectical feeling appears to Eisenstein instead to be the concretization of the artistic intuition of movement as such. He quotes the passage from Engels in one of his famous speeches at the

1935 Conference of Soviet Filmworkers, while advancing his discovery of the *Grundproblem* (the fundamental problem) of art. The *Grundproblem* exists, to put it schematically, in the conflict within any work of art between two tendencies of thought: the tendency toward conscious, logical abstraction and the tendency toward sensuousness, the prelogical, naïveté, primitiveness, all suppressed forms of mental life left behind by the civilizing process. In this schema of the split thought of art, it is the question of sensuousness and the prelogical that dominates Eisenstein's discussions of artistic form and construction. And thus what is in Engels's evolutionary narrative treated as an outdated structure of feeling, or a primitive dialectic of universal movement, assumes for Eisenstein an absolutely contemporary and modern valence. Art names for him precisely the domain in which the most progressive or evolutionarily advanced thought (reason, logic, science, analysis, the ideal of progress itself) coexists and struggles with thought's regressive tendencies. Art confronts the restraint of humanity's adult culture with a step back into the inhumane omnipotence of primary narcissism. The Heraclitean intuition of a world in becoming might not be scientifically legitimate; indeed, it may represent at best a proto-dialectical view of the world. For this very reason, however, it strikes at the core of what makes a work of art, which is why Eisenstein eventually condenses the passage from Engels into a single sentence that provides him with an effective and practicable principle of his artistic intuition of movement. First the movement, and then *what* moves.

To convey the practicability of the intuitive formula of movement to the audience at his 1935 speech—an audience of hecklers, we may add, who had already lost patience with his theorizing and formalizing—Eisenstein follows the quotation from Engels by translating its Heraclitean theme into a more specific problem of poetic expression. He questions whether the metaphysical intuition of reality as incessant flux he wishes to appropriate demands a specific form of expression or use of discourse. What type of sentence does the artistic intuition of movement call for? Eisenstein responds that the force of the intuition demands a sentence in which "the description of movement and action (the verb) precedes the description of who is moving or acting (the noun)."[8] In other words, the intuition of movement can be registered by subverting the structure of the ordinary sentence, by revolutionizing the typical form of our everyday speech: movement (represented by the verb) must be displaced from the position of the predicate and pushed in the direction of the sentence's subject, while *what* moves (the noun) must follow the opposite path and shift from its subject position toward the place of the predicate. The surprising effect of this new "juxtaposition of words" is that movement (verb) can no longer be read as merely the attribute of this or that substantive *what* (noun), while the substantive term in turn loses its fixity and firmness.[9]

Eisenstein presents a comparison between two sentences in German—

Die Gänse flogen (The geese flew) and *Es flogen die Gänse* (There flew the geese)—to illustrate the difference between an ordinary sentence and one that has been overturned by the artistic intuition of movement. The first of the two sentences, he says, strikes us as closer to the habitual way we order our words. Its tone is matter-of-fact, and it has "a dry, informational ring to it." The second sentence, however, surprises us. By reversing the common ordering of noun and verb, it carries "in its very turn of phrase," as Eisenstein puts it, "something lyrical, poetic that is not used in everyday colloquial speech."[10] What is it exactly that produces the lyrical effect of the second sentence? By starting with the *Es* (It, "There is") and the verb, the second sentence allows us first to seize the movement of flight as an impersonal and neutral event or action: movement (verb) not as something that predicates an already individuated identity (noun) but as a pure happening. "Movement is registered before the object is recognized."[11] Only after this initial effect, in which we feel movement without yet being able to assign it a recognizable shape, is the happening of flight related to a specific *what* that flies, as we perhaps feel our perception wishing to settle back into something more familiar and recognizable.

To the extent that the colloquial sentence *(Die Gänse flogen)* organizes our perception of the movement of flight, it stabilizes this movement by making flight an attribute of the individuated identity of the geese. But it also keeps our perception of flight rather general, because there is nothing to prevent us from attributing flight, represented in this way, to any number of other individuated identities (sparrows or airplanes, for instance). With the overturning of the colloquial mode of speech, there emerges the lyricism of the second sentence *(Es flogen die Gänse).* The poetic torturing of everyday discourse individuates the movement of flight and thereby gives us a dynamic sense of flight as a singular event, without first making it an attribute of this or that identity. In the lyrical sentence, movement itself becomes a "subject"—that is, if we are able to imagine the strange impersonal "subjectivity" of a movement that has been individuated for itself prior to any recognition of the thing that moves. The turn that separates the lyrical from the colloquial sentence and produces the shock of their juxtaposition—which is, of course, also the juxtaposition of art against our habitual experience—fundamentally changes our encounter with movement. Through the lyrical transformation of discourse, we pass from movement as a relational term that qualifies a subject to movement as absolutized, subjectivized for itself.

We may now wish to translate the effects of the lyrical intuition of movement, whose machination we have just observed in the case of the poetic sentence, into the domain of the image and plastic form, which are of primary interest to Eisenstein. Intentionally mixing and impurifying the two domains, we may say that ordinary speech always gives us a plastic figure (geese) first, to which then a generality of movement (flight) is attributed as a predicate.

The lyrical effect of the poetic sentence stems, on the contrary, from the fact that, in its disturbance of ordinary speech, the primacy of the plastic figure is abandoned. We are first confronted with movement (flight), without the support of a recognizable figure to guide us through this encounter. The recognition of the figure (geese) arrives only after we have "perceived" movement as something that has now become individuated for itself: movement not merely as an attribute of the figure's identity but as itself the thing whose identity concerns us, as itself what forms the very substance of our experience.

The term Eisenstein employs to describe this strange substance, a substance that has become indistinguishable from movement, is *plasmaticity,* which he opposes to the plastic identity of the figure perceived in its essential stability. Appearing with particular force in his *Disney* writings, "plasmaticity" signifies the attractive quality of a type of substance ("protoplasm," plasma) whose substantiality has become impossible to distinguish from the accidents of movement and change that affect it. "Plasmatic" are those figures whose defining substantial trait is the lack of any substantial continuity or self-identity. In place of plastic stability, *plasmaticity* stands for limitless malleability. In the context of Walt Disney's animated cartoons, Eisenstein describes the plasmatic as the behavior of "primordial protoplasm, not yet having a stable form, but capable of taking on any and all forms." Plasmatic phenomena exhibit "the endless possibility for diversity in form," and plasmaticity therefore implies an absoluteness of movement and change, an "'omni-potentiality,' i.e. the ability to become 'whatever you want.'"[12] In Eisenstein's conception of "plasmaticity" and Disneyesque lyricism, which he identifies with movement's innocent escape from the strict and logical forms of American industrial capitalism, no figure can be fixed and isolated as external to movement. Instead, crucially, it is now "the movement which describes the figure."[13]

The experience of plasmaticity allows Eisenstein to think movement as an intuition of limitless transformation. Movement signifies the possibility to become "whatever you want." It names the capacity to assume the shape of any-figure-whatever and, with equal ease, to abandon it. Lyrical emancipation of movement opens the figure to the dimension of pure figurability, in which interest in the attainment and stable maintenance of the figure is replaced by a fascination with the continuous emergence and dissolution of the figure in the medium of an essentially plasmatic reality. The task of the artist is to find a form that registers movement as the impersonal element of pure figurability—as a happening that animates our perception independently from our recognition of the figure and as such is capable of dramatizing for us the moments of the figure's appearance and disappearance. His understanding of movement as, foremost, pure figurability offers perhaps the most straightforward means of defining Eisenstein's relationship to the revolution of modern art. For does not the gesture of modern art in its opposition to classical art consist precisely of a refusal to make present the figure and to instead pose the very problem of its figurability? How is a figure figurable? What mattered to the moderns, in other words, was not the recognition of the figure in its visibility but the registering and exploration of the primacy of movement—of the dynamic condition and play of forces that make a figure visible in the first place.[14]

Eisenstein's Drawings

Movement must be thought as emancipated and must be made absolute, an element of pure figurability intuited against the stable presence of the figure. In all of Eisenstein's work, such intuition of movement may be seen most acutely in his drawings. The graphic line offered Eisenstein an opportunity for exploration and experimentation with movement. He filled many notebooks with drawings during his adolescent and teenage years and continued to develop his graphic skills through the 1920s in his plans for theater and film productions. But it was not until his time in Mexico (1930–32) that Eisenstein discovered what he considered his original approach to the practice of drawing. From his time in Mexico onward, he drew as though possessed by a compulsive graphomaniacal urge. Drawing provided Eisenstein with a veritable laboratory of movement, and in his experiments, he identified an intimate link between the graphic line and the dynamic process. The affirmation of this link between line and movement manifests also in the fact that, after his return to drawing in Mexico, Eisenstein does not—cannot, it seems—stop drawing. His is a line that never ceases and that cannot be arrested. It knows only the endless variability of its own repetition, which appears in series upon series of drawings, whose count in the Eisenstein archive runs in the several thousands.[15]

In Mexico, Eisenstein discovers the "paradise of drawing,"[16] which for him meant the introduction of a liberated and spontaneous graphic line. In his youthful drawings, the line could indeed be quite dynamic but ultimately remained subordinate to the tracing of physiognomies, the animal-types of Riga's bourgeois society. These early drawings offered caricatures of ultimately representational situations. During the 1920s, the line engaged mostly in the graphic sketching of theatrical and film works, playing the role of constructive design. In the early 1930s, however, the line establishes itself on its own account. Eisenstein writes in his memoir that in Mexico, he "began to draw again. This time in a proper linear way," adding that this was the moment in which his "drawing underwent an internal catharsis, striving for mathematical abstraction and purity of line."[17]

The purity of line Eisenstein writes of consists in its ability to register the process of movement. "What is a line?" he quotes a saying from the ancient

Chinese philosopher Wang Pi: "A line speaks of movement."[18] The graphic line is a literal realization of the formula "first the movement, and then *what* moves," because only after the line exists as a record of movement can it become a means of disclosing a certain something—a *what,* or a figure. The line, we may say, speaks of the process of pure figurability. It is a record of movement capable of becoming any-figure-whatever, but it is not in itself necessarily figurative. In the line, there exists always a surplus of movement over the stability offered by the figure. For Eisenstein, the line is thus, in essence, animated. One can see here the connection between Eisenstein's idea of drawing and his fascination with the lyricism of Walt Disney's "plasmatic" figures. All drawing is animation.

That the graphic line must before all else be related to the dynamics of movement leads Eisenstein to compare drawing to dance. "Drawing and dancing are branches of the same tree, of course; they are just two varieties of the same impulse."[19] He writes here not of any classical dance, for classical dance, which develops its movement through a "strict set of *pas*" that govern and determine its form with an "iron law," relies on figures or poses given in advance.[20] Eisenstein confesses his incompetence in classical dance, claiming his natural talent for a dance of an entirely different kind: "I still cannot manage a waltz, although I was able to pull off a foxtrot with great panache, albeit a jerky, black version in Harlem."[21] Unlike the classical dance, the jazz Eisenstein encounters during his passage through New York offers a lesson in free movement. Movement can be considered free if it is carried not by a reference to a set of figures meant to guarantee order and ultimately bring it to rest (re-pose) but by the regularity of its own rhythm. Just as the intuition of movement in jazz is freed from its subservience to poses, the graphic line can give itself to the tracing of its own dynamic rhythm, paying obedience only to itself and disregarding the figures that guided its movement in the classical conception of drawing. What the one who draws learns from the dancer is to support movement using nothing but the movement's own pulsation (the "there is," the *"es"* or "it" of movement) and to rely on rhythm "as a peg from which to hang any free, improvised movement."[22] "The free course of *all'improviso* [*sic*], flowing line of drawing or the free run of dance."[23] Only through improvisation does one become capable of lyrically individuating the line (as a trace of pure movement) independently of any *what* that this line might eventually come to figure.[24]

The artist takes the line for a dance. François Albera discusses Eisenstein's graphic work as sharing in the notion of drawing as a self-engendering process first suggested by Paul Klee, who, more soberly than Eisenstein, took his lines for walks. Rather than keeping an object in sight so as to circle it and produce its figure, the line abandons objective vision and allows the rhythm of the movement alone to determine its self-generating path. Eisenstein writes that, in the graphic line, he seeks only "the rhythm of expression," and that during the process of drawing he feels that "I do not see *how*—it flows. This is drawing not through vision, but through 'being.'" The drawing happens not through the perception of a figure but through an intuition of movement prior to it. "Without seeing, the hand begins to draw."[25] A certain basic blindness, or more actively a refusal of vision and its objectivity, characterizes Eisenstein's conception of the graphic line as the trace of pure, emancipated, free, and improvisatory movement.

Yet Albera importantly notes that in Eisenstein's case, the rhythmic line, the lyricism of emancipated movement, must be opposed to mere formlessness. The blind and intuitive freedom of movement, the improvisatory character of the line, emancipates us from the rigid rule of pregiven figures or poses but does not at the same time slip into a complete dissolution of form. According to Albera, who, following Georges Didi-Huberman, relates Eisenstein's practice to Georges Bataille's notion of the informal *(l'informe)*, one should see the Eisensteinian line perform the work of *deformation*. Crucially, deformation is distinct from formlessness: it "does not liquidate the form but allows for its overcoming."[26] It is, Albera explains, through deformation and not a plunge into sheer formlessness that Eisenstein liberates drawing from classicism and allows the line to register an independently improvised rhythm of movement.

The emancipation of movement from the static, substantive figure leads not to the annihilation of the figure but to a defiguration or disfiguration. For an example, one may look to Eisenstein's encounter with the distorted facial profiles on Mayan stone friezes at Las Monjas Palace in Uxmal, on Mexico's Yucatán Peninsula. "There is good reason to believe," he writes, "here in these blocks of stone, reflection is no longer stylized according to the true visibility of objects, but according to those horrible distortions of reality experienced by a brain in a drugged state."[27] A trancelike movement, blinded to the objective reality of vision and beyond the capacity of normal human imagination, does not lead to the abolition of the figure (the face, in this particular case). It must instead be observed in the horrific, disfiguring effects it produces on the surface of the figure. However, in formulating the description this way, it may still appear that a stable figure preexists the moment of disfiguration, when it is more correct to say that disfiguration comes first: if a figure might still be experienced in all of this, it will exist only as an effect, the consequence of disfiguration rather than its support. With the discovery of this new type of figure, accessible only through the work of disfiguration, we touch on something essential in Eisenstein's work.

While the modernist situation primarily sought to emancipate movement as pure figurability from the figure, Eisenstein's work nevertheless sought to raise, or rather to raise anew, the problem of the figure. It is no coincidence that in the formula with which we began our discussion of the intuition of movement ("first the movement, . . ."), Eisenstein makes a point not only to assert the primacy of movement but also to underline the *what,* or the figure, that comes in the wake of such absolutization of movement. Alongside its presentation of the lyricism of movement, his work suggests that it might not in fact be so easy to avoid the figure, to simply leave the figure behind and submerge oneself instead in the lyrical utopia of pure figurability, as though, right at the moment when the figure has been toppled by the intuition of movement and its blind lyricism, things turn again and there appears the necessity to nevertheless ask after the figure and inquire what the primacy of movement might look like from its perspective.

Something of the figure resists. Yet if Eisenstein asserts the need of the figure, it is not from a place of nostalgia for its classical serenity and its identity as a substantial form. Eisenstein's questioning of movement and the figure does not take place against the horizon of a stable world. Rather, Eisenstein seems to be aware that to replace the substantive figure with an exercise of the pure figurability of movement would cause us to miss the very dimension of movement itself. Were one simply to give up the figure in the name of the lyrical intuition of movement, what would be lost is not only the figure but the "purely protean thirst"[28] of lyrical movement as such. Without a trace left in the form of some kind of figure, the very force of movement that disrupts the primacy of the figure and emancipates us from its substantial weight itself vanishes into pure abstraction and emptiness.

Eisenstein can be seen as proceeding rather prudently, at once avoiding the annihilation of the figure and halting the consequences of the purely figureless suggested by the blind intuition of movement. We must accommodate the figure and engage the world of figures, he might say, while at the same time refusing to neglect the primacy of movement, the intuition of pure figurability or plasmaticity as an irreducible dimension in the production of artistic form. It is necessary to continue the production of figures, but we must insist in perfect confidence that artistic intuition always already unsettles and exceeds the experience of the figure. There is no question of returning to the figures of old. It is no longer possible to draw figures that would be self-possessed, stable, and secure. Eisenstein asks us to imagine a figure marked by a movement that exceeds the limits of figurative imagination, a certain *what* that has lost the stability or substantiality of its own contours in the wake of absolute movement—to think the figure as one thinks the elusive shape of a flame, a fiery figure, its coherence and unity indiscernible from dissolution and fragmentation, its legibility indistinguishable from a kind of fateful obscurity.[29] At stake, finally, is a figure that stages nothing but its own crisis—a *figure-in-crisis.*

The Figure-in-Crisis

PATHOS AND EX STASIS

If we at first interpreted Eisenstein's conception of drawing from the perspective of its lyricism, where the graphic line fulfilled its function as a trace of emancipated and absolutized movement, it now becomes necessary—but precisely so that we may hold on to the emancipated movement and prevent lyricism from turning into blinding abstraction—to approach the drawings and the question of movement from the other side: to assume the perspective of the figure, insofar as it is still possible to do so after its lyrical subversion. Which is to say, it becomes necessary to examine the question of movement as it relates to the figure we glimpse in moments of disfiguration and deformation, to analyze Eisenstein's graphic work (but also his conception of movement more broadly) as revolving around the figure-in-crisis.

Perhaps the most striking way Eisenstein presents a certain insistence of the figure in the wake of movement's emancipation is found in his suggestion that we might think the figure as a disguise or mask assumed by absolute movement. He explains this remarkable idea in relation to the figures in the Baroque paintings of Alessandro Magnasco, particularly Magnasco's paintings of monks that so significantly influenced the appearance of Ivan in *Ivan the Terrible.* In Magnasco's paintings, Eisenstein writes, we do not witness the

> movement of a figure caught by a brush, but a voluntary, affected movement of the brush, hastily disguising itself with the bones and flabby frames of ascetics with outstretched arms, bizarrely folded hands with long fingers.
>
> More often still it seems as though these ornate and fanciful flourishes are scattered among the monks' robes in order to warm up their own swirls and curlicues, loops and intersections, around the hearth.[30]

It is not, in other words, that the figure comes first and offers a limit in relation to which movement can be represented. We start with the movement, the dynamism of the painter's brush, which invents for itself the figure as a necessary disguise. It is as though in a moment of self-limitation, perhaps to ward off the threat of formlessness and empty abstraction, movement takes temporary refuge in the figure. The figure should be understood as a form of disguise that allows movement to appear in the picture. But not only does the figure make movement "visible" as something hidden that animates its agitated surface, it also reveals movement as something that might at any moment throw off the garb of its disguise and pass beyond the assumed figure, dissolve it, or go hunting for a new one.[31]

The drama of Eisenstein's drawings plays out in this tense and fundamentally unstable relation between movement as pure figurability (the "affected movement of the brush") and movement in figurative disguise (the figures of monks, for instance, who serve as masks that the "affected movement of the brush" assumes in order to make its appearance in Magnasco's painting). In this sense Eisenstein places himself in line not only with Magnasco but with an entire genealogy of painters with similar strategies of disguising the freedom of movement in the form of the figure: El Greco, Jacques Callot, Francisco Goya, Honoré Daumier. As he writes, in the works of these painters, the form of movement "makes a mockery of the theoretical nature of the bodies and clothing."[32]

Yet, while mocking it, movement requires the disguise of the figure in order to inscribe itself in the picture. As a form of disguise, the figure is continuously discarded or rearranged, repurposed and passed on. There is therefore something tentative about the figure, which must, even when seemingly finished, remain incomplete. This tentativeness or the constitutive incompleteness of the figure is thematized by Eisenstein in a late series of drawings, produced only two months before his death, entitled *Gifts* (Figure 1). In these drawings, the unclosed lines and loosely sketched contours of female bodies stretch and reach toward objects. They come almost to the point of touching, and yet the objects elude them. The gift is thus not associated with the act of possessing the object, nor is it tied to the figure's self-possession (because the figures in the series are clearly missing something; they abandon themselves to pursue the objects). Rather, the gift is on the side of movement, which takes on the fragile disguise of the figure and its precarious situation and thus makes itself visible. Movement is what prevents the figure from grasping its object; it is the reason the object remains suspended just out of reach. In place of the figure as completed movement or result, we see the *falling* of the object and the *reaching* of the female body. One gets a distinct feeling that Eisenstein meant to convey not one but two things with his choice of title for the series. Because of the primacy of movement, no thing is ever given, and it would be a mistake to think the figure as something that exercises possession—either of the object or of itself (self-possession). But also this: the figure, precisely because it is unable to possess, because it is itself possessed by movement, is what maintains the promise of the gift.

The figure does not guide movement but is produced by the movement's need to find a disguise or a mask, the need of the absolute movement to limit itself in the form of an appearance. It is as though, through a temporary appearance of the figure, the essentially blind and improvisatory movement stumbles into the domain of vision. Yet as soon as the disguise of the figure is assumed, the movement immediately seeks to overcome this moment of limitation that it posited for itself in the appearance of the figure. At no point

Figure 1. *Apple* from the series *Gifts,* December 19, 1947. Lead pencil on paper. Russian State Archive for Literature and Arts (RGALI), f. 1923, inv. 2, doc. 1573, s. 2.

in this process does the figure, the pretense to vision on the part of the movement's blindness, assume control over movement.

The primary relation the figure maintains to movement is that of *suffering.* A figure is above all what suffers movement. From the perspective of the figure, movement necessarily registers as violent *pathos.* In Eisenstein's drawings—but this holds for all of his work—pathos or the suffering of movement is the very element that makes possible the moment of vision disclosed in the figure. Nicole Brenez has something similar in mind when she writes that, in Eisenstein's case, "the capacity of a body to find itself affected by the violence of the world is affirmed as the condition of its representation."[33] There is no appearance of the figure, perhaps no appearance at all, that does not imply the reality of pathos or the violent suffering of movement. Before we too readily identify this suffering solely with forms of brutality, an aspect plainly evident in Eisenstein's films as well as in his graphic work, we should remember that, because pathos belongs first to movement in its absolute dimension, it must appear within the relative world of figures as entirely ambiguous. It is both pain and pleasure; rather, it is neither of the two and points to a beyond of pleasure. Movement enjoys itself in the guise of the figure—it even requires the guise of the figure for its own enjoyment—but from the perspective of the figure, this enjoyment necessarily appears as something incomprehensible, a strange and alien fate, pleasurable beyond pleasure and painful beyond pain.

Eisenstein finds the limit case of pathos—of movement beyond the pleasure principle, we could say—in the experience of *ecstasy (ex stasis),* because an ecstatic figure is in its most basic sense a figure seized by movement to the point of breaking, at which it divides and steps outside itself.[34] An ecstatic figure, which in Eisenstein appears in many guises—mysticism, religious rapture, sex, ritual forms of trance, the experience of the work of art, intoxication with narcotics—is a figure fully exposed to movement, quite literally exposed: thrown out of any pose or posture and pushed toward a transgression of its proper limit. "All my drawings are made almost in a trance . . . (from which I exit as broken, to use the vocabulary of Saint Theresa)."[35] Brenez points out that the Eisensteinian figure, characterized by the fact that it is fully exposed in movement, can be distinguished not only from the self-possessed classical figure but also from the "reserved, latent, undecided body in modern cinema."[36] The ecstatic figure is fully engaged, it appears as fully agitated and active—only it is not its own agency that exercises itself through it but the movement's. The maximum of activity and agitation coincides in the Eisensteinian figure with a fully passive and receptive disposition.

In the ecstatic figure—a figure beside itself, which, strictly speaking, is no longer a figure, but it also is not not one—one most fully sees the approach of absolute movement crafting for itself the temporary refuge of a mask.

Eisenstein therefore seems to believe—and this he imports from his study of religious ecstasy, despite the fact that he claims for himself the position of an atheist—that the transgression of the figure's limit found in ecstatic experience coincides with the self-limitation of absolute movement, which means that the moment in which a figure breaks and steps outside itself is also the moment in which it touches movement in movement's absolute dimension. Through this coincidence, the ecstatic disfiguration of the figure—the ecstatic loss of any figurative measure in the figure-in-crisis—provides a "measure" of absolute movement. Does Eisenstein not in this sense remain a humanist? His view is certainly not classical, but does it not belong to an essentially ecstatic, Christological humanism? Its claim, namely, seems to be that there occurs a self-limitation of the absolute and its violence that coincides with the transgression of the finite limit of the figure. Does not the suffering and the ecstatic seizure of the figure in some sense humanize the absolute, improvisatory inhumanity of movement? And is not the suffering of movement, by being made "non-indifferent" in the invention of the figure's ecstatic limit, this way also made meaningful?

Indeed, Eisenstein, whose graphic and filmic works proliferate a series of Christ figures and crucifixion scenes, finds the emblem of ecstasy in the figure of the crucified (Figure 2). In Eisenstein's Crucified, the ecstatic meeting between the figure and movement scrambles the body's anatomical coordinates (the limbs, for instance, become difficult to categorize; the head doubles). The body of the ecstatic figure is not anatomically correct: "enjoyment appears less as an expression of human psychology than it does as an effect of an anatomical explosion."[37] It is also rather difficult to tell whether we are encountering a moment of death (decapitation?) or a moment of excessive vitality (birth?). The ecstatic figure inscribes on the human body, demarcated by black lines, the large X and the stigmata of inhuman movement formally set apart from the body by the use of a different color, red. A figure of the crucified—yet made strange, because it does not offer us the suffering human face but rather a pair of masks, hovering above and below the body, with which Eisenstein perhaps wishes to stress that we are not to find in his figure the mysterious internal drama of humanity but humanity precisely as a mask, as a necessary disguise of something that remains inhuman. We may go on with our list of the different elements that the ecstatic figure of the crucified not so much reconciles or comprehends as simply exposes in their division. There is the corporeal contour and the letters (not so much words made flesh as words *and* flesh), the tracing of the line and writing, which suggest that we are to comprehend this ecstatic figure as an interaction between the imaginary unity of the body and the symbolic play of marks and traces, of doubling, of the game of filled and empty space, which involves the binaries of inside and outside, absence and presence, that hollow out and displace the body's

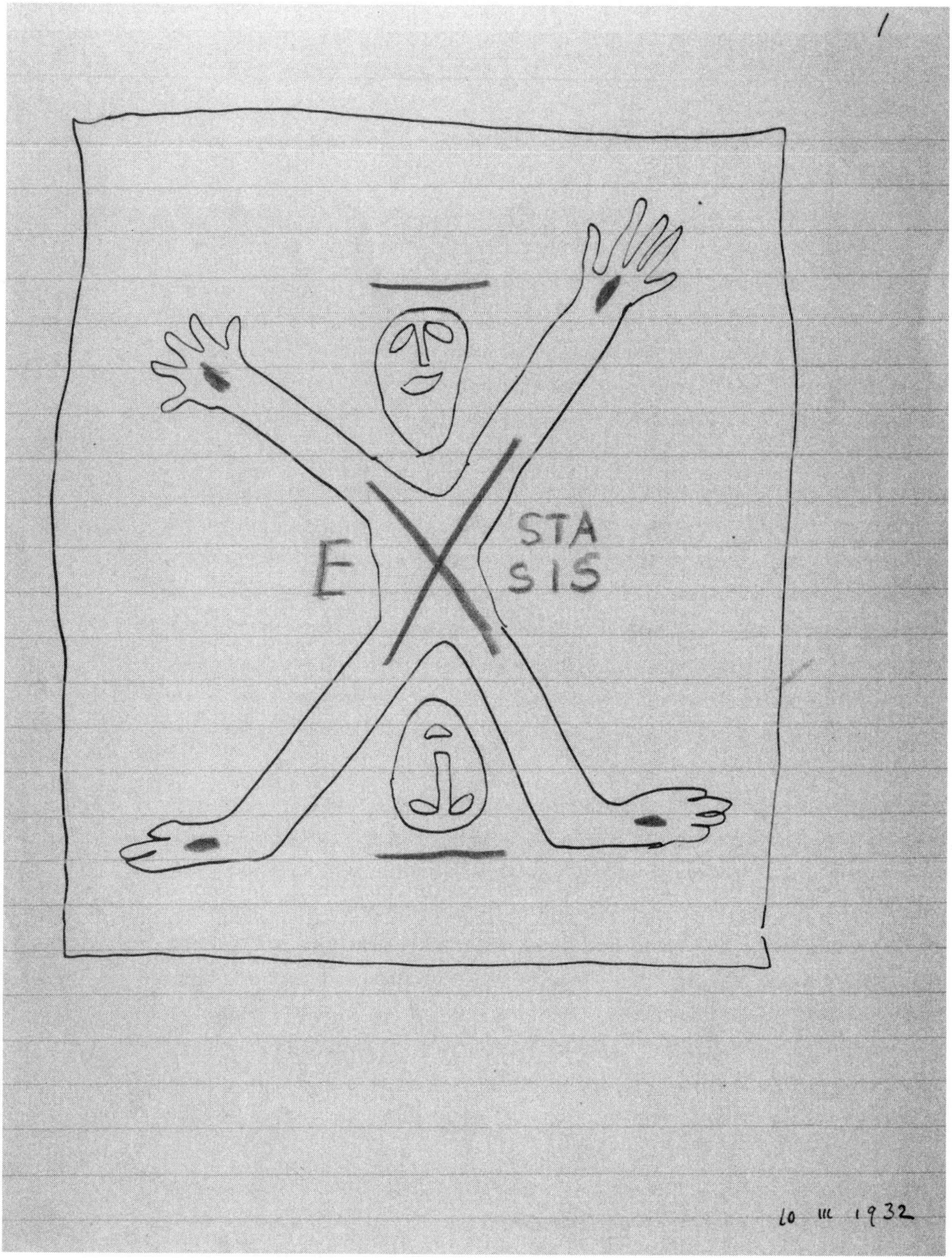

Figure 2. *Ex Stasis,* March 10, 1932. Ink and color pencil on paper. RGALI, 1923-2-1304-1.

imaginary unity. This is a figure fully beside itself but that, in this transgression of its proper limit, attempts to find the measure of absolute movement.

GROUNDLESSNESS

Vicente Sánchez-Biosca has suggested that, when it comes to the pathetic and ecstatic figure in Eisenstein's work, the question of ideological distinctions becomes of secondary importance because "a single destructive pulsion pervades everything. Violence . . . is a given."[38] Yet one may also observe how not all bodies are equally exposed to the suffering and ecstasies of movement in Eisenstein's world, which would mean that, for him, not all bodies bear equal relation to the appearance of the figure and that some distinctions do matter. Better than to describe Eisensteinian figures as though they somehow place bodies outside of ideological signification would be to say with Nicole Brenez that what the Eisensteinian figure seeks is to install a body where no body existed before, or perhaps even where there can be no body—where a body can have no being.[39] The Eisensteinian figure would in this sense be related to a body that is impossible to place and that for this reason may be considered an impossible body. It is after all not an uncommon experience while watching Eisenstein's films or looking at his drawings to become perplexed over the question of how exactly it is that this body we are seeing may be considered a body—how exactly it may be said to occupy its proper dimensions or its place—and to find the entire exercise of corporeality in Eisenstein's work rather disquieting. "We don't know what a body can do." To this famous slogan of Spinoza's Eisenstein might be tempted to add, "We have no idea in what impossible place a body might pop up and unsettle us."

Now, to describe the body installed by the Eisensteinian figure as impossible certainly means that the figure-in-crisis makes visible a body that does not fit easily within the preexisting (ideological) determinations of corporeality and its place in the world, but it does not mean that the suffering and the ecstasies of bodies that belong to the Eisensteinian figure find a place outside of ideology altogether. If there is a trait shared by all the figures in Eisenstein's work, it is this experience of making bodies escape their place without at the same time providing a new place where they could come to rest.

An example is the drawing *Sebastian* (Figure 3), one of a series of Eisenstein's Mexican Sebastians, which makes the body of the Mexican peon escape in the direction of the Christian martyr, yet without exactly arriving there because the drawing has simultaneously made the martyr's body approach the place of the peon facing a firing squad. "Sebastian" is thus a name for this double movement disguising itself in the torsions of the figure, which produces the effect of an impossible body, a body where there shouldn't be one, as though suspended between the two worlds we are typically asked to

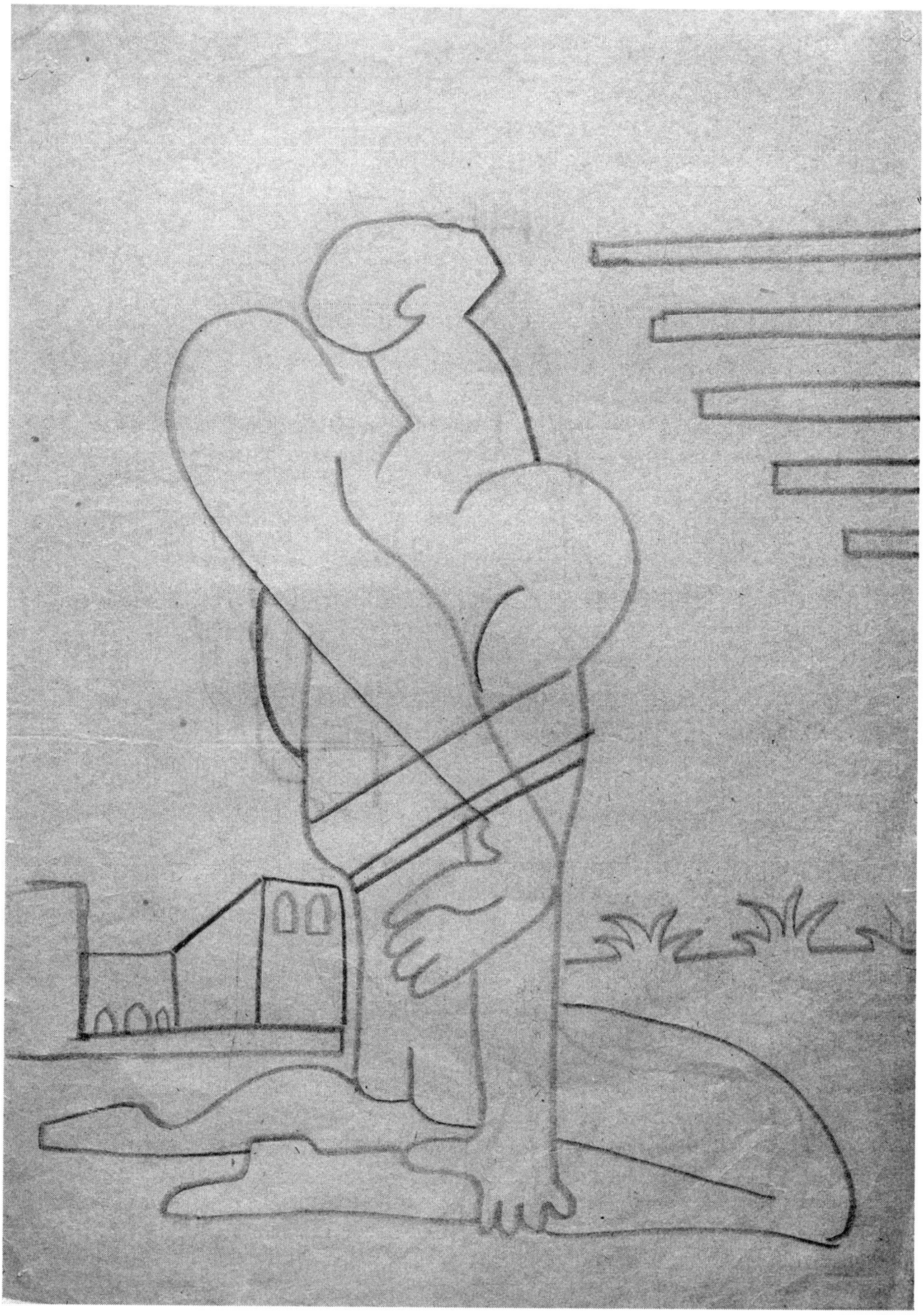

Figure 3. *Sebastian,* 1931. Lead pencil on paper. RGALI, 1923-2-1291-1.

keep separate: the world of the peasant and the world of a saintly martyr, the body of everyday labor and the body of faith, the physical body of common suffering and the sublime body transfigured into a religious symbol. All of which means that the disfigurations of the figure refer the body to an impossible space that exists only in the fiction of the drawing and in which one cannot discern between the profane and the sacred. An impossible space: especially so if one assumes that the very constitution of space and of spatial experience depends on an originary division that separates and thus makes discernible the sacred and the profane.

The absence of a proper placement of bodies that accompanies the appearance of the Eisensteinian figure—again, it is not that bodies do not have a place: they have it precisely where there should not be a body—is explicitly thematized by Eisenstein when he discusses the fact that his figures seem always to float in the "womb" or "'hover' in space; that is, the atavism in them belongs to the period before being set upon solid ground."[40] His perhaps most famous series of drawings, *The Death of King Duncan* (Figures 4, 5, and 6), explicitly plays with the absence of a proper place because it stages in more than 120 drawings (127, to be exact) the scene that in Shakespeare's *Macbeth* occurs offstage, a place that becomes radically dislocated from the space of dramatic action. Eisenstein's drawings of the murder of King Duncan imagine in a remarkable series of variations a scene that has no proper place and cannot be integrated into the drama to which it nevertheless belongs by haunting the events taking place onstage.

At a purely formal level, the *Duncan* drawings attest to Eisenstein's belief that his graphic work achieved the strongest effect particularly in those cases in which the line of pure movement was "used for drawing especially sensual relationships between human figures, usually in especially complicated and random situations!"[41] The series offers a remarkable exercise in the staging of the figure-in-crisis. The figure appears stretched and out of shape due to the violence of the action. Some of its parts expand to monstrous dimensions, while some are diminished. The figures devour, bite, suck each other, lie on top of each other in arrangements that tend toward a kind of angularity or geometrical regularity. They nest in each other. The king is stabbed, pierced by knives, left bleeding as his beard rises up into a scream. A stake is driven into Duncan's chest and used by Lady Macbeth as a pole upon which to perform an acrobatic dance. A cross is stuck from above into the eye of the reeling king. Duncan is decapitated and castrated, hung upside down, as the parts that have been cut from his body or ripped from inside of him circulate between Macbeth and Lady Macbeth. The murderers bathe in pools of blood that gush from the open neck of the decapitated king. They wipe themselves dry with the king's beard as though it were a towel, before they lie down and

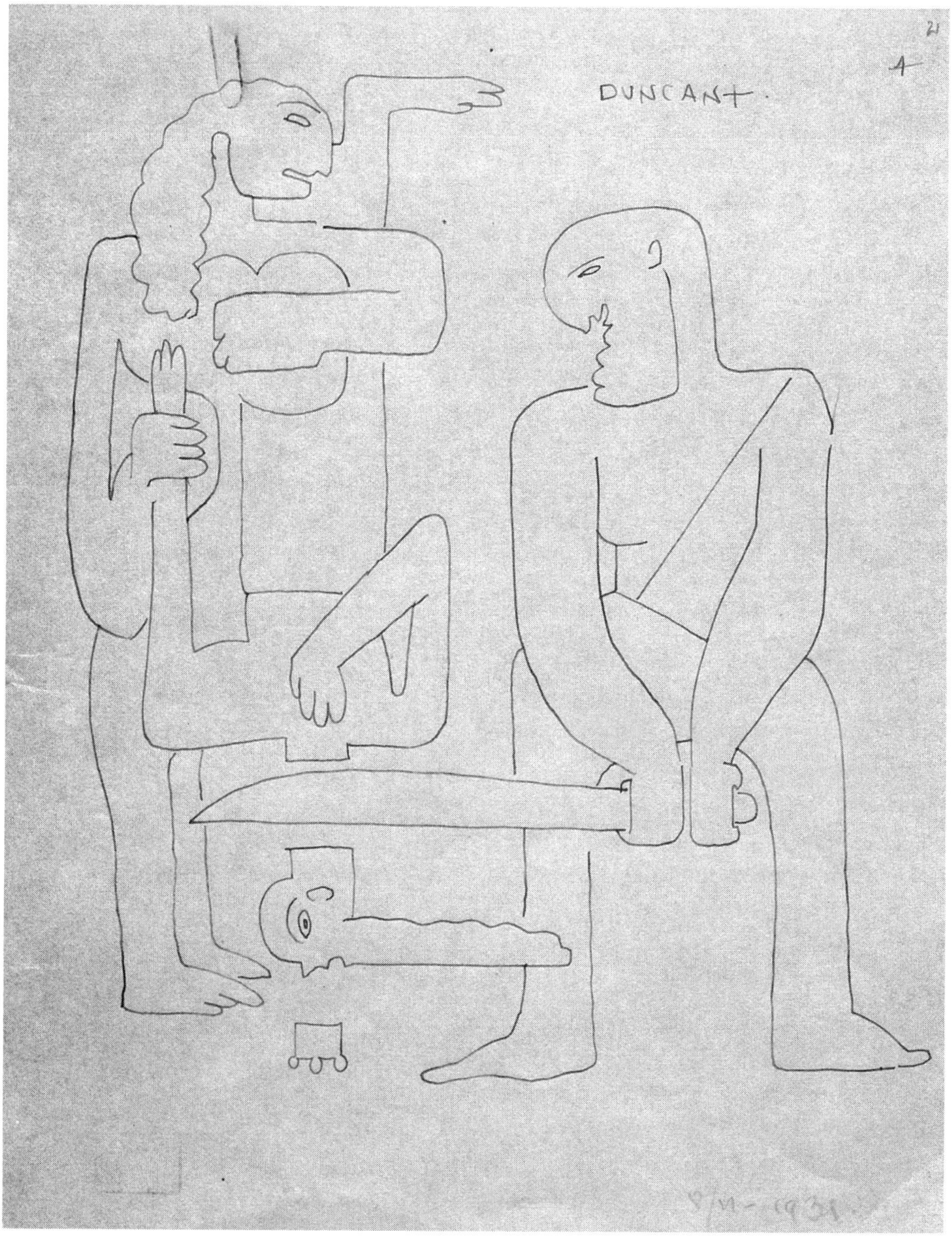

Figure 4. From the series *The Death of King Duncan,* June 6–8, 1931. Ink on paper. RGALI, 1923-2-1222-2.

Figure 5. From the series *The Death of King Duncan,* June 6–8, 1931. Ink on paper. RGALI 1923-2-1222-3.

begin their lovemaking during which the dead king's body serves as a bed or simply an inert piece complementary to the lovers' sexual play.

The series offers a remarkable phenomenology of oedipal cruelty in all its ambiguity.[42] For our purposes, however, *Duncan* serves as an illustration of the absence of proper placement and the evacuation of any figurative background surrounding the Eisensteinian figure. We must understand this absence as a necessary consequence of what was said earlier regarding the relationship of movement and the figure in Eisenstein's conception. For if the figure is produced out of a self-limitation of absolute movement, as a disguise taken on by movement that in itself is not figurative, then it is also the case that the figure can no longer be primarily related to its figurative environment and must therefore lose its link to the relative dimensions of the figurative space it would otherwise inhabit (left–right, up–down, foreground–background). There is no figurative space that could be given in advance and in which the pathetic and ecstatic entanglement of the figure-in-crisis could find its proper place, because it is precisely the improvisatory movement of the "line that creates its own path and defines its own spatial parameters."[43] A characteristic shared by Eisenstein's drawings and his films is that in both, the predisposition toward a figure-in-crisis, a figure that emerges only through the disfiguration performed by the nonfigurative movement, cuts bodies and objects out of their environment, disturbs their spatial coherence in order to displace and "deanecdotalize" them and re-place them within a different dimension.

Insofar as the figure may only be localized or placed in relation to the absolute movement of the line, it is essentially *groundless.* The dimension of the groundlessness of the figure is as crucial for our understanding of its relationship to movement in Eisenstein's work as are pathos and ecstasy. In the passionate suffering of movement, the figure does not merely break, go beyond its limit, and ecstatically jump beside itself. Its crisis also has to do with the fact that the figure loses its ground, the proper—that is to say, figurative—dimensions of its space.

The experience of pathos and ecstasy, which one may have initially read as a sign of a kind of positive charging of the figure by movement, must now be related to this essential negativity at work in the experience of the figure. In other words, if we miss the negative element of groundlessness, we may be convinced that a certain recovery or recomposition of the figure remains possible, that even in the midst of the figure's ecstatic transgression, the figurative space itself may have somehow remained unaffected and might thus once again provide a proper place for the figure. But this is not the case.

We have previously identified a certain humanizing (Christological) tendency in Eisenstein's conception of the figure-in-crisis, which consisted in the belief that the pathetic and ecstatic transgression of the figure's limit coincides

Figure 6. From the series *The Death of King Duncan,* June 16, 1931. Ink on paper. RGALI, 1923-2-1229-4.

with the self-limitation of absolute movement and can thus provide the inhumanity of the latter with its human measure or meaning. Now this suggestion must be qualified, and it must be said that at certain moments in his work with the figure, there nevertheless appears something different in Eisenstein's thought, which we will attempt to describe in the following way: Eisenstein associates the dimension of groundlessness, the abyssal background of the figure, with despair, delirium, and terror. These affects signal an anxious realization that, while the disfigurations of pathos and the ecstatic transgressions of the figure might indeed establish some kind of human measure for the inhuman violence of the movement of the world, there may at the same time be no measure, no clear limit, to suffering and ecstasy in themselves. We might be humanists and believe that, through the disfiguring of the figure, we impose a human measure on the inhuman; but we also cannot be humanists, because we know that there is nothing human in this act itself, that our suffering and our ecstatic transgressions, by which we give meaning to inhuman movements, happen against an absent ground, the absence of any proper human measure.

In the anxious groundlessness of his drawings, Eisenstein thinks the fact that the figure's humanization of inhuman movement, which takes the shape of the pathos and ecstasy of the figure-in-crisis, can itself not belong to the figurative or human space and remains constitutively out of reach for any humanizing operation as such. The decision to provide a figure (however distorted) for the nonfigurative movement can itself never be figured, and this impossibility must be inscribed as an absence, the nothingness of the background in the picture. The act of humanizing the inhuman violence of movement must itself be understood as a form of violence.

THE COMEDY OF *NICHTS*

For the reason that they explicitly bring out this abyssal dimension of the Eisensteinian figure, the most important drawings in the entirety of Eisenstein's graphic work are those that turn the anxiety-inducing absence of the ground into a figurative element within the picture. In the series *Nichts* (Nothing) from 1937—from the height of Stalin's Great Terror and Eisenstein's personal crisis precipitated by the banning of *Bezhin Lug*—it is groundlessness and negativity themselves that are drawn into the picture in the form of a simple circle, to which the figures of elastic and humanoid bodies also present in the picture are made to relate in a multiplicity of attitudes. In one of the drawings *(Ich schaue ins Nichts),* a figure is seen bending down and peering into the circle, across which the word "Nichts" is inscribed, while below it on the left another figure turns away, kneeling and covering its head, and on the right two headless figures tie themselves into a knot. In other drawings from the series *Nichts,* we see figures merging with the circle *(Wir entstehen im Nichts—Wir vergehen im Nichts),* falling out of the circle or dancing ecstatically below it *(Und Ganz und gar Nichts . . .),* passing it between each other *(Und immer Nichts)* or being trapped by it *(Es verrecke das blöde Nichts!),* and raising it up and drinking from it as from an enormous wine decanter *(Ich trinke das Nichts)*—none of which gives us any sense of things being handled adequately.[44]

The drawings of *Nichts,* in which the circle identified with nothingness becomes the central element, can be read as an attempt to make appear the negated ground of the figure and to thus allow this essential groundlessness, which characterizes Eisenstein's graphic work as a whole, to itself become reflected in the picture. The impossibility of placing the figure within a human, figurative space becomes, as though against all odds, inscribed within the figurative world itself. The drawings can, in other words, be read as literalizing the figure's essential groundlessness. They present an impossible situation, in which the figures are made to interact with the very thing that constitutively escapes them, their absent ground, as though the latter were itself simply one figurative element among others.

According to Eisenstein, such literalization is always a comic procedure: "Literalization—literalization of metaphors or anything else—as a 'technique of the comic.' Wonderful!"[45] The drawings of *Nichts* in this sense present us with the comedy of the figure and the nothingness of its ground. Pathos and ecstasy might be described as tending toward the tragic. They realize the approach of absolute movement through the disfiguration or the transgression of the finite limit of the figure. And there is undoubtedly something sublime in the pathetic and ecstatic figure as it finds itself broken, its finitude suddenly put into crisis (disfigured) by the force of seemingly infinite movement. The strategy of the drawings in *Nichts,* however, does something else. It does not offer us a transgression of the figure's finitude toward the sublime encounter with absolute movement but instead proposes to draw something infinite and absolute (nothingness) in the form of a finite figure (the circle). The comic effect of *Nichts,* perhaps the most devastating series among all of Eisenstein's drawings, stems from the fact that the element of groundlessness (nothingness, the abyss), which in principle should not be able to find a figurative embodiment, is nevertheless literally figured here, presented as something rather easily achieved by the drawing.

It is therefore possible to oppose in Eisenstein two modes of thinking the relationship between absolute, emancipated movement and the figure, two ways of thinking the figure-in-crisis: on one hand, a tragic humanism that operates through the disfiguration of finite figures by absolute movement; on the other, the series *Nichts* counters the tragedy of the figure with a comic inhumanism that figures the groundlessness of movement literally, within the

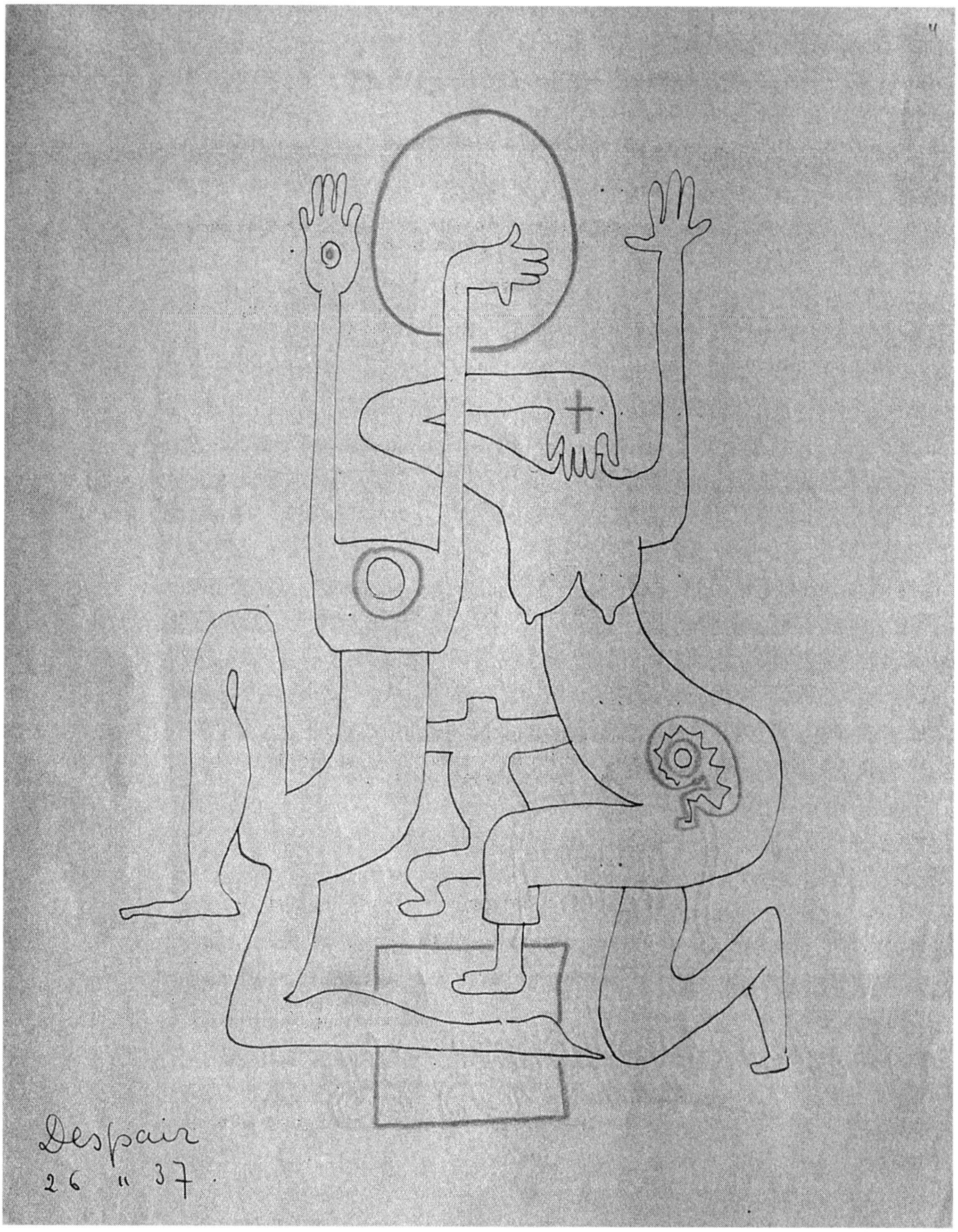

Figure 7. *Despair,* February 26, 1937. Ink and color pencil on paper. RGALI, 1923-2-1372-4.

figurative space of the drawing. It is striking to note that Eisenstein emphasizes the comic side precisely in the moment of the most acute political and personal crisis, when he attempts to depict phenomena of a truly horrifying nature—as though the tragedy of the figure (the humanism of pathos and ecstasy) would not suffice and only the comedy and literalism of nothingness could do justice to a desperately "tragic" situation (Figure 7).

Perceiving the Figure, Reading the Gesture (the Dialectic)

Let us sum up the findings of our brief excursion into the theory of Eisenstein's drawing. Eisenstein sees artistic intuition as intimately related to the emancipation of movement from *what* moves, the individuation of movement for itself, which amounts to an absolutization of movement. What matters is not the substantiality of figures but bringing to the surface the experience of figurability as such, movement as the capacity for any-figure-whatever. This is the element of lyricism, of musicality, in Eisenstein's thinking of movement. Yet the lyrical aspect alone does not describe what Eisenstein has to say about movement. A lyrical immersion in movement (as pure figurability or plasmaticity), simply opposed to *what* moves (the plastic figure), leads by itself only to formlessness and a kind of blindness. It is thus necessary to posit along with emancipated movement a certain resistance of the figure. The figure can, however, no longer be the substantial and stable figure of old but must instead become a new kind of figure, a figure-in-crisis, which emerges only through the work of disfiguration. Eisenstein's claim is that such a figure-in-crisis gives us access to the artistic experience of movement; it lets us "see" movement—or perhaps it would be better to say that it allows us to see what the blind movement itself sees—by allowing us to avoid both the absence of movement (classical, static figures) and its abstraction and emptiness (found in cases when a certain lyrical purity of movement is simply opposed to everything figurative). If there is an Eisensteinian invention in the thinking of movement, it is this: the absoluteness of movement, its nonfigurative dimension, is best thought from the perspective of the figure-in-crisis. What Eisenstein's drawings have helped us do is to describe this figure-in-crisis and to isolate three of its crucial aspects: pathos, ecstasy, and groundlessness. For Eisenstein, we sense the approach of absolute movement in the suffering of the figure (pathos), in the transgression of the figure's proper limit (ecstasy), and in the placing of the figure in relation to the topology of an impossible place (groundlessness). For Eisenstein, the path of movement leads from lyricism through the tragedy of the figure (pathos and ecstasy) and the comedy of the figure's essential groundlessness.

Now, there exists a term that unites the three aspects of the Eisensteinian figure. This term is *gesture*. The figure in Eisenstein is essentially gestural.

What, namely, is gesture if not the appearance of a movement that comes from outside and that we therefore suffer much more than produce ourselves? When we gesture, we are not simply acting but rather acting by becoming impassioned by movement that does not belong to us and that we are not able to contain. It is the movement of the world that disguises itself in our gestures rather than us acting out this or that movement. It is also clear that when we are seized by a gesture, the body is taken beyond its proper limit. To gesture is to become ecstatic, and perhaps the best way to distinguish simple action from a gesture is to ask whether being seized by movement has in some way ex-posed us, made us suddenly stand beside ourselves. If a performance of movement has indeed placed us beside ourselves, then we might assume that we have participated in the production of a gesture. And finally, if gesture means being seized by a movement that does not come from inside us but breaks our limit and transposes us outside of ourselves (the tragic aspect of gesture), then we can also say that the performance of a gesture necessarily involves a certain loss of ground. In gesture, we experience our body as groundless—and quite literally so, because any "essence," any meaning or signification a gesture realizes, appears only if the body at the same time figures something noncorporeal. To gesture is not so much to make a body vanish as it is to realize a body in relation to a dimension that constitutively escapes it (meaning, signification) and to therefore produce a body where it has no business being (the gesture's comic side).

Yuri Tsivian has stated that, "according to Eisenstein's theory, gesture is the prototype of all means of expressiveness that only human culture has at its disposal. According to this theory of a gradual development in stages, at the beginning was not the word but movement; after movement, as the movement's trace, emerged linear drawing; and only after that, as a verbal cast of movement, the art of rhetoric and literature."[46] Gesture, to which drawing seems to relate more intimately than other forms, is at the basis not only of dramatic and plastic arts but of verbal and musical creation as well. What the notion of gesture clarifies about the nature of expressivity is the fact that expression cannot be considered an externalization, a pressing outward, of something that previously existed within the figure. Gestural expressivity has nothing to do with the manifestation of interiority. On the contrary, expressivity only appears when something is seized and disfigured by the approach of movement, that is, when movement voids the content of *what* moves by pushing the latter to its limit and cutting it from its proper context. Expression, in this gestural sense, means putting something into crisis. Expressivity is not the outward appearance of an internal impulse but rather a dispossession of interiority by the appearance of an alien impulse of movement (Figure 8). Conversely, any turn toward interiority is precisely a result of a loss of capacity for gesture, as Giorgio Agamben, for instance, has shown in his

Figure 8. From the series *Gedanken zur Musik* (Musical ideas), April 12, 1938.
Ink and color pencil on paper. RGALI, 1923-2-1380-3.

remarkable short essay on gesture and cinema. According to Agamben, when the bourgeoisie lost its gestures at the end of the nineteenth century, this unsettled social class had no other way but to surrender to interiority and psychology, as a consequence.[47]

The dimension of gesture introduces a doubling or division into Eisenstein's concept of movement. On one hand, gesture requires the visibility and the perception of a figure that supports the performance of the gesture. On the other hand, however, it is also necessary that the figure disappear and that the performance of movement exceed mere perception if this movement were to be called gestural. There is always something more to gesture than the mere visibility of a figure's movement—a fact that finds confirmation in our feeling that a figure becomes "visible" in an entirely new way when it is seized by the performance of a gesture. We will clarify this distinction between the visible movement of a figure and gestural movement with the help of Vilém Flusser, who, in his definition of gesture and gesturality, relies on a similar division. The following passage from the opening of Flusser's book *Gestures* is worth quoting at length:

> Surely all movements of the body can in principle be explained by spelling out their causes. But for some movements, such an explanation is unsatisfactory. . . . Here, then, is the definition I suggest: "a gesture is a movement of the body or of a tool connected to the body for which there is no satisfactory causal explanation." And I define *satisfactory* as that point in a discourse after which any further discussion is superfluous.
>
> This definition should suggest that the discourse of gestures cannot end with causal explanations, because such explanations do not account for the specificity of gestures. Of course, causal ("scientific," in the strong sense of the word) explanations are needed to understand gestures, but they don't produce such understanding. To understand gestures, these specific physical movements that we perform and that we observe around us, causal explanations are not enough. Gestures have to be properly interpreted, too. If someone points to a book with his finger, we could know all the possible causes and still not understand the gesture. To understand it, one must know its "significance." That is exactly what we do continually, very quickly and effectively. We "read" gesture, from the slightest movement of facial muscles to the most powerful movements of masses of bodies called "revolutions." I don't know how we do it. . . . We need a theory of the interpretation of gestures.[48]

Flusser distinguishes two kinds of movement. On one hand, there is movement that maintains a body as visible within a causal series. One perceives a movement or an action of the body when one is able to follow it and relate it to a sequence of causes. On the other hand, there are movements characterized by the fact that they appear uncaused, as though a product of grace. Flusser calls such movements or actions *gestures.* The important point Flusser makes is that, because this second type of movement cannot be assigned a cause, it is not enough simply to perceive it. Gesture does not belong to the visible regime of causes. It must on the contrary be read, interpreted. We can say that there exists a *physics of the body,* of the body's movements and actions, that requires us to see, but that there exists also a *metaphysics of gesture,* which refers a body's movement or action to something invisible, and which must therefore be read and interpreted. The Eisensteinian figure finds itself at the intersection between these two dimensions.

Eisenstein conceives of the two types of movement Flusser identifies (visible, causal, perceivable versus gestural, uncaused, legible) as dialectically related, forming a unity of opposites or an internal division within the concept of movement itself. According to Eisenstein, who speaks of the "readable-perceptible form"[49] of a work of art, movement must somehow be taken as both: an "indivisible duality" of visible or perceivable movement, which places the figure in a causal series, and the legible or interpretable movement, which interrupts the chain of visibility and strikes the figure with the grace of a gesture. Conceiving the relationship dialectically means that a gesture arrives *through* the perception of the figure without ever becoming identical to this perception or reducible to the figure's visibility. To put it in Flusser's terms, the event of uncaused and free gestural movement inscribes itself in the mundane causal texture of the world of visible bodies and their actions. But we must also add that with the gesture's disruption (disfiguration) of the causal coherence of things, there emerges a new "visibility" of the (figurative) world, a new kind of seeing that pushes perception to its limit.

This is therefore a way to describe the elementary dialectic of Eisensteinian movement: a gesture that must be read *through and apart from* the visible or perceivable movement of the figure.[50] In this minimal sense, to think and work dialectically means to read, interpret, and establish the significance of free—uncaused—movement that "speaks" through and apart from the visible, perceivable, causally enchained movement that governs the world of figures. The dialectic is the approach according to which a free movement—which Eisenstein will alternately describe as thought, affect, or sensation—finds its bearings, its "thoroughness" and its "apartness," in relation to what for it is essentially a foreign figurative world:

> Ambiguous in its definition, variable in use, figuration appears in Eisenstein's theoretical economy mainly as a pole of repulsion, with which representation is deeply occupied to the extent that it designates a condition

> or a necessary substratum so that creation can conceive of itself as dialectical.[51]

The dialectic is that strange species of nonfigurative thought that requires the figure as a sort of unavoidable obstacle, without which the thought would itself become arrested on the path of its becoming.

Before moving on, let us add a note on another aspect of gesture identified in the passage from Flusser quoted earlier. There is something properly Eisensteinian in Flusser's description of the variable scales of gestural movement that can be read, as Flusser says, in the close-ups of faces or in the masses seized by a revolution. These are precisely the limits within which Eisenstein developed the scale of his gestural thinking. It is well known, for instance, that his conception of the *close-up* presents the face not only as something that increases the visibility of figures but as an operation that must disturb the world of visible causes and introduce into it a new quality, which is the becoming-expressive, becoming-gestural, of the face. For this reason, Eisenstein refuses the term *close-up,* a term that suggests merely getting closer to the object but in no way disturbing the regime of its visibility, and replaces it with *enlargement shot (krupnyi plan),* because he thinks that this other term better captures the discontinuity (the qualitative modification) introduced into the world of visible figures by the operation of the filmmaker.[52] We typically assume that the close-up merely adds something—some additional information—to the world already made visible by the film, when in fact its task is precisely the opposite: to withdraw something from the causal chain of our perception and introduce into it an irreducible element of obscurity, to perturb the visible texture of the world by inserting into it the effect of a mask, which then allows for the expressive and gestural appearance of the face.

At the other extreme of the gestural scale suggested by Flusser, we must mention Eisenstein's *filming of the masses,* which, especially in his early films, replaces the individual characters of bourgeois psychological realism as well as the individual heroes who might have been inherited from the epic tradition. Masses in rebellion, masses in flight, masses in battle, masses in carnivalesque celebration: it does not seem too controversial to suggest that what draws Eisenstein to the masses is not simply their figurative value, which allows us to recognize in them a crucial link in the visibility of historical causes that led to the accomplishment of the revolutionary situation. What makes the masses attractive—but also what makes them revolutionary in Eisenstein's works—is the fact that they are always seized by a gestural transformation of their visible movement. It is not so much that the masses possess movement as that a movement continuously enacts a sort of gestural dispossession of the masses.

Figure 9. Anonymous (attributed to Ma Fen), *The Hundred Geese,* circa 1250–300. Detail. Ink on paper, 17¹¹/₁₆ × 227¹⁵/₁₆ in. (45 × 579 cm); painting, 13³/₄ × 182¹¹/₁₆ in. (35 × 464 cm). Honolulu Museum of Art.

Figure 10. Photochronography of a gull (ten images per second), in Étienne-Jules Marey, *Physiologie du movement: le vol des oiseaux* (Paris: G. Masson, 1890), 145.

Movement, in Detail: From Kinematography to Cinema

How does the elementary Eisensteinian dialectic of gestural and visible movement at which we have arrived relate to cinema and the problem of cinematic movement? We will throw some light on this question with the help of another set of geese that one finds in Eisenstein's writing. This second set of geese comes from a Chinese scroll painting, produced sometime between 1250 and 1300 and attributed to the artist Ma Fen (Figure 9). Eisenstein analyzes the scroll, titled simply *The Hundred Geese,* in his essay "El Greco and Cinema."

Painted in ink, the scroll unfolds an image of a hundred geese engaged in various activities: flying in several directions, diving into and emerging from water, catching fish, nesting, and so on. The geese seem carefully individuated, but it is impossible for us not to see at least certain sections of the scroll as prefiguring Étienne-Jules Marey's chronophotographic records of the "animal mechanism" (Figure 10) or Edward Muybridge's animal locomotion studies, and to therefore assume that what the scroll describes could also be read as a continuous act of flight of a single goose, analytically separated by the painter into a series of immobile instants, which our eye is able to recompose into an impression of a continuous block of movement as it travels across the misty marsh encompassing the scene.

We can indeed see how Eisenstein is able to establish Ma Fen's *The Hundred Geese* as a place for the exploration of the nature of cinematic movement. His analysis treats the question of movement in cinema by displacing it into the domain of painting—a displacement that is further amplified by both the historical and geographical distance that separates Eisenstein from his example. Following the main points of Eisenstein's rather brief analysis of the scroll, which is embedded as an episode in a text dedicated to that great "filmmaker" El Greco, will allow us to see how the dialectic of gestural (readable) movement and the visible (perceivable) movement of the figure might be related to Eisenstein's thinking of the movement in cinema. More precisely, the example allows us to see how the dialectical division in Eisenstein's conception of movement, the division between gestural and figurative movement, can be mapped onto a distinction that is crucial for his thought, namely, the distinction between *kinematographic* reproduction of movement and what might be called the properly *cinematic* movement.

As he so often does when analyzing works of art, Eisenstein isolates from Ma Fen's scroll its most dramatic moment, which presents a sudden volte-face in what the picture represents as the flying movement of the geese. He picks what he considers to be the genuinely expressive part of the painting, the most artistically effective one, with an interest to analyze and understand its effectiveness. Eisenstein provides his own schematic and analytically annotated drawing of the section in question (Figure 11) and begins to describe its effect in the following way:

> Here is presented with utmost delicacy the turn of a flying bird, resolved by the three successive phases of a movement attributed to three independently flying birds. Between I and II, which are absolutely identical, the difference lies only in the wings, which pass from position (a) to position (b). We read this as the movement of the wings preparing for the turn.
>
> Between II and III, the turn of the entire bird is accomplished. Only the head remains identical (and it remains identical for all three birds). The body is abruptly thrown over to the other side, while the head remains immobile. With this, the body assumes a position that is the reverse image of I.[53]

Eisenstein is describing in the passage, which we have interrupted mid-paragraph, an operation that closely resembles the basic kinematographic process of analysis and synthesis of movement. The continuous movement of the

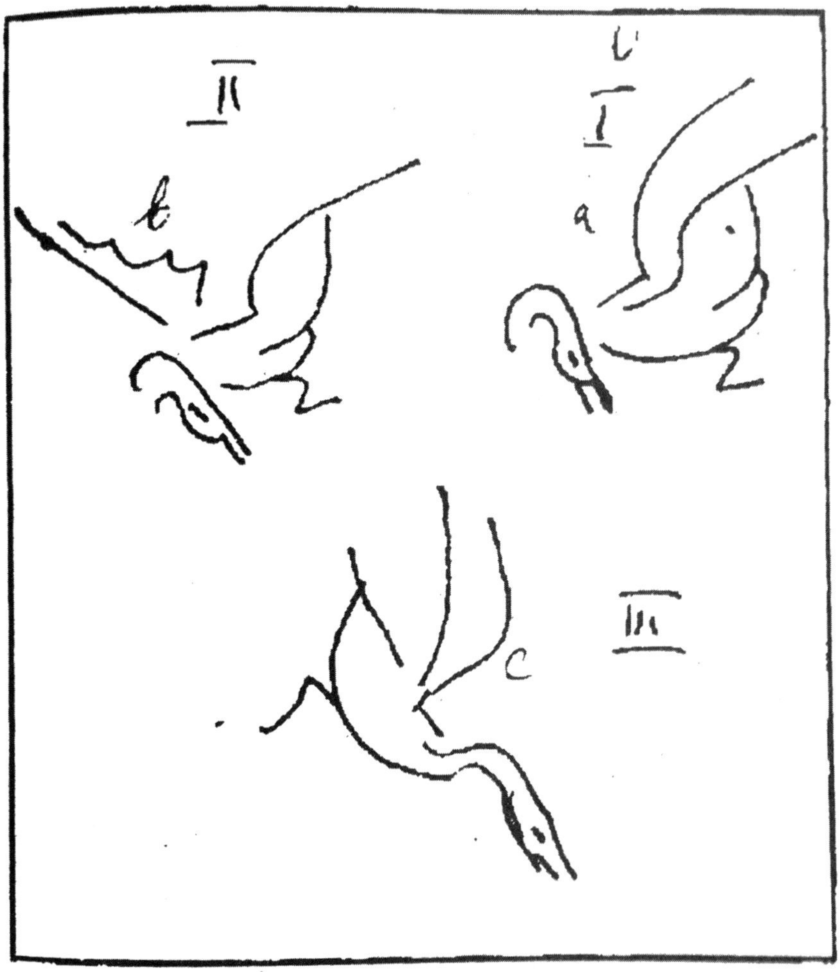

Figure 11. Eisenstein's drawing of the detail of the turn from *The Hundred Geese.* The drawing appears in the edition of Eisenstein's essay "El' Greko i kino" (El Greco and cinema), published in Sergei Eisenstein, *Montazh,* edited by Naum Kleiman (Moscow: Muzei kino, 2000), 427.

turn is first said to be "resolved" into three successive phases, as though it were captured chronophotographically. Between themselves, these individual immobile instants modulate a series of simple operations: repetition (the position of the body between I and II; repetition in the position of the head in I, II, and III), change of position (the lowering and spreading of wings between I and II), and mirroring (the body in III inverts the body in II; the wings in III reflect mirrorlike the position of the wings in I). Out of these mechanical and successively arranged modifications of visible traits, our perception recomposes a single movement of the turn: "the turn of the bird is accomplished." Eisenstein thus presents the basic kinematographic operation, which simultaneously gives us the movement of the turn and the unified figure of a single goose composed of three geese, which our perception seems to organize in such a way that the movement of the turn becomes attributed to the unified figure.

According to Eisenstein, Ma Fen's picture mimics the rudimentary mechanism of the kinematographic apparatus, which is distinguished by its ability to create a synthetic perception of movement out of a set of successive immobile instants. According to André Gaudreault, the most basic problem of kinematography is how "to create linear progression out of the momentary,"[54] or, as he puts it in a more technical formulation, how "to create vectoriality out of punctuality."[55] In Eisenstein's analysis of the dramatic moment in *The Hundred Geese,* the kinematographic question is precisely how a punctual series of three still depictions can produce the sense of the vectorial unfolding of the turn of a unified figure of the goose.

Showing how the Chinese scroll anticipates chronophotography and the kinematographic synthesis of movement is, however, not the main goal of Eisenstein's analysis. For him, the description of the kinematographic effect, identified in this case in a distant Chinese predecessor, does not yet properly address the question of cinematic movement. The basic kinematographic operation gives us a perceptible figure in movement. What does not yet appear, however, with this perception supported by the kinematographic apparatus is the movement of the turn for itself—the turn not as something predicated on the identity of the figure but precisely as an autonomous gesture. Importantly for Eisenstein and his idea of cinema, the kinematographic transformation of punctual instants into a vector of movement is in itself not enough to explain the dramatic or properly artistic effect of the turn of the goose in the Chinese scroll. What makes the fragment of Ma Fen's painting expressive and artistically effective is that it allows us to sense another kind of turn, the turn as it exceeds the visibility of the unified figure and takes place in the domain of gesture. We may generalize a bit and say that, in Eisenstein's case, the problem is always how to create, through and apart from the kinematographic movement of a figure, a thought and a feeling of another kind of movement that is gestural and expressive and that, in its tension with the movement of the kinematographic figure, constitutes the domain of cinema. *Cinematic* movement must, in other words, be found in its distinction from *kinematographic* (re)production of movement.

And so Eisenstein needs to continue his analysis of the dramatic moment in the Chinese scroll painting:

> Yet one seizes here another movement. Remarkably, this other movement is read slightly after the "turn" of the figure: we are thinking of what happens to the head. Fixing our sight on it, we suddenly see that,

> rather than being bent in the form of an arch, the neck is . . . strenuously extended.
>
> This happens so unexpectedly, just when it seems that the necessary movement has already been accomplished, that it produces simply the sensation of a jolt. And this jolt immediately begins "to put on the garb of the plot" [*odevaetsia siuzhetom*]—we perceive it as a jolt of the bird's head forward after the bird has turned around mid-flight. (The heads of the first two birds, which are turned squarely in the opposite direction of their bodies, carry the tendency toward the change in direction of the flight.) Such an effect, which corresponds completely with the dynamics of an organic process of movement in which a jolt to the entirety of the body projects the head forward on a long [extended] neck, is obtained by the subtle nuance of the perception of movement of the details in time, which I have marked above as noteworthy.[56]

There we have it! In addition to the perceived movement of the figure's turn, there appears "another movement," which arrives with a slight delay, after we have already (kinematographically) recomposed the turn of the goose. We perhaps assume we have seen it all. And in a sense we have, because what happens next does not belong primarily to what can be seen. We have perceived the movement of the turn in its entirety. Yet it is then that "another movement" strikes and surprises us, affecting us with a "sense of a jolt."

What is crucial here is that the effect of "another movement," which gives us the shock of a gesture and of the expressiveness of the turn, is produced by an entirely different logic than our initial, kinematographic perception of the turn.[57] In this other movement, we do not encounter the sense of a figure's continuous movement produced out of a series of successive phases but rather the shock of a violent immobilization, a punctuation produced by a fixation of a detail—the strenuously extended neck—that appears as though cut out from the vectorial continuity of the turning figure. It is this punctual intervention that then produces the sense of another movement, an altogether different vectoriality from the one that belongs to our perception.

The kinematographic figure allows us to perceive the turn's continuous movement. Then, however, as we linger on the picture "after the 'turn' of the figure," which is to say, as we extend our perceptual activity beyond the limit necessary for us to see the turn, something different emerges, as though entering from out of sight. We fixate on a detail—the tortured neck of the third goose—which escaped us at first, as our perception, relying on the presupposition of a unified figure, strove to recompose the movement of the turn from the sequence of successive phases. In the act of kinematographic perception, the detail had to be subsumed by the figure's continuity of movement. Now, however, as we perhaps no longer feel the pressure to maintain the perceptual integrity of the figure, the detail jumps at us from the picture with an undeniable punctual force. We "fix our sight" on it, blow it up in size in a manner analogous to making a close-up (or rather an "enlargement shot"). We isolate the decontextualized part as though it were the picture in its entirety.

It is not difficult to recognize in this "subtle nuance of the perception of movement of the details," as Eisenstein calls it, the operation of disfiguration, from which an entirely different figure must be deduced. Something arrives and puts the figure of the goose in crisis. The strenuously extended neck points to the elements of suffering and ecstasy, the strained figure demonstrating that it has been seized and displaced by a movement it cannot contain, or that it can contain only at the price of breaking or snapping. At the same time, the fixation of the neck as a detail, the moment of decontextualization of a part ripped out of a continuous whole, and the way this partial object comes to occupy almost the entirety of our attention all point to the fact that we no longer find ourselves exactly in figurative space, that the figure-in-crisis we deduce through the strained neck no longer shares ground with the figure we just saw perform the movement of the turn. What occurs, in some sense, is the disappearance of the initial figure through the work of disfiguration, which turns the body of the goose into a purely gestural matter. Suddenly, after we have perceived the turn of the bird, we get something like the experience of the turn as such, not as it might refer to the integral unity of the figure but as it might be thought and felt for itself. A turn with a capital *T*.

The Turn is not simply seen; it is felt and thought in the presence of a gesture and must for this reason be read through and apart from the visible turn of the goose. We could say that the disfiguration of the kinematographic figure, the goose suddenly put into crisis by the inhuman straining of its neck, presents us with a striking detail, which refuses reintegration back into the continuity of kinematographic movement and thus requires a different approach—that of reading and interpretation. Does this not give us a rather fortuitous and beautiful definition of cinematic movement as something different from kinematography? Cinematic movement in this sense appears whenever the simple kinematographic perception of movement is disturbed by an element that shatters the integrity of the kinematographic figure and the space it inhabits. Cinema emerges to help us read and interpret the crisis suffered by the kinematographic figure, turning the latter into a garb, as Eisenstein puts it, a mask, a disguise, under which the shock of another movement can begin to plot its way in the world. Which is to say, cinema appears whenever the kinematographic figure becomes enigmatic, a bit obscure, when it appears to be hiding something or seems to be falling apart, that is, whenever its significance ceases to be accessible by sight alone. And with this, cinema transposes the kinematographic figure into a different space, a topology of its own, that does not have to obey the figurative dimensions that govern kinematography.

The problem of cinematic movement is, for Eisenstein, the reverse of the one identified by Gaudreault in relation to kinematography. If the task of kinematography lies in the accomplishment of a passage from punctuality to vectoriality, from a series of momentary instants to a perception of continuous movement, then the task of cinema lies in knowing how to interrupt or punctuate the continuity of the kinematographic movement, opening it up to the possibility of a different kind of vectoriality than the one kinematography offers to our perception. What can be called *cinematic* is the vector of this other movement—of thought and affect—which appears with the help of the graceful intervention of a gesture that puts into crisis the visible continuum of our perception.

Gaudreault himself does not make this type of distinction between the kinematographic movement and the movement of cinema. Although he, for instance, claims that "the kinematograph was transformed into cinema by means of a radical metamorphosis, a true mutation,"[58] he seems to nevertheless maintain that the kinematographic problem of movement (the passage from punctuality to linear progression) remains the material basis of cinematic movement as well. Eisenstein, too, seems at times to posit an organic continuity between kinematography and cinema. Yet one can easily show that he is at those moments distant from the more fundamental wager of his work, which in its entirety presents a strong argument against any such organic continuity.[59]

What Eisenstein allows us to see is how the introduction of the idea of cinematic movement as something different from mere kinematography transforms the material basis of movement as such. Though a certain ahistorical materialism might maintain that the material basis of the kinematographic apparatus remains unchanged throughout the various "superstructural" determinations of its use, among which we would have to locate that of cinema, a more properly *historical* materialist perspective realizes that what mutates and radically changes in the shift from kinematography to cinema (from the visibility of figures in movement to the *dialectic* of gesture and visibility, from perception to the *dialectic* of perception and reading) is the material basis itself. Although it might appear that cinema deploys the basic kinematographic apparatus while leaving it unchanged, this is not the case. The appearance of cinema—of the properly cinematic conception of movement—transforms the meaning of and gives an entirely different function to the material basis that supported the situation of the kinematograph. Cinema puts the kinematographic figure into crisis, disfigures it, makes it suffer, step outside itself, and ultimately lose its proper ground. With this, cinema imposes on the kinematographic figure the materiality of its own gesture—no less material, despite the fact that we may not be able to simply identify it with the technical apparatus of kinematography.

■ ■ TWO

The Form-Problem

THE GROTESQUE AND THE EPIC IN ACTION

> If we try to find truly epic productions in the most recent times, we have to look around for some sphere different from that of epic proper. For the whole state of the world today has assumed a form diametrically opposed in its prosaic organization to the requirements which we found irremissible for genuine epic, and the revolutions to which the recent circumstances of states and peoples have been subject are still too fixed in our memory as actual experiences to be compatible with the epic form of art.
>
> ■ G. W. F. Hegel, *Aesthetics: Lectures on Fine Art*

> STALIN: Have you studied history?
> EISENSTEIN: More or less.
>
> ■ "Stalin, Molotov and Zhdanov on *Ivan the Terrible*, Part Two"

The Impurity of Cinematic Movement: Theatricality

We concluded the preceding chapter with the idea of a fundamental discontinuity between kinematographic and cinematic movement, which suggested that cinematic movement emerges only at those points at which the visibility of the kinematographic figure is put into crisis. Only when the moving figure produced by the kinematographic apparatus is seized and disordered by a gesture of movement that does not properly belong to it—a gesture that turns the visibility of the figure's movement into a symptom that must be read and interpreted—do we enter the domain of cinema. "Eisenstein," "Hitchcock," "Godard," "Akerman," "film noir," "the classical Western," "the slapstick comedy of Chaplin"—all these may be names of individual auteurs and great genres. But more fundamentally, they are names for different and singular ideas of cinema, different ways of putting into crisis the visibility of the kinematographic figure—names, in other words, for singular gestures in which it is possible to read the presence of some properly cinematic materiality.

Yet, as it takes leave from the kinematographic figure, cinematic movement does not establish itself in any kind of purity. On the contrary, it is a fundamental characteristic of cinematic movement that its proper materiality remains always and essentially impure. Cinematic movement, in search of its freedom from the kinematographic figure, on the lookout for its own proper gestures, is always mediated by something else, and this something else pushes cinema along, supporting it in the quest for the autonomy of its movement. What comes to mediate and help establish the idea of cinematic movement in this way are the ideas of other arts. We find in Eisenstein's work a voracious need to refer to other arts as he attempts to determine his idea of cinema: painting and sculpture, poetry and the novel, theater, music, architecture, dance. His engagement with the arts does not serve the purpose of mere illustration, where other arts are used merely as examples, demonstrating and legitimating something cinema would be perfectly capable of demonstrating by itself. Rather, other arts—as we saw with the example of painting in chapter 1 (Ma Fen's *The Hundred Geese*)—offer themselves as necessary in making sense of cinematic movement, especially insofar as this movement must be distinguished from the one guaranteed by the technical properties of the kinematographic apparatus.

Eisenstein's discourse determines the meaning of cinema through displacements, making it circulate between different artistic domains, as though what cinema is can only be conveyed with words borrowed from elsewhere—as though the language of cinema can only be spoken by speaking through other arts. It is somehow proper to cinematic movement that it becomes established in the impurity of this indirect construction. Eisenstein's work thus exhibits a remarkably promiscuous relationship to other arts, which all seem to be waiting in the wings, ready to appear at any time on the stage of theoretical construction and assume their temporary role in this great spectacle of mediation that is the becoming of Eisenstein's idea of cinema. Drawing on all the arts as he asserts cinematic movement's autonomy from the kinematographic figure, Eisenstein at the same time acts as a great impurifier of artistic autonomy. When he claims he is interested in everything except the cinema, he is talking about nothing but his idea of cinema.

Of all the mediating instances, it is theater that might be considered the most immediately engaged in this spectacle of mediation through which Eisenstein constructs his idea of cinema. Theater offered Eisenstein the first concrete possibility to consider himself an artist. It was in relation to theater that he began to theorize—not only in his first famous texts on "Montage of Attractions" (1923) and "Montage of Film Attractions" (1924), but even earlier, already during the Civil War that followed in the wake of the October Revolution, in his "Notes Concerning the Theatre" (1919–20).[1] From theater, Eisenstein moved to film direction, which meant that the elaboration of his idea of cinema inevitably had to take into account the difference as well as the commonality between the two arts.[2] Finally, theater provided a master—Vsevolod Meyerhold—in relation to whom the young Eisenstein was able to assume his apprenticeship of great art as a distinct subjective or existential possibility.[3]

More than any other art, it was theater—and specifically Meyerhold's idea of *theatricality (teatral'nost')*—that played the crucial mediating role in Eisenstein's creation of his conception of cinematic movement. By theatricality, we have in mind something rather specific: the period of Meyerhold's experimentation as both theater director and theoretician between 1906 (his staging of Alexander Blok's *Balaganchik*) and the October Revolution of 1917. This is the period during which Meyerhold developed his original idea of theatrical performance, based primarily on the experiences of *commedia dell'arte* and the grotesque, which he explores most exhaustively in his 1912 essay "Balagan" (The fairground booth), the central text of his major theoretical achievement, *O Teatre* (On theater), published in 1913.[4] Meyerholdian theatricality is bound closely to his conception of *stylized theater* or, as it may also be called, the *theater of convention (uslovnii teatr)*, which he opposes to the "naturalism" of bourgeois drama while proposing it as the name for a new kind of theatrical space that might allow for a constant reconfiguration of and experimentation with the very conventions of theatrical performance.[5] Theatricality names a practice of theater that, unlike the illusionism of bourgeois "naturalism," makes visible and, by bringing them to the surface, displaces its own conventional limits, without at the same time leading us out of theater altogether. In its opposition to the bourgeois theater of the nineteenth century, Meyerhold's theatricality can further be distinguished from two other attempts at revolutionizing the theater. First was the dominant strain of Russian symbolist theater that sought its opposition to bourgeois drama in the revival of the mystery-play and the cultic function of spectacle. In response to this tendency of Russian symbolism, Meyerhold follows Andrei Bely and insists on the need to separate theatrical performance from religious or cultic ritual.[6] Second was the later, postrevolutionary, productivist extreme of Soviet constructivism, which imagined the artistic movements of theater dissolved within a larger, industrial orchestration of collective movement. In this sense, we may also distinguish, but with less absoluteness, the theatrical Meyerhold of the prerevolutionary years from Meyerhold's own post-October development, during which he invented his biomechanical method of actor training and moved closer to the Taylorist metaphor of movement characteristic of the constructivist and productivist avant-garde.[7]

Eisenstein met Meyerhold as a student in the early 1920s, the moment of "constructivism in theater." However, it was not so much the Meyerhold of the 1920s as the encounter with the earlier Meyerhold and his pre-October idea of grotesque and comedic theatricality that imparted to Eisenstein the decisive lessons of movement. The prerevolutionary theatrical conception of movement he appropriated from Meyerhold crucially mediated for Eisenstein his idea of "revolutionary" cinema and, even more specifically, his idea of cinematic action.[8]

The present chapter revolves around the question of how a certain Meyerholdian theatrical conception of movement and action—which, as we will see, belongs to a very precise definition of the *grotesque*—comes into conflict with Eisensteinian action's other desire, which is *epic* in its character and scope. The hypothesis examined in what follows is that the fundamental formal problem of Eisenstein's filmic work may indeed be found in the dialectical contradiction between the *theatrical–grotesque* and the *epic–heroic* conceptions of action. With this term—the *formal problem*—we borrow a concept that Fredric Jameson has adapted from Georg Lukács's theory of the novel in the following way:

> To identify the formal contradiction at the heart of a work is not to criticize it but to locate the sources of its production: it is in other words, following Lukács's useful formula, to articulate the form-problem the work attempts to solve. Without confronting such a form-problem, without in other words grappling with a genuine contradiction, it is hard to see how a work could have any distinction or win any value. The form-problem (and not necessarily its solution, for contradictions are "solved" only by being articulated) secures the work's position in history: in the history of form, first of all, and by way of that, in the various levels of social history, of subjectivity, and of the mode of production.[9]

To articulate the form-problem, or the basic contradiction of a work, is to locate this work *in* history. But, we may add, because it is not at all clear that history makes sense apart from the interventions of form, one must also say that it is only through a description of the work's basic formal contradiction that we discover the "location" of history in the first place. Only by tracing the work's formal problem can we isolate what gives history shape and makes it intelligible, so that the work might then find a place *in* it. In our case, the formal contradiction between the theatrical–grotesque and the epic–heroic—a contradiction that traverses the entirety of Eisenstein's filmic output (it is, in this sense, the work's "source of production")—not only tells us how Eisenstein's work fits in its historical context (the place his films occupy in the Revolution) but helps us "locate" the sense of history and historical action as such (to find in his work the "place" of the Revolution itself).

The Plasticity of Movement, the *Cabotin,* and the Mask

An obvious question presents itself: how was Meyerhold's conception of theatricality capable of assuming the crucial role of mediating Eisenstein's construction of cinematic movement and action? Its capability lies undoubtedly in the fact that for Meyerhold, theatricality had to be developed and constructed in opposition to any naturalist or empirically verisimilar idea of movement. That is, for Meyerhold, theatrical movement and action could not simply resemble movement and action as we perceive them outside of the theater. In this, Meyerhold's idea of theatricality opposed not just the naturalist illusionism of bourgeois drama but also the kinematography of early cinema. Writing in 1912, Meyerhold objected to what he perceived as early cinema's extension of naturalism in movement, opposing his conception of theatricality to the kinematographic (re)production of natural movement:

> Far too much importance is attached to the cinematograph, that idol of the modern city, by its supporters. The cinematograph is of undoubted importance to science as a means of visual demonstration; it can serve as an illustrated newspaper depicting "the events of the day"; for some people it might even replace travel (horror of horrors!). But there is no place for the cinematograph in the world of art, even in a purely auxiliary capacity. And if for some reason or other the cinematograph is called a theatre, it is simply because of total obsession with naturalism . . . everything mechanical was enrolled in the service of the theatre. This extreme obsession with naturalism, so characteristic of the general public at the end of the nineteenth and the beginning of the twentieth century was one of the original reasons for the extraordinary success of the cinematograph. . . . Electricity came to the aid of the naturalists, and the result—a touching union of photography and technology—was the cinematograph. . . . The cinematograph, that dream-come-true of those who strive for the photographic representation of life, is a shining example of the obsession with quasi-verisimilitude. . . . Just as the theatres which are still trying to propagate naturalistic drama and plays fit only for reading cannot stay the growth of truly theatrical and totally non-naturalistic plays, so the cinematograph cannot stifle the spirit of the fairground booth. . . . The fairground booth [*balagan*] is eternal.[10]

This remarkable statement expels early cinema precisely from the domain in which it has been placed by most subsequent film history, namely, the domain of the fairground booth and popular forms of entertainment and attraction. Indeed, while film history situates early cinema in relation to the circus and the music hall—the inheritors of *commedia,* which form the essential background for Meyerhold's idea of theatricality—Meyerhold wishes to strictly separate the two domains. He must have at that point not seen much that could convince him of the possibility of a genuine emancipation of movement from a subservience to the spontaneous naturalism of the kinematographic figure, which offered only a type of electrified naturalism. The task of art and theatricality lay, on the contrary, against the kinematographic effect in an antinaturalism of movement. One had to disturb and displace the kinematographic figure, which for Meyerhold represented no difference from the tired figures of bourgeois drama, in the direction of a greater and more imaginative plasticity of movement.

Meyerhold's statement allows us to see exactly how his idea of theatricality—and of theatrical movement as something opposed to mimetic verisimilitude and naturalism—was able to catalyze Eisenstein's break with the continuity of the kinematographic figure by pushing movement in the direction of its properly cinematic gesture. Meyerhold's idea suggested to Eisenstein that a different plasticity of movement—something of an entirely different order than the crude "naturalism" of the kinematograph—was required were cinema to become established as an art capable of a genuine rivalry with Meyerhold and his theatricality.[11] At the beginning of the twentieth century, the search for a new plasticity of movement belonged much more to the theatrical revolution—of Meyerhold, but also of Adolphe Appia, Gordon Craig, Max Reinhardt, and Georg Fuchs, whose *The Stage of the Future* (1904–5) itself significantly influenced Meyerhold—than it did to early kinematography, whose fascination depended, according to Meyerhold, not on a new plastics of movement but on something else entirely: the remarkable technical capacity to capture and reproduce, with great fidelity, the movement of empirical reality. Theatricality taught Eisenstein the imperative of a fundamental dissatisfaction with the "naturalism" of the kinematographic figure. And precisely because it demanded a greater, nonnaturalist, and nonempirical plasticity of movement than kinematographic reproduction of reality could supply, theatricality was able to open up a space in which a genuinely cinematic idea of movement was able to emerge, distinct from movement's kinematographic capture.

Meyerhold began to develop his conception of theatricality already in 1905, when for the first time he affirmed the plasticity of movement and gesture as autonomous elements in any performance of theater, making movement assume an increasingly divergent relationship with respect to other elements of theatrical art, primarily that of speech (word, dialogue).[12] "Plasticity itself is not new, but the form I have in mind is new. Before, it corresponded closely to the spoken dialogue, but I am speaking of a *plasticity which does not correspond to the words. . . .* The essence of human relations is determined by gestures, poses, glances, silences. Words alone cannot say everything. . . . The difference between the old theatre and the new is that in the new theatre speech and plasticity are each subordinated to their own separate rhythms and the two do not necessarily coincide."[13] In the text of "Balagan," Meyerhold pushes the divergence between the series, movement, and speech, to a certain limit, asserting the primacy of the *design of movement* over the word, which, according to him, stands for narrative and psychological content (individualism) and "literary" representation of action (illusionism). Opposed to focusing on dialogue, he recommends that every playwright compose "a few pantomimes. The pantomime is a good antidote against excessive use of words. . . . He will be permitted to put words into the actor's mouths, but first he must produce a *scenario of movement.* How long will it be before they inscribe in the theatrical tables the following law: *words in theatre are only embellishments on the design of movement*?"[14]

A direct line connects Meyerhold's statements and Eisenstein's affirmation of the primacy of movement, which we discussed in the preceding chapter.[15] The primacy of movement taken in its plastic autonomy is the most constant feature of Meyerhold's idea of theatricality, the strongest weapon in his attack against the illusionist and individualist tradition of bourgeois theater. From it, a new conception of the actor emerges. By surrendering the actor to the primacy of movement, Meyerhold seeks to liberate acting from the task of psychological and narrative representation, turning it toward "play-acting" and improvisation.[16] The new actor should not be so much an actor as a juggler, an acrobat, a mime, a virtuoso performer of the kind that used to wander across Europe in the traveling troupes of *commedia dell'arte,* or the kind that may be found in the theatrical forms of the Far East. In "Balagan," Meyerhold affirms *cabotinage* (the practice of the strolling, traveling player) as the term around which to build this new conception of theater. He calls on the theater's proletarian dimension—the virtuosity of the actor's performance—as the engine of all theater and introduces the *cabotin* as the subject of theatrical labor on which any form of theater, regardless of how much it wishes to hide this fact, effectively rests. "If there is no cabotin, there is no theatre either."[17]

Eisenstein was very much struck by Meyerhold's description of the *kuroko,* the black-clad stagehands of the Japanese Noh theater, who perform the typical tasks of a running crew and appear onstage during the performance "in full view of the audience." For both Meyerhold and Eisenstein, the *kuroko* signaled the antinaturalism of Noh acting: "When the costume of an actor playing a woman's part became disarranged at a tense moment in the drama, one of the *kuroko* would quickly restore the graceful folds of the actor's train and attend to his coiffure. . . . After the battle, the *kuroko* would remove fallen helmets, weapons and cloaks. If the hero died on stage, the *kuroko* would quickly cover the corpse with a black cloth, and under the cover of the cloth 'the dead actor' would run off the stage."[18] Theatricality, embodied in this case in the appearance of the *kuroko,* means bringing the hidden labor of spectacle production to the spectacular surface where it may be enjoyed as part of the performance. Theatricality does not dispel the fiction of the performance but includes and makes visible the conventional means required for its staging.

Meyerhold therefore affirms "theatricality" also in its pejorative sense: a performance that, because of a lack of substance, points to itself in an excessive manner and becomes overly "rhetorical."[19] Indeed, his idea of theatricality reveals the extent to which such pejorative meaning rests on a specific class position and can, in fact, be understood as an attempt to dismiss the question of labor from the dimension of performativity. Endowing "theatricality" with a pejorative sense transforms the labor of performance into substanceless superficiality, so that it may become easier to separate it (as something "merely" theatrical) from theater's proper essence. In place of the moralistic bourgeois distinction between the "empty" surface of theatricality and "genuine" dramatic content, Meyerhold insists that the substance or the "depth" of the new theater has to coincide with its laborious and excessively rhetorical surface. The essence of action must be sought in the proximity of and not in the opposition to the superficiality of any theatrical exercise.

The key instrument in the transformation of the actor into a virtuosic vehicle of movement is the mask. Under the clear influence of *commedia dell'arte,* the idea of theatricality announces a *"new theatre of the mask."*[20] For the mask immediately "mutes" the actor's body. It takes away the conventional tools of psychological realism, such as the expressivity of the face. With its immobility, the mask forces expression to become distributed across the entirety of the actor's corporeal movement. The mask is a peculiar form of reduction that introduces the possibility for an "extreme diversity of character."[21] If the variability of the face represents a certain psychological capture of movement, then the mask, with its immobility, its invariance, enables multiple articulations and disarticulations of gesture and movement. The mask might be immobile, but it propels the body toward a remarkable plasticity of movement and possesses, as Meyerhold strikingly puts it, a "chameleonic power . . . concealed behind the expressionless visage of the comedian."[22]

One finds the exact same affirmation of the mask in Eisenstein.[23] In Eisenstein's cinema, the experience of the mask forms the core of his theory of *typage*—the production of typical characters, capable of representing not individual protagonists but rather the protagonicity of social categories and structural class positions at play in the process of history and revolutionary struggle. Typage submits the characters to a logic of selectively applied traits. In this way, individuals are reduced to social personae and to the external appearance of the symbolic mandates they occupy in a situation. On the basis of theatricality, Eisenstein develops the subversive insight of the comedic art of the mask, according to which the set of external characteristics and limited traits that describe our appearance in the social field—our mask, precisely—is far closer to the real core of our "personality" than the infinite interior or psychological richness we imagine ourselves as possessing. The mask is our "personality" in action (the word *person,* after all, comes from the Latin word *persona,* "actor's mask"), and what determines and individuates us essentially is not what lies within us but our relational position in the world, the place we occupy in the situation in which we act and which is populated by others:

> When a traditional mask emerges, the audience knows straight away who it is and what it is. The specific character of the comedy of masks depends not on the revelation of character but on the treatment of it, because a person comes on [stage] with a defined character passport. And *commedia dell'arte* plays on situations between traditional characters.[24]

The reduction of our access to the psychological richness of character operated by the mask pays off a hefty dividend in the form of the new possibilities it offers to scenic movement, an entirely new "kaleidoscopic" universe of combinatorial play with events and situations, which an intense focus on psychology and interiority would certainly block.[25]

On Stabbing without Touching: The Puppet and the Grotesque

For Meyerhold, all the elements of theatricality we have briefly sketched—plasticity of movement as primary, disassociation of movement and speech, a new visibility of theatrical labor, the depsychologizing effect of the mask—come together in the figure of the puppet or the marionette. Under the influence of Heinrich von Kleist, whose "On the Marionette Theatre" inspired many modernist theatrical innovations, Meyerhold viewed the actor of the illusionist and individualist theater as a puppet that had suffered the misfortune of becoming human. The actor in bourgeois theater is a puppet that has been made to assume the semblance of a human being—captive to empirical reality (positivism, naturalism), ignorant of the fact of its own labor (capitalism, commodity fetishism), and blinded by a sense of its own irreducible inner richness (psychologism): a puppet made to perform the role of a human being so often that it has become possible simply to replace it with human actors. Such is the project of bourgeois theater: to humanize the puppet.

Apart from pointing to the fact that the anthropomorphism of bourgeois drama is neither the native land nor the inevitable fate of theatrical art, this remarkable idea leads Meyerhold to assert an opposing and affirmative project of theatricality as one in which "the puppet stood up for itself and did not yield to the director's efforts to transform it."[26] We are asked to picture the following situation: if theatricality, in the figure of the *cabotin,* emancipates the actor's labor and virtuosity from the naturalistic and psychologizing constraints of bourgeois theater, this is possible because the new actor at the same time turns into a vehicle for the emancipation of the puppet.

This mutual becoming of the actor and the puppet suggests that there will be something uncanny about movement and action as they appear in the disposition of Meyerholdian theatricality. Action will, for instance, begin to oscillate between the inhuman and the human, the inorganic and the organic, the artificial and the natural, the mechanical and the corporeal, angularly fixed and plastically pliable, and so on. At the extreme, however, theatrical action may also cease to resemble any recognizable idea of action and appear as somehow both movement and nonmovement, action and absence of action:

> When the puppet weeps, the hand holds the handkerchief away from the eyes; when the puppet kills, it stabs its opponent so delicately that the tip of the sword stops short of the breast; when one puppet slaps another, no color comes off the face; when puppet lovers embrace, it is with such care that the spectator observing their caresses from a respectful distance does not think to question his neighbor about the consequences.[27]

There is something curious about these puppet-actions. Something in them is withdrawn or held in reserve: the movements are more suggested than fully represented, and when they are represented, there remains something incomplete or rather doubtful about their presentation. It is as though action could somehow include inaction—as though action could, in the very moment of its happening, go against itself, against the very principle of action.

We are told a puppet weeps, but because it holds the handkerchief away from its eyes, how may we be sure it is indeed weeping? Usually, the puppeteer would present the action of weeping by bringing the hand that holds the handkerchief to the head of the puppet and using the gesture of wiping that would simulate the presence of tears coming from the puppet's eyes. But with the distance that separates the hand holding the handkerchief and the puppet's eyes, which by themselves are unable to produce tears, where exactly is the action of weeping to be found here? The problem is, of course, that it is perfectly possible to accept that the image described by Meyerhold indeed produces in us a powerful impression of "weeping." Seeing what Meyerhold describes ("the hand holds the handkerchief away from the eyes"), we know what we have just encountered is the action of weeping, its pathos perhaps even strengthened by the unusual gesture. But the gesture is unusual precisely because the action of weeping itself (at least in its common, naturalistic form) is withdrawn from representation. We "see" the puppet weeping without seeing it weeping.[28]

Similarly, when a puppet stabs another puppet, Meyerhold's passage presents this action without representing the act of stabbing itself ("the sword stops short of the breast"), which gives rise to a contradictory or oxymoronic sense of a "delicate" stabbing. When a puppet slaps another puppet, we now see the action of slapping, and yet, because "no color comes off the face" of the slapped puppet, it is as though the action has been presented without taking place. Because there is no visible trace of the action, no apparent damage to the other puppet, it is as though the movement has happened and yet has not happened, as if action has taken place and yet perhaps it has not.

There emerges the strange sense of action constructed by theatrical movement: an action presented by its withdrawal from representation (the weeping puppet), an action that is realized by being withheld and thus has to pass through its opposite or through some paradoxical or oxymoronic determination (a "delicate" stabbing, a stabbing that stops short of stabbing), to which we may also add an action that happens yet leaves no trace and therefore installs in us the idea of a doubtful happening (a slap that does not affect the face of the other puppet). When puppets embrace, Meyerhold writes, they do it with such care "that the spectator observing their caresses . . . does not think to question his neighbor about the consequences." We may, in other words, not feel embarrassed by what a caressing embrace usually leads to. But this is meant to suggest a more general lack of concern for consequences and a certain innocence of theatrical action performed by the puppets in Meyerhold's remarkable passage with regard to the empirical, natural reality of movement. For if the question of the consequences of action does not arise, then the status of action as a cause of something is also in doubt. And indeed, there is something miraculous—uncaused—in the effect produced on us by the action of puppets: action appears as though its sense were subtracted from the dimension of the causal series, which is to say, subtracted from movement insofar as we usually understand movement that carries the sense of action as constituted precisely by a set of causes leading to a determinate set of effects.

Action, then, at odds with our sense of empirical, natural movement. With the puppets, Meyerhold is describing theatrical action that manages somehow to impress itself fully, shock and move us, while at the same time remaining in the modality of the "as if." We perceive the sense of this action, yet the performance rebels against our idea of what constitutes action proper, which means that the performance of the puppets produces a sense of action that remains to some extent an open question. It takes place without settling into something accomplished or something that we would be able to consume and move on from. Escaping the empirical, natural course of movement (a series of causes and effects), theatrical action not only surprises us (the miraculous aspect) but also leaves us suspended in this moment of surprise (its inconsequential aspect). A paradoxical sense of action emerges without the clear limit that we would require if we were to recognize in action the finality of an event. This is why an encounter with a puppet may be troubling, and why, following such an encounter, which has often served as the figure of the uncanny, our return to "normality" turns into a rather precarious undertaking. For if the dagger never touches the torso of the puppet that is nevertheless stabbed, is it not possible, then, that this action of stabbing has no proper finality, that it has no end and may indeed go on forever in some strange temporal modality that seems to go against empirical time itself? The theatricality of puppet-action makes the sense of action appear in time, yet as something that is not temporally finalized. A sense of action thus rises against the finality implied in the unfolding of the action's temporal sequence.

Meyerhold's other name for the kind of theatrical action we have been trying to describe is *grotesque.* What he calls grotesque is a device or a formal element that has to do with the very structure of the work of art. The grotesque, Meyerhold says, quoting from Andrei Bely, offers us an experience of a reality that we are able to access only indirectly. Grotesque refers to the work of art's ability to present reality as a whole without being able to fully represent it as such. Meyerhold calls such grotesque presentation-without-representation the operation of *schematization.* In the case of theatrical action, what is grotesque about it is that it gives us a forceful impression of action ("weeping," "stabbing," "embracing"), yet does so without unfolding the action in the totality of its representation. Theatricality and the grotesque do not operate through the development of action in its representational fullness but by presenting action in the form of its schematic reduction, a form of synthesis that gives us the sense of action not in its realistic, but only in its *typical,* unity. "When the puppet weeps, the hand holds the handkerchief away from the eyes." In the example, the action of weeping is presented as something whole, yet this sense of the whole does not depend on the full representation of action in its realistic entirety, reproducing and resembling its empirical movement, but rather on the construction of this action in its typical, most fully reduced form. The grotesque offers action in its emblematic design rather than in the form of an exhaustive representation. It produces a sense of action that impresses us more as a *form* of action than action developed in the fullness of its content. In doing so, the reductive and laconic schema of action reveals something about the being of action that is far more intense than what a realistic or empirically faithful representation of action is capable of conveying.

Montage of Attractions

Eisenstein's famous idea of "montage of attractions," his first great theoretical invention advanced in the first half of the 1920s, belongs fully to the Meyerholdian, theatrical–grotesque conception of movement and action.[29] Admittedly, a statement like this might at first appear as rather dubious. Does not Eisenstein's "attraction," unlike Meyerhold's theatricality, which is characterized by a certain indirectness of action (presenting action by withdrawing it from representation), name precisely the opposite: action as direct blow? Does not "attraction" name a type of circus performance that, rather than making us doubt, leaves us certain about its effectiveness, because its aim is to produce physiological shock in the spectator? With the term *attraction,* Eisenstein describes a performance of action capable of realizing a certain emotional or intellectual content directly rather than representing it illusionistically. In the theater of attractions, the "nobility" of a hero, for instance, does not stand as a theme outside the actions taking place onstage but is directly embodied in the erotic effect of the actor's presence and movement. Similarly, the "sublimity" of religious pathos is not to be treated as a subject independent of the performance of action but must be incarnated in the actions of sadistic torture enacted by and on the bodies occupying the scene. Attraction is a performance in which a theme ("nobility," "religious sublimity") becomes fully immanent to the "mechanics of movement" performed on the stage (the eroticism of the actor playing the hero; the sadistic violence exercised by one set of bodies against another). Theater of attractions is emotional and psychological, but "in the sense of direct reality as employed, for instance, in the Grand Guignol, where eyes are gouged out or arms and legs amputated on stage."[30] Eisenstein's concept of attraction, with its stress on the acrobatic and the physiological, is thus meant to return some faith in the capacity of action and movement to realize immanently whatever might be the subject of performance; it is an attempt to affirm the possibility of certain great themes and subjects of theater (sacrifice, heroic nobility, religious enthusiasm, human wretchedness), which we usually think of as transcendent realities existing beyond the world of action and movement, themselves becoming active in our physical world: the suffering and erotic bodies no longer merely hinting at the idea or suggesting it as its representational bearers but becoming capable of embodying it directly.

Despite Eisenstein's affirmation of direct action in his notion of attraction, he does not, strictly speaking, conceive of such a thing as attraction purely in itself. He never speaks of attraction without raising the question of the *montage* of attractions. Attraction that would stand by itself, unrelated to anything else, would not be attraction proper in Eisenstein's sense but merely a stunt. Eisenstein conceives of attraction as a new basic unit of construction within a larger unity of theatrical and filmic composition. Unlike stunts, which may stand purely autonomously, attractions are relational elements and thus only relatively autonomous. As such, they are inseparable from the notion of "associative chains," into which they are combined. Attractions point to the necessity of conceiving theatrical and filmic work as an "effective structure," in which they become articulated. In a manner identical to the logic of the Meyerholdian theatrical–grotesque, Eisenstein speaks of "attractional *schemas*": actions must be organized according to a precisely designed formal schematism that is not contained within individual attractions themselves. "The downfall of the majority of our Russian film derives from the fact that the people who make them do not know to construct attractional schemas consciously but only rarely and in fumbling fashion hit on successful combinations."[31] In his early texts, Eisenstein defines the task of the director as creating schematic reductions, selecting and organizing fragments of movement and action—a type of work that must, according to him, be distinguished from script writing and filming from a prewritten script. The influence of the Meyerholdian theatrical–grotesque is thus evident in the shift from words to the design of movement and action, and in the stress Eisenstein thereby places on the director's task of inventing schemas:

> Transposition of the theme into a chain of attractions with a previously determined end effect is the definition we have given of director's work. The presence or absence of a written script is by no means all that important. I think that, when it is a matter of operating on the audience through material that is not closely plot-based, a general scheme of reference that leads to the desired results is enough, together with the free selection of montage material based on it. . . . In the selection and presentation of this material the decisive factor should be the immediacy and economy of the resources expended in the cause of associative effect.[32]

Individual attractions offer a break from illusionism. Eisenstein calls them "real artificialities" (as opposed to the "depictive" or illusionistic artificialities of bourgeois theater). But what is truly significant is that the concept of attraction opens up the possibility for a new type of whole (associative chain, attractional schema), where action no longer serves the aim of psychological or plot-driven representation. Rather, the montage of attractions serves a new kind of "cinema of action that is useful to our class" but which is at the same time a cinema "free from narrowly plot-related plans."[33] Attractions announce a new type of performance, in which the structure or the schema of the whole can now emerge in relation to direct bits of action. Still, this structure or schema, insofar as it necessarily plays a mediating role, introduces a form of indirectness—indeed, a new form of indirectness, which is different from the illusionist indirectness of nineteenth-century bourgeois theater, because it is possible to think of it as though emanating from the attractions themselves. But it is a form of indirectness nevertheless. By being articulated (or schematized) into a larger relational whole, individual attractions become linked to each other, but they also become indirectly related to the effect a performance as a whole has on the spectator.

Herein lies a remarkable similarity between Meyerhold's theatrical–grotesque and Eisenstein's montage of attractions: in both cases we find an affirmation of a new unit of direct action—in Meyerhold, the acrobatic performance of the cabotin; in Eisenstein, the individual attraction—which is asserted against the "naturalism" and "psychologism" of action in bourgeois theater (the paradigmatic case of which, for both Meyerhold and Eisenstein, is the great Stanislavsky). Both Meyerhold and Eisenstein affirm in this sense the surface of action or an action that realizes and exhausts its meaning on the surface of bodies in movement. Both affirm that the theme of action or the subject of action should be immanent to the performance of this action itself. Yet what this initial naming of liberated fragments of direct action is meant to give us is a new form of indirectness, a way of structuring performance into a new type of whole, a new method of constructing the sense of action (the theatrical–grotesque schema in Meyerhold; the attractional schema of montage in Eisenstein's case). This new construction does not try to subdue the fragments of direct action and return them to the safe, representational distance of illusionist performance; instead, it seeks to amplify them, to sharpen their effect, to affirm them in their directness, while at the same time overdetermining the individual units with an effectiveness that belongs to the whole and thus transforming them into parts of a larger structure. The true novelty of Meyerhold's conception of the theatrical–grotesque as well as Eisenstein's montage of attraction lies in this new form of indirectness, which belongs to the activity of the structure or the schema. It is not simply by affirming the directness of theatrical action but rather by relating this directness to a new way of structuring and schematizing the performance that Meyerhold and Eisenstein most forcefully break with the illusionist and representational treatment of action characteristic of the nineteenth-century tradition of bourgeois performance.

It should therefore not surprise us that in Eisenstein's famous text "Montage of Film Attractions," we find an example of presenting action remarkably similar to Meyerhold's description of puppet-action discussed earlier. Eisenstein demonstrates his method of montage of attractions with a properly theatrical example, which might have been taken straight from Meyerhold's writing on the grotesque:

> Let us take . . . murder as an example: a throat is gripped, eyes bulge, a knife is brandished, the victim closes his eyes, blood is spattered on a wall, the victim falls to the floor, a hand wipes off the knife.[34]

Like Meyerhold's puppets, Eisenstein's example presents action (murder) without its representation in the form of a fully developed totality: at no point do we see a "shot" of the knife making contact with the body of the victim. The sequence is composed almost entirely from close-ups or Eisensteinian enlargement shots, the only exception being the medium shot of the victim falling to the floor. The crucial moment of action, the moment that would represent the action that gives the entire ensemble its name and would in some sense stitch the series of details or enlargement shots into a unity, does not appear. The scene is presented as a multiplicity of actions (gripping of the throat, bulging of the eyes, brandishing of the knife) with a missing centerpiece. The sense of action ("murder") arises therefore not out of a representational totality but out of a delinked multiplicity of represented actions. What we get is precisely murder presented in the form of the theatrical–grotesque: the action of murder is rendered schematically. The schema, rather than some fully unfolded representation, itself supports the emergence of a remarkable effect of sense. We get an action of murder that is presented more as a design or a form of murder than murder that would develop fully as the representational content of the scene (it would be easy to draw here a parallel between Eisenstein's example and the famous shower scene in Hitchcock's *Psycho*—another scene that gives us less the representation of murder than a presentation of the *form* of murder).[35]

Strike and the Eisensteinian Grotesque

In its finale, Eisenstein's first film, *Strike* (1925), offers a remarkable example of the sense of action we have been trying to describe by associating Eisenstein's montage of attractions with the Meyerholdian conception of the theatrical–grotesque. At stake in the arrangements of a montage of attractions is action organized according to a schematism (operations of selection and reduction, impoverishment and formalization), where it is precisely the schematic gesture of form that impresses on us the sense of action, despite action's dissolution into a decentered multiplicity of fragments at the level of representation. In describing the final sequence of *Strike* (Figure 12), we may want to adopt Eisenstein's style of describing the scene of murder: "a butcher's knife is brandished; the masses flee in all directions; the knife hangs suspended in the air; the knife falls and strikes the head of a bull; the bull leaps, convulses, and falls to the ground; a group of hands stretches upward; a butcher approaches; hands stretch; a tsarist military regiment marches in strict formation; the bull's throat is slit."

What makes the sequence important to us, and what relates it to Meyerhold's puppets, is that the massacre is constructed from an assemblage of fragments that presents action by withdrawing it from any representational unity or totality. The sequence produces the violent sense of a tsarist massacre of workers; yet, it does so indirectly, in the mode of a grotesque schematism. We are given five distinct series of fragments: (1) the proletarian masses in flight (consisting of eleven shots); (2) the tsarist soldiers (seven shots); (3) the slaughterhouse/slaying of a bull (eleven shots); (4) close-ups of hands stretching toward the sky (two shots); and (5) two intertitles. Only in one shot in the entire assemblage do we briefly see the fleeing mass of people and the soldiers sharing the frame. Importantly, however, even in this shot, which appears in the final third of the sequence, the soldiers are not seen firing their guns at the people; that is, even in this shot, in which the two groups whose confrontation is at the heart of the sequence appear jointly, we do not get a direct representation of the massacre. The only other moment in which the workers and the soldiers appear simultaneously on-screen occurs following the sequence's antepenultimate shot, when, for a brief moment, a dissolve transition superimposes the image of the massacred workers, their bodies strewn across the field, and the marching soldiers, filmed from waist down, to suggest the metaphor of the tsarist army trampling over the victimized mass of human beings.

The central shot, the centerpiece of action, is missing in all of this—just as the moment of the knife touching the chest was absent from Meyerhold's description of the "delicate" stabbing of the puppet, and just as the knife piercing the body did not appear in Eisenstein's description of a murder scene. Rather than striving to represent it fully, Eisenstein relays the action of a violent suppression of worker rebellion by the tsarist army by introducing a second, incongruent series—the series of the slaughterhouse. If judged simply by the number of shots it occupies in the sequence, the series of the slaughterhouse equals in importance the series of the fleeing and massacred people (both contain more fragments than the series of the tsarist army). A montage of attractions at work in the final sequence of *Strike* operates thus not by unfolding for us the action of the massacre in its representational totality but by short-circuiting such representation and installing in its place an attractional schema of comparative juxtapositions—or, as Eisenstein puts it, an "associational comparison [of the massacre] with a slaughterhouse,"[36] which assembles the different series without unifying them. With the already mentioned exception of a single shot—which may perhaps for this very reason be considered a mistake, a moment of inconsistency in an otherwise remarkable mastery exhibited by the young filmmaker in the use of his device—the individual series never touch. We may even venture a hypothesis that the repeated appearance of the close-up of hands stretching upward under an empty sky—certainly the most surprising fragments in the entire sequence, which seem to enter from a space all their own, heterogeneous to both the city outskirts (the scene of the massacre) and the slaughterhouse (another scene of killing)—forms a separate series precisely to mark within the assemblage

Бойня.
The carnage.

Figure 12. The massacre of the workers in the finale of *Strike* (1925).

the presence of difference as such and to emphasize the distance maintained throughout between the individual series of action within Eisenstein's attractional schema. The two-fragment series of hands reaching skyward serves, in other words, as a reminder of nontouching, the crucial formal feature of the entire sequence's design.

To make the distinctiveness of Eisenstein's approach clearer, one should, for instance, compare it to Griffith's method of montage that alternates between two series of actions. In Griffith, the two parallel series of actions are intercut, with their inter-action motivated in the direction of unity. They are supposed to meet in the end, to touch in the moment of a duel, which offers resolution and a sense of action tied to the effect of its total (resolved, concluded) representation. In the case of Eisenstein, the sense of action is, on the contrary, not tied to any such unitary representational effect. While Griffith's "parallels" ultimately meet on the plane of represented reality, Eisenstein's series run in an infinite parallelism. A unity of sense ("carnage," "defeat") thus emerges in Eisenstein's case as delinked from representational totality. What supports the sense of action is not representation but rather the attractional schema produced by the work of montage. The sense of action is a result of a selective and reductive formalization (in this case the form of comparison that governs the schema of montage) that is capable of maintaining the interaction of the different series within a multiple or detotalized assemblage.

It is also through this delinking of action from its development within a representational totality that there emerges the real violence of the sequence. The monstrosity of the finale of *Strike,* in other words, has little to do with images of bull slaughter and everything to do with the violence of the schematic form, which disallows any attribution of action to a unitary instance of representation. The disturbing thing about Eisenstein's attractional schema (comparative in form) is that it does not tend toward a totality within which the fragments of represented action and their series could somehow be recollected. On the contrary, the sequence operates by maintaining what Eisenstein called a "juxtaposition of monstrous incongruities," an assembly of "disintegrated phenomena."[37] Individual representational fragments of action are combined into different series, and these series are then configured according to a precise schema, yet in such a way that the sense of the whole action emerges as distinct and somehow in excess of what the sequence manages to represent. What happens—and what produces the impression of great violence—is the violation of any kind of "objective" relation between the sense of action and its representation in the sequence. As Eisenstein would say, the task of a montage of attractions is to make emerge something in excess of the "objective" link between sense and representation and thus to discover the "subjective" orientation, the *"purely semantic purpose"* of sense.[38] The violence achieved by this sequence in *Strike* has to do therefore with a certain becoming-autonomous of sense, the severing of the tie that might otherwise ground the sense of action "objectively" within a representational type of assemblage.

Eisenstein's development of the method of attractional schematism reaches its limit in the late 1920s in his famous idea of intellectual montage (or, as he also calls it, *montage of intellectual attractions*):

> The old filmmakers, including the theoretically quite outmoded Lev Kuleshov, regarded montage as a means of producing something by describing it, adding individual shots to one another like building blocks.
>
> . . . According to this definition (which Pudovkin also shares as a theorist) montage is the means of *unrolling* an idea through single shots (the "epic" principle).
>
> *But in my view montage is not an idea composed of successive shots stuck together but an idea that* DERIVES *from the collision between two shots that are independent of one another* (the "dramatic" principle). ("Epic" and "dramatic" in relation to the methodology of form and not content or plot!!) As in Japanese hieroglyphics in which two independent ideographic characters ("shots") are juxtaposed and *explode* into a concept. THUS:
>
> Eye + Water = Crying
> Door + Ear = Eavesdropping
> Child + Mouth = Screaming
> Mouth + Dog = Barking
> Mouth + Bird = Singing
> Knife + Heart = Anxiety, etc.[39]

What Eisenstein calls his "dramatic principle," but what is more precisely understood as the limit case of the theatrical–grotesque schematization, is a montage method of presenting action which makes the sense—what Eisenstein at this point called the "concept"—of action ("crying," "eavesdropping," "screaming," etc.) emerge out of a purely indirect form of representation. The juxtaposition or collision of two incongruent and seemingly conflictual fragments that do not in themselves contain a reference to action produces the sense of action as a pure event (an explosion). The sense of action emerges through the deployment of a conflictual schema that organizes the juxtaposition of representational fragments, but without grounding this emergence in a representational way. For this reason, Eisenstein's idea of montage in "Dramaturgy of Film Form" has been summed up with the following equation: A × B = C, where A and B stand for the representational fragments, × stands for the conflictual schema of their arrangement, and C is the new sense that emerges as the product of the schematic arrangement.[40] The "dramatic" principle of conflictual juxtaposition is slightly different from the comparative schema we observed in the finale of *Strike,* where Eisenstein still maintained some representational content related to the sense of action. The "dramatic" principle pushes to the extreme and offers something like an ideal type of the very gesture of theatrical–grotesque presentation of action, because it tends toward a complete divorce of the sense of action from its representation.

Eisenstein opposes his "dramatic" conception of montage to the "epic" principle (identified with the montage methods of Kuleshov and Pudovkin). "Epic" stands for a type of montage that does not seek to fundamentally—qualitatively—separate the sense of action it produces from the unfolding of action in a series of representational fragments. The logic of the epic can therefore be illustrated in the following way: A + B = AB. In the absence of a dramatic or theatrical–grotesque schema, the epic filmmakers rely on the simple operation of addition, placing representational fragments not in conflict with each other but one on top of another "like building blocks." What this means is that, in the epic, the sense of action is essentially tied and subordinated to the successive "unrolling" or unfolding of the representational fragments of action within the film's totality. This means that within the epic, the sense of action may never be experienced as an event in itself, qualitatively different from the representational texture of the film, as is the case in Eisenstein's examples of dramatic montage, where the sense of SCREAMING suddenly explodes out of a schematic juxtaposition of two representational fragments—CHILD × MOUTH—that in no way represent "screaming."

Eisenstein's dramatic and conflictual schema carries a certain risk: the divorce of the presentation of action as an explosive event from its representational basis renders the sense of action radically unstable. How may we, for instance, be certain that the sense of "anxiety" emerges out of a collision between two representations: knife and heart? Is it not quite possible that out of such a collision an entirely different sense might emerge, or that, seeing the colliding representational fragments, we will simply draw a blank, that no sense of action will be suggested to us? Even if a sense of "anxiety" is produced, how may it not appear as utterly disorienting, senseless in its complete detachment from the represented reality out of whose antagonistic ordering it emerges? There is a risk that the theatrical–grotesque tendency takes on when Eisenstein pushes it to its "dramatic" limit, as he tries to do in "Dramaturgy of Film Form." His attempt to completely emancipate the sense of action from representation leads sense toward becoming an almost purely contingent event, in which it is difficult to distinguish between sense and a certain delirium of sense or non-sense.

The Pressure of the Epic

The tendency toward a pure contingency of sense autonomous from its "objective" relation to representation (and therefore difficult to distinguish from a kind of "subjective" delirium or non-sense), which Eisenstein theorizes in his utopian vision of intellectual montage in the late 1920s, is present already in *Strike* and in his first experiments with attractional schemas of montage. How else might one otherwise explain the reaction to Eisenstein's first film by the "epic" Lev Kuleshov, who, in 1926, objected precisely to the lack of unity in *Strike,* the lack of a more "objective" relationship between the sense of action and its representation in the final sequence of the massacre:

> The montage of *Strike* is significantly weaker. . . . Everything is too chopped up, there are places that lack all sense of connection and, what's most important, any unifying line of action, any unifying line of the *siuzhet,* is often missing. For instance, in the very weakest final section of the massacre. The associative montage—the slaughterhouse and the parallel slaughter of the workers—hardly has any right to be employed in its present form. This scene in the slaughterhouse, unprepared by a second, parallel line of action, is deficient.[41]

Eisenstein's penchant for the theatrical–grotesque, for the monstrous juxtaposition of dismembered series without representational unity, disturbs the possibility of an epic comprehension of the work as a narrative unity or as the embodiment of a unified line of action. For Kuleshov, the final sequence of the massacre is the weakest, because it is at the furthest remove from his own epic principle, according to which it is the unity of representation that should ground the sense of action produced by a film, and according to which the production of sense that would be autonomous from such representational unity is simply a risk not worth taking. Eisenstein is therefore not entirely mistaken when he identifies Kuleshov as the name of a certain pressure toward the epic, the pressure of a genre different from the theatrical–grotesque and a vision of cinema that, according to Eisenstein, limits the "dramatic" capacities of montage.

Another look at *Strike* may, however, reveal that the principled opposition between the theatrical–grotesque ("dramatic") and the "epic" in Eisenstein's case is not simply an external one, an opposition between Eisenstein's own poetics and the poetic methods of other singular figures of Soviet cinema. Rather, it is also something internal, very much intimate to Eisenstein's work, a tension that animates it from within. The fact not only that he uses "epic" to describe Kuleshov's and Pudovkin's methods (themselves already quite different) but that in another place he also calls a filmmaker as distinct as Dziga Vertov an "epic" filmmaker suggests that we should consider "epic" not so much an objective category as a specifically Eisensteinian oppositional term—that is, a term that remains utterly vague in its meaning, unless it is taken from within the singularly Eisensteinian perspective.[42] This, however, suggests in turn that the opposition between the theatrical–grotesque ("dramatic") and the "epic" is not merely one through which Eisenstein may be distinguished from other Soviet directors, but one through which he tries to come to terms with the pressure of the epic in his own filmic work. In this case, it might be possible to stage the contradiction between the two genres of action—one tending to "dramatically" liberate the sense of action from representation, the other to develop it "epically" within a comprehensive representational totality—as something itself formally decisive for Eisenstein's cinema.

We may remember that *Strike* was initially planned as the first of a six-part series of films on the workers' movement in Russia, a massive epic project called Towards the Dictatorship of the Proletariat (of which Eisenstein managed to complete only *Strike* and half of another film that became *Battleship Potemkin*). The purpose of the project was to relate the post-October present to the longer history of revolutionary struggles of the workers' movement in Russia. Though *Strike* does not refer to a concrete historical event, it does make concrete the situation and the activity of struggle under the prerevolutionary regime of autocratic capitalism. As it was produced to make the post-October audiences integrate the revolutionary past into their new present, the film also places this new Soviet present within a larger historical continuity. *Strike* implicitly attempts to turn the present into the fulfillment of past struggles, which are thereby contained in the present in the form of a memory. The global task of the film, along with the entire six-part series of Towards the Dictatorship of the Proletariat, was an epic recollection whose function was to keep alive the claim of the past on the present, to produce a living memory of the past that could serve as a call for revolutionary vigilance to be maintained after the success of the October Revolution.

The unifying perspective of the present recollecting the past and the past living on in the present is inscribed into the film with its opening motto, a statement by Lenin: "The strength of the working class is organization. Without organization of the masses, the proletariat is nothing. Organized, it is everything. Being organized means unity of action, the unity of practical activity. Lenin. 1907." Insofar as the film is a film about the failure and violent defeat of the workers' strike in pre-Revolutionary times, it demands of the viewer to experience the remarkable multiplicity of actions and their failure through the question of unity, specifically an organized unity of action whose historical significance becomes fully elucidated only with the triumph of the Bolshevik Party in the October Revolution. Without the form of unity supplied by party organization, a form that ties together and represents the multiplicity of mass activity as an effective totality, the proletarian mass is nothing. Without party unity, the proletariat is unable to act at the level of its world-historical, heroic, and revolutionary task—a fact demonstrated in *Strike* by the defeat and violent massacre of the workers. Eisenstein's attractional schema in the final sequence of slaughter might therefore be interpreted as an attempt to impress on us at the level of form itself the remarkable sense of mass activity, which is doomed to defeat precisely because it does not find a proper unity and remains dismembered. The carnage of the workers and the absence of its unitary representation would in this sense belong together as two sides of the same coin, both demonstrating the necessity of the unifying figure of the party.

Yet the failure of the past must not only be explained according to its historical meaning (defeat as necessary without strong party organization). It must also be recollected and remembered so that the historical meaning of the past might live on in the specific form provided for it by the present. For this reason, the film does not actually end with the sequence we have been calling the finale of *Strike,* the devastating massacre of the workers, but with a brief coda, a sequence of shots whose purpose is precisely to convert what we experience as a remarkably open sequence of dismembered series of actions into a completed and accomplished event.

In extreme close-up, we see the eyes of Strongin, the worker whose suicide earlier in the film triggered the rebellious strike of the factory workers. The angry eyes of the proletarian are interrupted by an intertitle that sets up the film's concluding effort to negotiate the relationship between the prerevolutionary past it has represented and the present it itself occupies: "And like bloody unforgettable scars on the body of the proletariat lay the wounds of Lena, Talka, Zlatoust, Yaroslavl, Tsaritsyn, Kostroma." The intertitle attempts to name the anonymous mass of workers and to gather them up into the unified proletarian body (a task perhaps contradicted by the serial form of the list), as well as to construct something like an idea of a living memory by instructing the spectator to see in the "scars," traces visible in the present, the presence of "wounds"—a past which, though overcome by the present, may still be sensed as an open question, somehow not fully "healed," under the layer of the present time, thus intensifying the latter's revolutionary exigency. After the intertitle, there follows another extreme close-up of Strongin's eyes. The frowning folds of his face now suddenly open into an expression of alarm. And finally, the two intertitles that conclude the film: "Remember" and "Proletarians" (Figure 13).

The action of the carnage, the remarkable theatrical–grotesque openness with its dismembered attractional series, is given closure and in this sense appears as re-membered in the present as both something overcome (the victory of October) and a warning or reminder (the mistake of the past—disunity of action—as a constant threat). There is undoubtedly something theatrical and grotesque about this moment of the film, if we observe it simply by itself, with its violently incongruous juxtaposition of the extreme close-up of the eyes and the written text. But against the preceding sequence of the

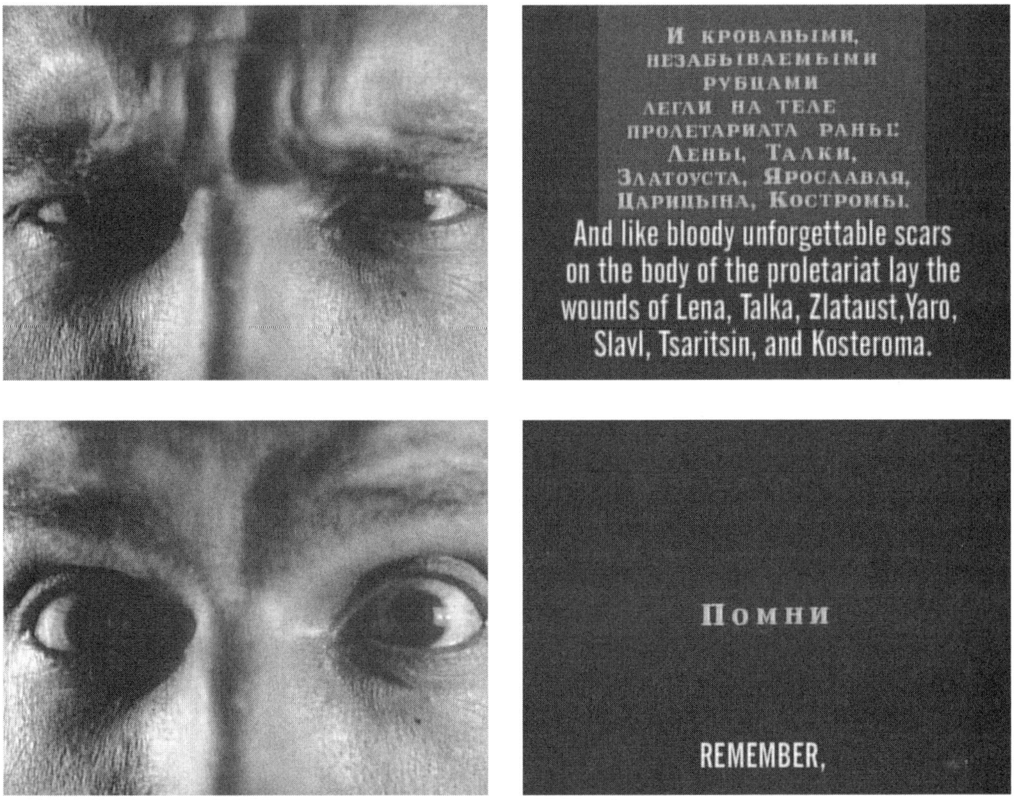

И кровавыми,
незабываемыми
рубцами
легли на теле
пролетариата раны:
Лены, Талки,
Златоуста, Ярославля,
Царицына, Костромы.
And like bloody unforgettable scars on the body of the proletariat lay the wounds of Lena, Talka, Zlataust,Yaro, Slavl, Tsaritsin, and Kosteroma.
Помни
REMEMBER,

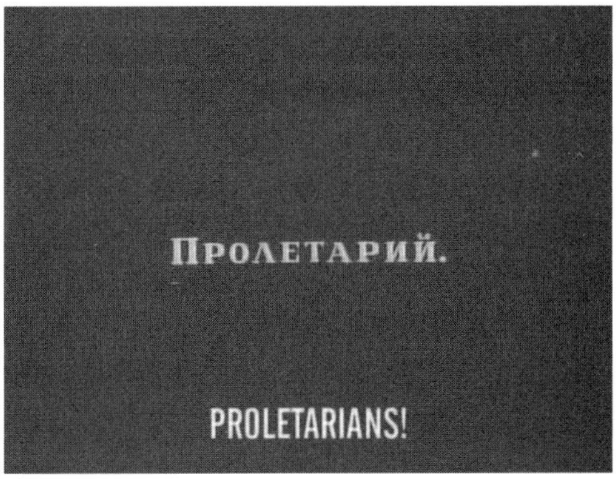

Figure 13. "Remember, Proletarians!" The concluding shots of *Strike.*

massacre, this little bit of grotesquerie nevertheless produces an epic effect of closure. It suggests what will occupy our critical focus below, namely, that the theatrical–grotesque ("dramatic") and the epic in Eisenstein's filmic work not only stand in opposition to each other but form a veritable contradiction, whose presence may be observed in the fact that one genre may be at work in and through the other. Here in *Strike,* for instance, two pieces of theatrical–grotesque ("dramatic") montage of attractions, placed one after another, produce an effect of the epic.

What takes place between the finale (the massacre) and the coda ("Remember!") is an attempt to convert a dismembered series of actions organized according to the attractional schema of comparison into a re-membered representational unity (the necessity of party unity, the demand of revolutionary memory). The sense of the action of carnage, which has been delinked from the pressure of a representational unity, becomes now a representative part (a didactic example, even) within a larger totality: none other than the long epic of the Revolution itself, from its underground days to its taking possession of history. A presentation of action, which in the sequence of carnage was missing its centerpiece, becomes now itself precisely such a centerpiece within the construction of revolutionary memory. In the theatrical–grotesque finale, we saw the sense of action emerge without reference to a unified representational cause—the attractional comparative schema serving precisely as a way of doing away with the causal unity of action. Yet the film ultimately reinterprets this sense as a moment in the progressive realization of a single and unitary Cause of revolutionary history, the relationship to which is, according to the film, maintained by the form of the Leninist Party and the watchful collective memory of the Soviet people.

Between the finale of *Strike* and the film's coda, there occurs a transformation of the sense of action produced by the theatrical–grotesque form of montage of attractions into an event that is no longer "dramatic" but rather epic in nature. It was Hegel, in his lectures on *Aesthetics,* who described as characteristic of the epic precisely such passing of action into the purposeful form of a narratable event *(Begebnis)* or into "the *fact* [*Begebenheit*] of an action."[43] The epic produces a sense of action not so much as it is encountered in its "subjective" happening but as something complete and concluded. Through this, action is given a certain degree of "objectivity" and representational unity. As Jean-Pierre Dubost writes, the narratable event or *Begebenheit* is action treated as a "prearticulated given," worthy of being "taken into account by the narrative."[44] The epic transforms the *casus,* the occurrence of action, into a *casus narrativus,* action that has assumed a form appropriately predisposed for its inclusion within a larger narrative whole. In *Strike,* the case of an open and emancipated sense of action—produced by Eisenstein's handling of the massacre of the workers in the finale of the film—assumes, in the perspective of the coda, the status of a *casus narrativus,* of a narratable event, which allows it to become integrated into the larger epic whole: the sense of action that proceeds from the representation of the unitary historical cause of revolutionary struggle.

Here, drawing further on German terminology might prove useful, for it allows us to distinguish two different conceptions of the event and consequently to identify two distinct ways of giving form to action. Action purposefully (pre)articulated into a narratable event *(Begebnis),* which belongs to the epic, can be juxtaposed to something that we will call the *event of action itself,* the theatrical–grotesque occurrence of action as such, for which that other, philosophically notorious, German name for event—*Ereignis*—may be used. As a term, *Ereignis* may not very easily be extricated from Heidegger and his poetic philosophy following his famous Turn, where, translated variously as Event, Appropriation, Enowning, it plays a central role in thinking the historicity of being.[45] Perhaps this, too, is not to our disadvantage, and some Heideggerian resonances of the term might in fact be maintained and even made useful in clarifying this different—nonepic—treatment of action that we find in Eisenstein's theatrical–grotesque method of montage of attractions. The principle of the attractional schema that montage follows does not give us action in the form of a narratable event *(Begebnis),* but neither does it present action as "mere happening," what Hegel would have called *blosses Geschehen,* a term that suggests a certain formlessness of action. What the montage of attractions tends toward and what it wishes to construct is the *Ereignis,* the event of action itself. What is at stake in the theatrical–grotesque handling of action is the attempt to manifest, to place before our eyes *(Eräugnen),* the structures (the schemas, the designs, the forms) proper *(eigen)* to action itself and therefore different from action as it may appear from the perspective of the epic in which it is (as a narratable event, *Begebnis*) inevitably made to adapt to the pressure of some larger unity or cause. What the theatrical–grotesque handling of action attempts, in other words, is to present action not as an accomplished fact articulated in advance but as it might reveal itself in its own proper way, as it may seize us—or, precisely, attract us—in its own proper visibility, independently of our attempt to give it the shape of an event within a story. The difference is one between action that is itself the subject of an event (the theatrical–grotesque) and action that has become an event represented as a given fact, the object to be taken up by the subject of a narrative or plot development (the epic).

In the gap and the shift between its finale and its coda, *Strike* accomplishes the transformation or the passing of an *Ereignis,* the event of action itself, into action as a narratable event *(Begebnis)*—the passage from action, which manifests first in search of a form or schema properly its own, into something that takes place in the form proper to the epic and its memory. To put it another way, the film moves from action maintained in its own visibility to the abandonment of this visibility in the name of a telling and remembering of the action's heroic meaning.

More than simply accomplishing this passage, the remarkable feature of *Strike* is that it exhibits the difference between these two radically different genres of action and the two distinct forms of presenting the event. History, Eisenstein seems to be saying, takes or appropriates *(Ereignet)* its place in the dismembered form of an action, which montage is able to present according to its own proper schema, before we get to embody it, remember it, comprehend it as an event within a story *(Begebnis).* What seems to be at stake for Eisenstein is the assertion of both the need and the pressure for the revolutionary epic as well as the fact that the presentation of revolutionary action does not necessarily have its source or its ground in the form of epic representation. Even if we assume, as Eisenstein in some way does in *Strike,* the epic form as the horizon of revolutionary action, there remains the question of the event of action itself, without which the epic horizon would appear empty, devoid of much active sense, its heroic figures reduced to immobile shadows.

What matters therefore is not to decide between the theatrical–grotesque and the epic, between the event of action itself *(Ereignis)* and action recollected in the form of a narratable event *(Begebnis),* but to grasp them in tension—an internal tension that characterizes Eisenstein's formal work in his films. That we are indeed dealing with a contradiction characteristic of the very form of Eisenstein's work can, for instance, be illustrated by the fact that it is possible to observe the tension both at the level of *Strike*'s macrostructure, the conception of the film as a whole, and its microstructure, the operations at work in individual moments and episodes of the film.

We have seen the extent that action in the film as a whole, from Lenin's opening motto to the closing injunction to remember, becomes embraced by a strong pressure to assume the shape of an epic event, an exemplary expression of the unified cause of a larger revolutionary history. Yet, Eisenstein's own statements regarding the film articulate a very different idea of the film, which we may describe anachronistically as the idea of *Strike* as a work of a militant *enquete* or inquest (a term that belongs to a later, Maoist stage of twentieth-century revolutionary politics). The approach of *Strike*—which "allows us to conceive of arranging something other than 'little stories' and 'little romances' with a 'little intrigue'"—is conceived by Eisenstein as an investigation into the *"technique of the underground."* It is the attempt, as he says, to "provide an *outline of its* [the revolutionary underground's] *production methods* in individual characteristic examples."[46] Rather than epic unity, this description suggests an interest in exploring the strike as a multiplicity of instances of militant action and repressive counteraction. What must be investigated through the work of montage are the dismembered series of actions, arranged according to the schema that the event of the strike appropriates for itself: in what forms does the event of a strike think itself? What design belongs properly to the subjectivity of a strike? This is a question markedly different from the epic problem of situating the strike within the story of the Revolution.

Next to this "macro" question of the overall structure and purpose of the film, the formal tension between the theatrical–grotesque and the epic may also be observed at the film's "micro" level, as something that characterizes and motivates the formal decisions at every point within the film. Let us, for instance, observe the moment of Strongin's suicide, the first dramatic peak in the film's plot, which serves as the tipping point for the strike itself. Eisenstein presents Strongin's suicide by hanging, the desperate worker's response to an unjust accusation of thievery, in a way comparable to the final massacre of workers: the action of hanging itself is missing from the assemblage of actions that Eisenstein machines together in presenting to us the sense of the action. Rather than showing us the hanging, Eisenstein handles the action of the suicide through a set of details that never directly depicts the suicide itself: a despondent Strongin sits on a machine; a close-up of Strongin's hands making a noose with his belt; a close-up of a stool that falls from underneath Strongin's feet; a close-up of the belt attached to the top of a machine that tightens; a close-up of Strongin's feet dangling in the air (Figure 14).

Only then, after this dismembered presentation of action in its details, which Eisenstein intercuts with shots of other workers going about their business on the factory floor, do we see an image of an already dead Strongin, his head cut off by the frame as he hangs from a machine, with a group of workers who finally notice him and begin to rush toward him in order to dismount his hanging corpse. At this point what has been a remarkably reduced and intimate presentation of the suicide—the schema of which followed Eisenstein's favorite device of synecdoche or the *pars pro toto,* the partial details presented in close-up standing in for the event as a whole—begins to turn into a narratable, public event. In fact, the happening assumes the shape of what is perhaps *the* narrative event of all narrative events: the crucifixion and the descent from the cross. For this is the iconographic reference and the tradition into which Eisenstein wishes to insert the sense of Strongin's suicide (Figure 15).

The worker's suicide, which took place at a remove, obscured and unbeknownst to other workers, is now suddenly endowed with a plenitude of representational meaning, far exceeding the singular sense of the action's initial schematic presentation. The event of the suicide itself is transformed into an event suitably prearticulated for a (re)telling, according to which we can now read the appearance of the collective of workers circling around the dead body of Strongin, lowering and lamenting the corpse, as part of the epic (Christian) story of the sacrifice and redemption of humanity.

Figure 14. Strongin's suicide in *Strike.*

This brief examination of the formal tension at work in the sequence of Strongin's suicide allows us to point to another dimension at stake in the difference between the theatrical–grotesque and the epic, that is, the event of action itself and action as a narratable event. The passage from the theatrical *Ereignis* of the suicide to its recollection as an epic *Begebnis* involves a refocusing from a form of presentation in which action occurs not only without the central piece of action, but also without the representation of the human figure, to a form of action in which the human figure becomes primary, the center of representation. The shift from theatrical–grotesque to the epic–heroic includes the anthropomorphization of action, which in the form of its own proper event, the initial event of the suicide, is not anthropomorphic. Eisenstein's presentation of Strongin's suicide by hanging is striking precisely because it works without the integral human figure, which it replaces with a series of details, the spare parts of the human body cut off by the frame, escaping centrifugally, equal to other objects that populate the scene. Seeking then to inscribe the sense of Strongin's suicide into the epic narrative of sacrifice and redemption (revolution or the emergence of the revolutionary collective) by attaching it to the iconography of the Descent, Eisenstein places the human figure squarely in the center of his representation of action.

If, as we discussed earlier in the chapter, for Meyerhold the human actor was a vehicle for the emancipation of the puppet, and the idea of the theatrical–grotesque involved a certain inhumanization of action, then one could say that Eisenstein, with the shifts between the theatrical–grotesque and the epic as exemplified in *Strike,* envisions the possibility of the human reemerging from its erasure by the theatrical–grotesque and the attractional schema of montage. Epic forms of action are essentially anthropomorphic. "It is the wrath of Achilles which is to be found in the Iliad and to provide the unifying point."[47] The theatrical–grotesque presentation of action, on the contrary, does not need the human figure to serve as the center. Precisely because it seeks an essentially decentered schema of action, the theatrical–grotesque of the montage of attractions does not demand that action be put on an anthropomorphic ground and be made to converge on the human figure. Instead, the event of action itself *(Ereignis)* appears as an assemblage of various actions, without touching on the human as the focal point in the middle. In Hegel's terms, this absence of the human center would mean that in the theatrical–grotesque and the montage of attractions, actions relate to each other in a purely external way, which is precisely how he defines "mere happening" *(blosses Geschehen)*: action as pure externality, uninformed by the interiority of human intentions and passions. (This, incidentally, is also how we may translate Kuleshov's reaction to the finale of *Strike*: "There is no human unity here, things are merely happening—*blosses Geschehen*!") Yet the lesson of the theatrical–grotesque and of the Eisensteinian montage of attractions is

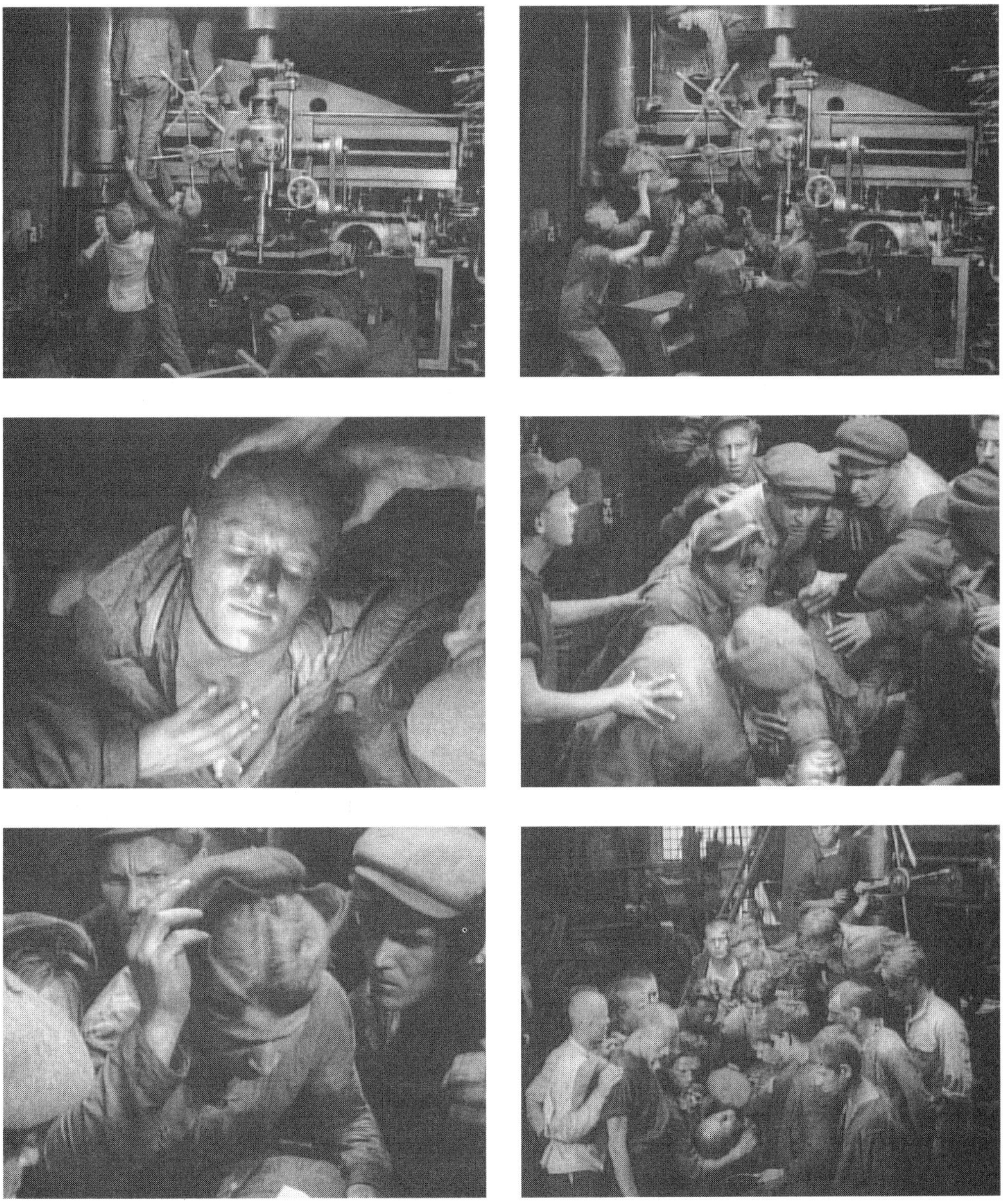

Figure 15. The iconography of the descent from the cross as the factory workers dismount Strongin's hanging body in *Strike*.

precisely that what appears as "mere happening," as a pure exteriority of actions devoid of human meaning, might in fact hide the event of action itself, the form or the design of action that takes its place without giving privilege to the human and within which the humanity—which is also to say, history and politics—must first look for the possibility of their appearance.

The Form-Problem and Eisenstein's Filmic Work

To show that what we are describing is not merely a tension but a veritable contradiction, it is necessary to demonstrate not only how the two genres of action—the theatrical–grotesque and the epic—are present in Eisenstein's filmic work but also that each is somehow always already at work in the other. This more precise sense of the contradiction is intimated already by *Strike,* where it is, for example, the theatrical–grotesque quality of the montage of attractions in the final massacre of the workers that opens the possibility of its transformation and representation as an epic event, a *casus narrativus* belonging to the long story of revolutionary history. It is the event of action itself *(Ereignis)*—action appropriating for itself its proper forms in the work of montage—that opens up and harbors the possibility as well as the need for its retranslation into the stuff of epic narrative *(Begebnis).* But what must then be shown as well is how this epic absorption of the evental sense of action produced by the theatrical–grotesque in Eisenstein's films also comes at a certain price. For the epic representation of action which offers us something like the event memorialized—an event without its evental aspect—does not manage to control or subdue the theatrical–grotesque, evental sense of action, which means that precisely through the operation of making the event of action become part of a larger epic, narrative movement, the filmic work opens the epic–heroic representation itself to a radical disturbance and a potential overturning from the side of the theatrical–grotesque. The confidence of the epic itself prepares the ground for the reappearance of the evental sense of action and the theatrical–grotesque on a higher plane, the plane of the narrative making sense of history.

FROM GROTESQUE TO EPIC AND BACK: *THE GENERAL LINE*

Early in Eisenstein's *The General Line* (1926–29), we encounter a scene of the political becoming of the film's protagonist, the peasant woman Marfa Lapkina. The scene depicts the birth of Marfa's political or militant consciousness, which turns her into the epic heroine of the film, whose actions then come to embody the new collective subject of Soviet farm labor and help us traverse the new situation of the Russian countryside in the throes of the process of mass collectivization and Stalin's violent upheaval. It is time to plow the

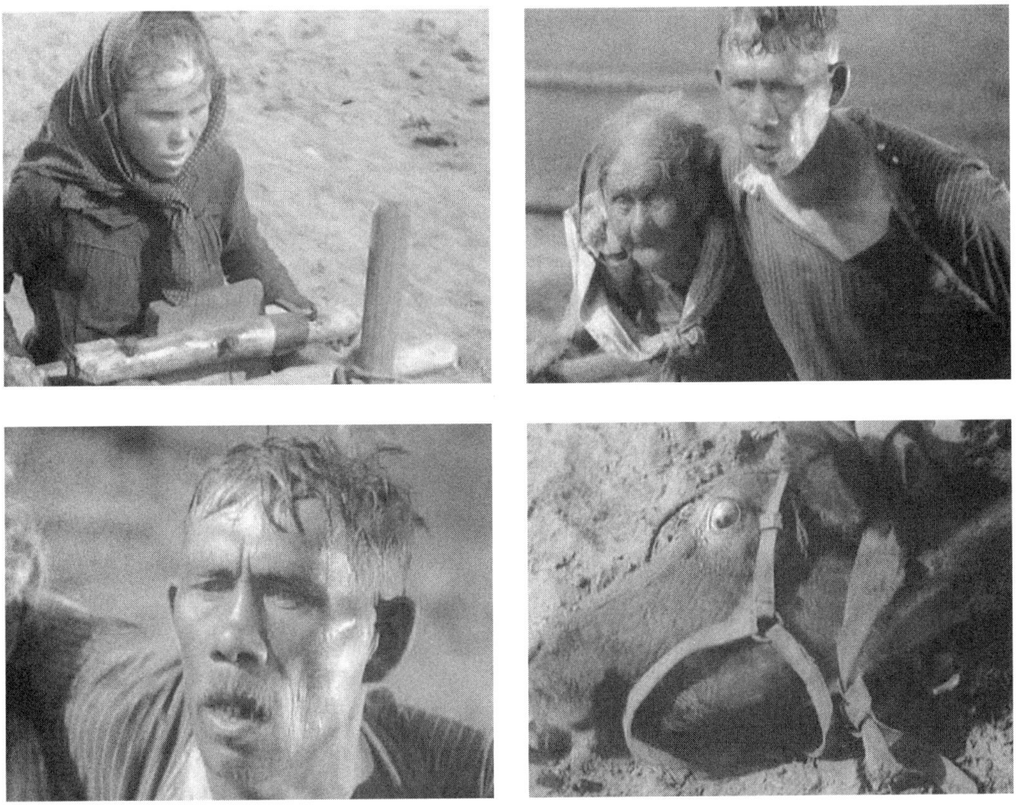

Figure 16. The toiling peasants compared to exhausted animals in *The General Line* (1926–29).

fields, yet Marfa, along with other impoverished peasants, cannot afford to buy a horse. Without the aid of a strong horse, the task of plowing her field and preparing it for planting is impossible. Refused help by the kulaks, Marfa and her emaciated cow are made to pull the plow to the limit of exhaustion. Eisenstein organizes his montage in such a way that he compares or makes equivalent the exhausted animals pulling the plow and the exhausted peasants (Figure 16).

In the moment of drudgery, however, Marfa suddenly lifts the plow and angrily drops it to the ground. She then repeats the same violent gesture with her arms, striking the handles of the plow with her fists and exclaiming, "It is impossible to live this way!" (нельзя так жить!; *Nel'zia tak zhit'*!). Eisenstein cuts up Marfa's sentence and intercuts it with shots that repeat her gesture of refusal—the downward striking movement of her arms. As the gesture becomes intercut with the titles that convey Marfa's exclamation, we are suddenly transported from the field to a very different place. Allowing us, first,

Figure 17. From the gesture of refusal to the discourse of collectivity. The displacement of Marfa from the field to the village assembly in *The General Line.*

to recognize the change of location only by the transformation of Marfa's clothing, Eisenstein then pulls away to reveal Marfa now standing atop a podium addressing her fellow villagers—an entirely different situation than that of her solitary toil in the field. With the series of disconnected words (three, *"Nel'zia!"* + one, *"tak"* + one, *"zhit'"*) that become assembled into a sentence, the sequence transports Marfa from her privately owned plot of land to the communal place of the village assembly (Figure 17).

With this, the initial gesture of refusal becomes transformed and its purely negative content (her refusal to continue) filled by something a bit more positive: the demand for a collective or farm cooperative—a demand that takes the form of a political slogan ("It is impossible to live separately"; "We must do it together"). What Eisenstein stages in these images is the becoming-militant of the peasant woman, the sudden appearance of a political animal in the place, but also in the displacement of the place, occupied by the animal-

peasant. The sequence presents the birth of political speech and of political being, which emerges through the "No!" announced by the toiling and suffering body, whose act of refusal opens up the possibility for the demand of a new collectivity.

What interests us here is the form with which Eisenstein stages this event, in which we encounter the very birth of political speech and action. Eisenstein employs a device that combines the repetition of a single gesture—the violent downward movement of Marfa's arms—with the operation of displacement that transports the gesture to a new place. Repetition (of a gesture) + displacement (of the same gesture): one may count this device among Eisenstein's other theatrical–grotesque schemas of action (the comparative schema of the finale of *Strike*; the conflictual schema of "The Dramaturgy of Form"; the schema of *pars pro toto* that presents us the suicide of Strongin). Eisenstein uses the schema of "repetition + displacement" to stage the very event of political speech and action, a sudden birth of politics in the place or in the displacement of the place of animal suffering. What is remarkable about the sequence and the formal schema with which it stages this event is the suggestion that the appearance of politics must be related to the ability to displace the negative gesture of refusal, the gesture of an animal that has simply had enough of its private suffering. The event of politics depends, in other words, not on a gesture that would be somehow other than the one offered by an animal's resistance to suffering but, on the contrary, on the ability to displace precisely the gesture of animal refusal as such, to find for it a place in public and thus give it a chance to develop as a discourse, and to thereby introduce the surprising and elusive moment of the repetitive gesture's negativity as a site for new collectivity.

As striking as Eisenstein's attempt to think the event *(Ereignis)* of political speech and action, however, is the pressure exercised within the film by the epic side of the film's ideological enterprise. It is well known that Stalin censored the film and ordered Eisenstein to reshoot and reedit some of its parts to make it conform to the official narrative of the Soviet conquest of the countryside during the process of mass collectivization. Following Marfa's refusal, the question becomes how to incorporate the remarkable form of Marfa's political birth into the narrative of conquest, to integrate the event through which the toiling body turns into a body of militant discourse into a building block for the epic story of the state's conquest of the countryside. To answer this question, the film suddenly displaces Marfa yet again: this time from the podium, where we had just seen her address her fellow villagers, into the audience. In her place at the podium now stands a Bolshevik agronomist, clearly resembling Lenin, who picks up from Marfa's speech to continue within his own proper discourse (Figure 18).

Jacques Aumont has compared the function of Marfa's character in *The General Line* to the linguistic function of the "shifter," a concept introduced by Roman Jakobson, who defined it as a term whose meaning can only be determined in relation to the context of the message communicated between sender and receiver.[48] A "shifter" is therefore a term that does not carry any determinate meaning by itself and whose shifts in meaning point not to its internal semantic richness but to a movement between different contexts that provide it with meaning. Perhaps nowhere as much as in this particular moment of the film does Marfa—displaced from the podium into the audience—appear precisely as such a shifter.

Her displacement signals that we all of a sudden find ourselves in the context of a rather different message than the one communicated by the event of her political becoming. From Marfa's discourse—which the backward villagers laugh at violently, since they obviously find it rather incongruous that the place from which the public address is made would be occupied by the militant peasant woman—we now move to the discourse of state policy. Marfa's role in this new context is not to speak but to affirm the party line, not to exercise her newly found militancy but to vote in favor of the new cooperative. She casts what is practically the sole vote of acquiescence to the state proj-

Figure 18. Marfa as shifter. From the podium into the audience in *The General Line.*

ect, while the rest of the villagers, who want nothing to do with the collective farm, abandon the site. Moving from Marfa to "Lenin," we have moved from an emerging slogan to the state decree, from the event of militant politics in the countryside to the arrival of the militant representative of institutional power, from the schema of political becoming to the figure of the leader.

Eisenstein, of course, feels the need to reunite the two messages brought to light by Marfa's shifting, which articulate quite precisely the ambiguity of the *subject* of politics: a term that somehow means both the one who subjectivates a new political truth and the one who acquiesces to this truth as though it came from outside. In the desire to unite the two meanings, the sequence ends by returning Marfa to the podium, where she now joins "Lenin" as they proclaim the farm cooperative open and observe the rest of the village community scatter and disappear.

It would be rather easy at this point to castigate Eisenstein for the blatant manipulation with which he seems to want to make us believe in the continuity between the political becoming of the peasant and the official discourse of the state as personified in the "Lenin" figure. But it is also possible to read this final reunion as a sign of genuine utopian belief. In the late 1920s, it was still possible to somehow coordinate the two meanings of revolution: revolution as the event of politics and history in places and among people long thought incapable of becoming subjects of such an event and revolution as the conquering project of state power (whose ultimate and disastrous gesture would be precisely to evacuate any evental dimension from the revolution itself). It is possible to raise the option of such a utopian reading because it is not at all clear that *The General Line* manages to reconcile the two meanings of the revolution, or the two places it has provided for Marfa: the theatrical event of her militancy and her role within the epic–heroic of collectivization. In fact, the film's attempt to produce an epic of the Soviet collectivization of the countryside (a narrative of the conquering movement of Soviet power) is haunted throughout by the evental appearance of this new political subjectivity staged in Marfa's act of refusal and the displacement of her gesture within the discourse of militant collectivity.

In the central part of *The General Line,* which presents us with the film's epic movement of conquest—from the first success of the newly established cooperative farm in the backward environment of the Russian countryside to the height of modern, industrialized Soviet agriculture embodied by the Corbusian *sovkhoz*—it is the conquering expansion of space itself that takes place in what is effectively Marfa's dream. The conquering movement is shown in a manner that makes it rather difficult to distinguish the new reality of collectivized agriculture from what takes place in the sleeping mind of the peasant, thereby investing the newly conquered reality itself with a certain excess of subjectivity, a destabilizing excess that suggests to us the inability of the epic movement of the film to fully integrate and contain the event of politics it has so effectively staged in the subjective figure of Marfa's character.

The sequence we have in mind begins at the moment Marfa falls asleep. The new farm collective has just made its first money, which, after a brief threat, is now securely in her possession, stored in the box on which she lays her head. In the series of images that belong to Marfa's dream, Eisenstein shows us first a great bull, an image of virile productivity, rising in a superimposition over a herd of cows—a metaphor of mass impregnation. This is then succeeded by a combination of images of milk bottles filled in an automated dairy factory and a set of more abstract patterns of dynamic, rushing movement of liquids, milk, and white river water, which signal an explosive burst of production we are to understand as both natural and man-made. From there, Eisenstein weaves into the sequence images of farm animals: piglets suckling and wandering the yard of the *sovkhoz,* little chickens hatching in an industrial incubator, and pigs idyllically swimming in the river. And following this, the images jump immediately to the slaughter of pigs and the processing of their meat in the abattoir, which Eisenstein intercuts with a repetitive shot of a spinning porcelain pig figurine. Finally, a tractor appears, coming around the corner and opening a vista onto the modernist architecture of the *sovkhoz* (designed for Eisenstein's film by Andrei Burov, a Soviet follower of Le Corbusier). The *sovkhoz* is a utopian combination of rural idyll (animals moving freely among humans) and scientific laboratory (hygienic, geometric), teeming with activity that is to represent to us the project of the new Soviet collectivist and industrial agriculture.

We have come very far within this dream-movement from the moment in which Marfa's weary head fell in stupor to the utopian space that strikes us as utterly unprecedented in the world of the film. It is only at this point that Eisenstein inserts an intertitle—"Perhaps you think this is all a dream?"—which is followed by a close-up of Marfa turning her head and smiling, her eyes taking in the new utopian reality. As the intertitle raises the question, we have not yet been given a definite sense whether what we see belongs to Marfa's dream or to reality. The realization produces a rather disorienting effect, because it allows us to interpret this moment in two different ways. First, we may suppose that the intertitle and Marfa's reappearance signal a return to reality. We were wrong to think of ourselves as still within the dream. Marfa is no longer dreaming; it is through her wakeful eyes that we now enter the utopian *sovkhoz.* Therefore we should understand this new space as something that might have begun as a dream but is now reality. Yet if that is the case, we may also begin to wonder: at what point exactly did this conquest, this tremendous expansion of space that led us from the modest room of the small collective farm to the magnificence of the *sovkhoz,* turn into something real? We must admit that the question cannot be answered with any satisfaction. And so there immediately opens the possibility of a second reading, namely, Marfa has entered her own dream. What we encounter is not the *sovkhoz* as it might be seen through her wakeful eyes, the reality as she sees it, but rather this place as she dreams herself seeing it—an interpretation supported by the fact that the close-up of Marfa appears against an empty background, separating her from the space of the *sovkhoz.* But this would mean that the new reality of collective, industrial agriculture has itself become derealized.

At this point Eisenstein introduces another intertitle. In response to the question posed by the previous one ("Perhaps you think this is all a dream?"), we read, "Nothing of a kind." A door opens, and we see Marfa enter the pristine barn from which she will select the collective farm's new bull, at which time Eisenstein then adds two more intertitles: "This is"; "a SOVKHOZ!" The intertitles are meant, of course, to assertively assuage our anxiety as we find ourselves oscillating—at the point, we should remember, at which a certain epic conquest of the new historical situation should have reached a moment of completion—between reality and dream, or rather between a dream that has become reality and the sense of a reality that has become derealized. What Eisenstein wishes to relieve us of is precisely the undecidability attached to the u-topic sense of what we are seeing: the *sovkhoz*—the emblematic place of new collective farming—as a place caught between dream and reality but belonging to neither, and thus a nonplace that may only be glimpsed in the chiasmus that makes us circulate between the two equally impossible interpretations.[49]

The utopian dimension, the sense that what we are seeing has no proper place, is at odds with the epic movement of conquest also attempted in the remarkable sequence of Marfa's dream. If the epic movement seeks to reduce the dream's excessive subjectivity and reality's objectivity to a single level, that of the conquered objective reality itself, then what might we call the aspect of the sequence that resists such reduction? Eisenstein himself offers the following possibility:

> Upon what is the fascination of the grotesque constructed? It is constructed upon *unclosed lines.* What is the basic motif of the grotesque? The combination of reality and fantasy, the combination of two opposite levels. . . . A *non-reduction of levels,* an absence of synthesis, are also a mark of the grotesque. Elements which are usually merged and synthesized are present in the grotesque without fusing together. . . . The material and non-material levels are present not as a unity, which shows one side and then another, but the opposite: there is a creeping of one level into the other and *an emphasized collision of the real and the unreal.*[50]

Grotesque is therefore a synthesis without synthesis and can in our case refer to *The General Line*'s synthetic attempt, which, however, does not allow us to fully decide between dream (the unreal) and reality in its representation of the *sovkhoz.* The u-topia, the absence of the place at which dream and reality could meet and reconcile, throws into profound doubt the epic narrative of progress that the film defends at its most explicit, manifest level. For if we may not be certain of the new reality as an integral or at least a decidable reality, then we must also doubt the synthetic vision of the temporal progression that led us to it; consequently, we are also forced to question the epic reduction of distinct temporalities within a single temporality of the film's narrative movement.

The nonreduction of distinct times—what we may call the grotesque schema of time—prevents the narrative of *The General Line* from settling into the temporal continuity characteristic of epic narrative. Even when, as is often the case, the various episodes of the epic are presented in a nonlinear order, this relative freedom of epic construction confirms rather than negates the unifying vector of temporal continuity that organizes the sequence of actions and events. In the case of *The General Line,* however, something rather different is at work: the status of the vector of progress appears utterly ambiguous. It is not a straight line at all but rather an "unclosed" one, a line split and diverging from itself. The new (Soviet industrial agriculture) does not overcome the old (the cosmos and the communal forms of the archaic Russian peasantry), as much as both are made to cohabit a present divided into two irreducible temporal levels, itself and the past—what Ernst Bloch famously characterized with his concept of *Ungleichzeitigkeit* ("non-same-timeliness"; synchronicity of the nonsynchronous). The Blochian *Ungleichzeitigkeit* is perhaps most visible in the status of animals within the film. For the animal is, on one hand, presented as it exists within industrial society: as raw material, meat, to be processed into an industrial product. On the other hand, animals signify something far more archaic: the sacred animal, a totem or a fetish, functioning as the symbol that unifies the village community. The film presents with equal artistic freedom both the indifferent industrial slaughter of pigs and the memorable death of the bull that has become a totemic embodiment of the cooperative—certainly one of the most remarkable scenes of animal death in the entire history of cinema, in which it is the sadness of the cosmos itself that is drawn into mourning for the dying animal. Animal is irreducibly both totem and commodity. Rather than using transition as something that merely serves the narrative movement as it passes from one stage to the other, say, from the archaic peasant cosmos (totem) to the industrial order of modern society (commodity), it is as though *The General Line* made transition itself into an autonomous temporal figure. The film finds everywhere not a progressive vector of time but transitional movement in which time divides: transition no longer as the in-between in the service of a progressive epic temporal continuity but as all there is, creating a sense of temporal disorientation of the present in which different developmental stages can coexist without subsuming or mastering each other.[51]

OPENING THE EPIC EVENT: *BATTLESHIP POTEMKIN* AND *OCTOBER*

The grotesque, whose theatrical and evental sense of action the film had tried to incorporate into a narrative of epic conquest, returns at the narrative level in the form of the nonreducibility of distinct temporal levels that resist the film's attempt to give a purely epic shape to the historical present. The sense of the present constituted in this way—as an articulation of nonsynchronous temporalities, as consisting of nothing but transition—brings a profound disorientation into our sense of time: the historical present is constituted as something destitute, dispossessed of an effective unity. The reappearance of the grotesque thus signals a certain lack or failure of the epic grasp of the present, which in turn introduces a sense of crisis into the very meaning of revolutionary or historical action. The recurrence of the grotesque at the level of the film's narrative—as the impossibility of constructing the sense of the present that would be reducible to a single unified temporal figure (progressive heroic conquest)—suggests that the epic task of revolutionary, historical action constantly finds itself in danger of being carried into a vey different sense of time than the one it itself wishes to construct.

Battleship Potemkin (1925) is often identified as the exemplary revolutionary epic. Yet, strictly speaking, *Potemkin*'s epic movement occupies only the first three parts of the film (everything that takes place before the famous Odessa steps sequence), which lead us from the conflictual situation of the ship to the heroic rebellion of the proletarian sailors and the expansion of the event—the liberated battleship's conquest of the shore—in a festival of solidarity and fraternization between sailors and citizens. This epic movement follows a Christological matrix, the key element of which can be found in the sacrifice of the heroic sailor Vakulinchuk (who is carried out of the sea in a set of shots that iconographically refers to the pietà). The transportation of his corpse from the ship to the shore allows for the emergence of a new collectivity: the citizenry of Odessa, which pours as a mass into the port and gathers in mourning the dead hero. We see their affect undergo a remarkable movement from mournful sorrow to righteous anger and, finally, to revolutionary enthusiasm, symbolized by the raising of the red flag on the battleship. In the first three parts of the film, we observe the heroic action of the rebellious sailors who react to a fundamentally unjust and conflictual situation and, through this action, produce a new one, along with a new figure of collectivity.

But then—*suddenly!*—this first, epic and triumphant conclusion to the film is violently interrupted by the famous sequence of the massacre at the Odessa steps: the surprising entrance of a wholly different kind of movement, coming from some radical elsewhere and difficult to relate to the epically constructed movement of action that brought us to this point. What enters is less a movement supported or carried out by action as movement that overwhelms action and destines it to a certain helplessness or nothingness. In what unfolds, no action is able to react to the movement, take it upon itself, embody its conflicts, and thereby bring it to an end.

Eisenstein stages the futility of human action amid the chaos in the moment of the anguished mother who carries her dead son up the steps to confront the tsarist army and make a plea for an end to the violence. The scene is another Eisensteinian pietà, yet one that fails to produce any new situation or a new figure of collective solidarity. The respite in the infernal movement of the sequence, the pleading mother who tries to act by opposing the descending motion of the tsarist regiment, is fleeting. There is no genuine conflict here, and she is summarily executed, her small boy trampled by the soldiers resuming their descent. It becomes clear at this point that what has suddenly invaded the world of human action and the festival of a newfound solidarity is not another human group but a group of marionettes. It is the terrifying, puppetlike movement embodied by the tsarist regiment that destines all human action to futility. There is no successful heroism, no nobility of combat, no dynamism of action and counteraction, only the automatism of the military puppet-machine and its annihilating power.

In *Potemkin*, the grotesque, which we earlier identified with the event of action itself, returns within the epic narrative of the film as something that overwhelms action, a sheer cruelty of movement against which no human action may be opposed, and which therefore has to be renegotiated and given a form other than the epic–heroic. In the case of the Odessa steps sequence, Eisenstein responds to this problem by introducing another of his schemas.

Here the epic sweep of the situation is abandoned in favor of a schematic organization that follows the dialectical logic of graphic conflict. First, the vertical lines (the flight of the people and the direction of the military march) conflict and oppose the horizontality of the steps themselves. That conflict is then set against, and indeed sublated within, forms of diagonal lines seeking to reconcile the opposition of horizontality and verticality. Yet the diagonals themselves, by producing their own divisions within the frame, work to reintroduce graphic tension and conflict. It is following this further set of conflicting graphic orientations that the famous baby carriage appears. From the point of view of human action, the carriage is a perfect illustration of helplessness, the futility of the epic: it figures the nothingness of action. Its circular wheels do, however, offer the possibility to Eisenstein of somehow motivating anew all the graphic conflicts that he schematically distributes throughout the sequence as the circle form unites in itself all other lines: horizontals, verticals, and diagonals (Figure 19). Yet even here, what ultimately takes place is not the affirmation of the conciliatory figure of the circle as a figure of the dialectical sublation of conflict, but instead a final assertion of the diagonal cut in the gesture of the "Cossack," whose violent swipe of arm and sword from top right corner to bottom left of the frame strikes at the carriage.

If the sequence of the Odessa steps (part 4 of *Potemkin*) offers us the temporal experience of suddenness or surprise so overwhelming in its movement that it cancels out all possibility of epic representation of action, then the film's fifth and final part offers a different but equally anti-epic figure of time. After the surprise of the steps, we are thrown into the experience of anxious suspense as Potemkin, once again at sea, approaches the squadron of the royal navy. Eisenstein organizes suspense as an accelerating movement involving both the action of sailors preparing for the confrontation with the squadron and the mechanical movements of the battleship's engine. In a more common episode of anticipation, the device of suspense would be used to increase the intensity of action, which would then be released with the final arrival of the event. In the case of the end of *Potemkin*, however, anticipation,

Figure 19. The dialectic of graphic conflict in the Odessa steps sequence in *Battleship Potemkin* (1925).

the franticness of action in preparation for the confrontation, results in the absence of an event. What was awaited in suspense (confrontation with the squadron) never comes to pass, and Eisenstein's counterfactual resolution of tension into a moment of solidarity and mutual recognition between Potemkin and the squadron is somehow unsatisfying, a letdown that fails to give us an experience adequate to the sense of the event we have conjured up in our anticipation. Unlike the solidarity between the sailors and the citizens of Odessa in part 3 of the film, this final moment of fraternization between Potemkin's sailors and the sailors of the royal navy seems unearned, hardly a genuine event.

The epic finale of *Battleship Potemkin,* which we have located right before the Odessa steps sequence, is thus supplemented in the film by two other endings that take the form of suddenness (surprise) and anticipation (suspense). If the epic movement of the first three parts of the film manages to reconcile event and its action (in the sense that it is the action of the sailors that produces the event of rebellion, which is then further embodied by the actions of the human collective), then the surprise ending offered in part 4 and the suspenseful ending of part 5 present two different ways of disaligning event and action. In the case of the suddenness and surprise of the Odessa steps sequence, we encounter an event whose movement completely overwhelms action. The suspense in the final part of the film, on the contrary, confronts us with action (even dynamic and frantic action), yet where the event itself (the confrontation) is missing. It is as though Eisenstein wanted to show us what suddenness (event without action) and suspense (action without event) looked like in themselves. The disalignment of event and action in the case of surprising suddenness and anticipative suspense produces a very different sense of temporality from the epic temporality that governs the first three parts of the film. As a consequence, the film does not simply offer an epic representation of a rebellion. Rather, an epic event (an event that appears as heroic and collective action) is supplemented by two alternative "readings" of what an event might also look like. First, as surprise or suddenness, a pure event destines all action to nothingness; then, as anticipation or suspense, pure action fails to reach the occurrence of a genuine event.

If, in the case of *Potemkin,* epic representation is supplemented by two radically different interpretations of the event, *October* (1928) presents an event (the great revolution itself) that never reaches the status of epic portrayal in the first place but is instead divided from within by the existence of incongruous and "nonreducible" temporalities.

We may begin our discussion of *October* with Eisenstein's remarkable presentation within the film of the July Days of 1917, in which he interweaves a series of actions: the massacre and the dispersal of the mass protest on Nevsky Prospect; the capture and torture of a young Bolshevik, another among Eisenstein's many Sebastians, who is violently attacked by bourgeois women, who pierce his torso with their umbrellas; the rising of the bridge that includes the iconic image of the suspended white horse; the bourgeoisie cruelly enjoying itself by throwing issues of *Pravda* into one of St. Petersburg's canals. This is a remarkably complex interweaving that distributes action into distinct series that are somehow rhymed together. The murdered protestors, the pierced proletarian St. Sebastian, the dead horse, the confiscated and destroyed issues of *Pravda*: all of this signals the event of the revolution's temporary defeat and the advancement of the counterrevolution, which reaches its alarming climax in the approach of General Kornilov. But the sense of this temporary defeat as a narrative event, the counterrevolutionary push against the momentum of the revolutionary year, dissolves within the interweaving of fragments whose montage fails to produce a clear impression of unity. Or rather, the unity of the event is so faint, so difficult to grasp in the first couple of viewings, that what one gets instead is the sense of an intricate tapestry of fragments without a common thread. There is no sense of unified, let alone individuated and heroic action emerging against this interwoven tapestry of actions.

The sequence is all historical background. "*The Strike* and *October* are undeniably canvases that lack a major historical figure."[52] This is how Eisenstein characterizes his film more than ten years after its release, looking back at *October* from the perspective of the late 1930s, when the epic–heroic historical film became a central genre in the Stalinist attempt to create a distinct genre system of socialist realist cinema modeled after classical Hollywood. According to Eisenstein in the late 1930s, *October* weaves together a portrayal of the historical situation realized in its epic richness and creates a "colossal resonance of the epoch" that renders the "historical scale of the events." Yet at the same time, the film leaves this epic situation a depopulated landscape, devoid of historical action of equivalent epic–heroic stature. Even the figure of Lenin can hardly be seen as occupying any kind of central or heroic place in *October.*

What the film presents is a vast historical tableau without action, an epic landscape into which no heroic figure has managed to enter. And next to this heroless epic canvas, Eisenstein places humorous games with figurines and little ceramic statuettes, metaphoric play with all kinds of objects, which his intellectual montage organizes into forms of judgment that satirize and evaluate the historical events. In particular, the humor of a montage of objects—yet another version of puppet theater—is there to stage and ridicule the enemy: Kerensky and Kornilov face off as two Napoleon miniatures; the head of the provisional government enters into a mechanical peacock's behind; the reactionary slogan "For God and Country" is mocked in the famous sequence of the gods; Menshevik speeches are dismissingly compared to the playing of harps; and so on. The epic and heroic action missing from the historical canvas is transposed into its inverse in this miniaturized world of play and satire, with objects that fill in for the film's lack of individuated human action. The film's action thereby lacks any unitary or epic scale, and this despite the fact that *October* was to present the great Revolution on the occasion of its tenth anniversary and was thus itself announced as an epic event.

In "Our *October*: Beyond the Played and the Non-played," a text written shortly after the film's appearance, Eisenstein acknowledged the split in the film: the division between epic revolutionary action, created for the mass scenes, and the experimental humor and puns of "intellectual cinema" in the parts of *October* meant to demonstrate the historical outdatedness of the "enemy" (Kerensky, Kornilov, and the Mensheviks). The film "speaks with two voices,"[53] Eisenstein writes: on one hand, it harkens back to *Potemkin*'s pathos of the masses (except that it fails precisely to give us the epic image of a mass-in-action that *Potemkin* approached); on the other, *October* looks forward toward a fully realized cinema of "intellectual montage" (the utopia of filmic movement that could realize conceptual thought directly in the very fabric of images). Eisenstein defends the lack of unity in *October,* mockingly calling the film's schizophrenic split a "tragic fault," as the mark of a transitional film, in which what is at stake is the elaboration of new montage methods whose precedence necessarily pushes unity into the background—a most remarkable statement, especially when one remembers the amount of pressure Eisenstein's project was under as an "official" commemorative project of the Soviet state.

October does not give us a univocal sense of the Revolution but instead opens up the event to a polyphonic arrangement of voices. The formalist film critic and theorist Adrian Piotrovsky, in his contribution to the controversy that embroiled the film immediately after its release, described the film in terms of its

> lack of coordination between three or four essentially different stylistic devices. The film comprises newsreel (the first reel, the shots of fraternization, etc.), the heroism of enthusiastic direct action (in the scenes of the storming of the Winter Palace), extended phrases of high cinematic metaphor (the raising of the bridges, Kerensky's ascent), and lastly elements of aesthetic symbolism (when the statues, the porcelain and the crystal become the center of the picture). This stylistic diversity is not just a matter of form, it is rooted in various artistic traditions and the world-view that they each conceal.[54]

Piotrovsky describes the overall structure (or lack of structure) in *October* in the same terms Eisenstein used to describe the grotesque. As a "non-reduction of levels," the film is composed of a series of distinct devices and genres. One may even find in it a coexistence of distinct and anachronistic artistic traditions (Russian symbolism hiding under the constructivism of montage, for instance[55]). Yet whatever the level one is considering, the film does not impose on this multiplicity of voices any single instance capable of unifying them.

Piotrovsky's response to this formal multiplicity of Eisenstein's film is double. On one hand, he stresses the film's failures: not only the lack of formal unity but also the fact that some sequences appear too long and the script contains a number of mistakes—it creates great dramatic tension before the storming of the Winter Palace but then squanders that drama as it drowns action "in an intrusive display of details."[56] Piotrovsky also points out the omission from the film of certain events (the growth of the workers' movement, the collapse of the war front). And finally, there are the "individual formal failings of the film,"[57] such as the choice of Nikandrov for the role of Lenin and the "extremely mean" portrayal of Lenin, who is not given a role adequate to his centrality in the Revolution itself.

On the other hand, Piotrovsky's enumeration of the film's faults leads him to a rather striking solution when he proclaims, "*October* must be reedited." What makes Piotrovsky's proposal (made after Eisenstein had already reedited the film once following its initial release) so striking is that his demand to reedit does not rest, despite his criticism of the film, on the idea of one single and true version of *October*. Rather, he imagines the possibility of an infinite series of remontages of the film's material. Which is to say, he imagines a multiplicity of *Octobers*. In this, it is worth quoting him at length:

> The basic raw material from which the film was made is material of exceptionally high quality. . . . The weaknesses of the film do not lie there but in its arrangement, in the montage which, side by side with individual achievements of enormous power and innovation (the raising of the bridges, Kerensky's ascent), simply transgresses in the shortcomings listed above. The reasons of the failure of the montage are understandable enough: they lie in the enormous quantity of film shot without a distinct plan, in the absence of a precise initial script and, lastly, in the short time left to the director after a particularly strenuous shooting schedule to systematize his material. So there can be only one conclusion. Work on *October* cannot be considered finished. We have a second version of the film on our screens now. It differs greatly from the first version, which was shown during the tenth anniversary celebrations, and this is both good and bad. Now we have a right to ask for and to expect yet another version of *October* or, more concretely, several new versions. . . . *"October" must be reedited. That is the conclusion we draw from the first results of its showing and that is the request which we have a right to address to the authors of this monumental and grandiose work.*[58]

The possibility of several new versions of the film—of the film as a process of constant reediting—is here not simply a sign that one may have several perspectives on the historical event of the October Revolution and that it may take time before the true account of the event is finally produced. In Piotrovsky's text, it is rather a certain openness of the event itself that registers in the demand for a constant reworking of the film's montage structure. The multiplication of *Octobers* must here be read as a sign that there is something in Eisenstein's presentation of the revolutionary event that opens up the multiple possibilities of its realization in the form of filmic montage. Eisenstein successfully presents the Revolution as exceeding actualization in any particular representational form—and therefore also refuses to represent the Revolution merely in the form of an epic and the unified temporality of a narratable event. In other words, it is the achievement of Eisenstein's film itself to have opened up the gap between the presentation of the Revolution and its possible representations, the gap that makes the real of the event itself appear through the experimental work with the film's form.

HISTORICAL EPICS: *ALEXANDER NEVSKY* AND *IVAN THE TERRIBLE*

Compared to Eisenstein's four finished silent films, *Alexander Nevsky* (1938) and the two parts of the unfinished trilogy *Ivan the Terrible* (part 1, 1944; part 2, 1946/1958) require a shift in perspective. If his earlier films exhibit an open conflict between the epic–heroic and the theatrical–grotesque, then these last films belong more firmly to a distinct epic genre: the Stalinist, patriotic and national epic of the late 1930s and 1940s. This means that the contradiction we have been tracing must here be considered as something immanent to the epic–heroic film itself. Evgeny Dobrenko has persuasively argued that, despite what may be anachronistically called Eisenstein's auteur status, we miss something crucial about his last films if we simply oppose them, in the name of great art, to the conventionality and predictability of the Stalinist historical epic. On the contrary, *Alexander Nevsky* and *Ivan the Terrible* engage with the genre and transform it from within, thus putting into crisis the genre's ideological function.[59]

Of Eisenstein's two last films, *Alexander Nevsky* seems to fit less problematically into the genre of the Soviet historical epic, whose popularity it also helped establish. In his book on the epic tradition, *Epic and Empire,* David Quint usefully historicizes Eisenstein's film as the final example of the nineteenth-century romantic revival of the national medieval epic that began with James MacPherson's publication of the *Poems of Ossian* in 1760 and included the popularization of the Norse eddas, the *Nibelungenlied, Chanson de Roland, The Song of Igor, The Poem of the Cid,* and so on. The ideological function of the medieval epic was to provide a legitimating narrative for the emerging nations and nation-states of the nineteenth century.[60] As perhaps the last example in the sequence, *Alexander Nevsky* stands, according to Quint, at the point at which the genre turns upon itself in a moment of self-reflection: "*Alexander Nevsky* may represent itself as belonging to an epic genre that has run its historical course—to the point where the genre reverses its original political and class suppositions."[61]

The reversal that *Alexander Nevsky* performs in relation to the conventions of the epic tradition has to do with an overturning of some of the crucial binary oppositions that support the traditional construction of epic action and narration. The film conveys its message "by the manipulation of epic conventions that, the film suggests, have now played out their historical destiny. For if we return to the ideological dichotomies of the shield of Aeneas—West victorious over East, Male over Female, Reason over Nature, the unified One over the disorganized Many, Permanence over Flux—*Alexander Nevsky* can be seen to reverse the entire Virgilian imperialist pattern."[62] Most of these reversals have to do with Russia and the Soviet Union's geopolitical position (caught between West and East, Germany and Japan) as well as echoes of the October Revolution itself (which pushes the film toward the anti-imperial gesture of national liberation). But they also provide for some of the film's most remarkable dramatic and formal solutions. Thus it is the German bishop, the representative of the Holy Roman Empire, who proclaims the traditional epic ideology of imperial conquest (representing, of course, Nazi Germany). It is the German imperial army that is epically all male, possesses technological superiority in its robotic appearance, and exhibits great and terrifying order in its formations (echoes of the soldiers from the Odessa steps). The Russians, whose national Orthodoxy the film stresses against the universalist Catholicism of the imperial German army, ride into battle with women and children, appear in flux, and have to rely on the crafty designs of guerilla warfare rather than technological superiority. The masculine figure of heroic action is also to some extent reversed by the film. "The very strategy of the battle on the ice, where Alexander has his army construct a V-shaped trap to receive the onslaught of the German wedge, 'feminizes' the Russian soldiers,"[63] Quint observes, which means that the victory of the cunning Russian army—Alexander crafts the strategy of the V-shaped trap after hearing a vulgar joke at the military campfire—is presented by Eisenstein as the victory of Eastern hordes over a Western imperial army, a revenge of nature against technocratic civilization.[64]

Despite the film's ability to reverse some of the foundational binaries of the epic tradition, *Alexander Nevsky* does not step outside of, let alone destroy, the genre. The "film can portray Russia as a balanced mean between two politically undesirable extremes," between West and East (order and flux, unity and multiplicity, masculinity and femininity), contesting in this way the "Virgilian ideological categories." But this contestation is a way "to keep them alive as well."[65] "The film remains an epic of empire, for the emperor, the strongman Alexander, has not disappeared."[66] In fact, Eisenstein intended to end the film with the death of Alexander, betrayed and killed by the Mongols after humiliating himself in front of the Mongol ruler. The hero was to be sacrificed, with the Russian army then defeating the Mongols at Kulikovo, the site of Alexander's death, under the command of his grandson. Eisenstein thus initially proposed the continuity of empire (from Alexander to his grandson) at the expense of the emperor; indeed, his initial intention was to present the necessity of the emperor's humiliation and sacrifice for the maintenance of the empire's historical continuity. Stalin, however, refused and decreed that the film must end with Alexander's rout of the Germans, with the leader triumphant ("Such a fine prince could not die!"). In the existing version of the film, therefore, "the prince—and the Stalinist regime he allegorizes—seems a necessary condition for a film 'epic' itself. . . . His film is emblematic of the ways in which this 'new' epic could still evoke ideological categories and patterns of thought that had proved surprisingly tenacious across two millennia: like the 'fine prince,' epic could not die."[67]

Except perhaps in what is the film's most famous sequence—the sequence that has at times been made into an emblem of the film as a whole—where montage reasserts the fragility of the constructed epic vision. The short sequence in which Russian soldiers anxiously anticipate battle at Lake Peipus is the one moment when the film suspends the epic–heroic exigency in its construction of action and instead harkens back to the symbolist vision of "static drama." In his conception of "static drama," which, far more than with human actors, he associated with the powers of the marionette, Maurice Maeterlinck imagined the theatrical potency of an old man who sits perfectly still, slumped in his chair, recording the silence of his room. In that state, the character comes in touch with the cosmic course of life inaccessible to humans engaged in dramatic intrigue.[68] Stasis allowed for completely removing from the stage the movement of narrative and dramatic action in order to register, in the achievement of empirical motionlessness, the presence of a supersensible, universal movement deeper than the movements of human passion and action. Meyerhold adopted Maeterlinck's idea of static drama, according to which it is precisely the withdrawal of the representation of action that allows a deeper reality of movement to appear onstage. In his early writings, Meyerhold thus affirms works of "static theatre" and their lack of external as well as psychological action: "static theatre," according to Meyerhold, aims "at a deft mastery of line, grouping and costume color, which even when static creates an infinitely stronger impression of movement than the naturalistic theater. *Stage movement is achieved not by movement in the literal sense,* but by the disposition of lines and colors, and by the ease and cunning with which these lines and colors are made to cross and vibrate."[69]

In the moment of anticipation at Lake Peipus in *Alexander Nevsky,* all epic and dramatic action—all movement in its "literal sense"—ceases. What surges in its place, supported by the schematism of Eisenstein's montage, is the feeling of another kind of movement, of movement's pure plasticity, whose gesture manifests, in Eisenstein's claim, in the graphic shapes of frame composition and the corresponding "actions" of Sergey Prokofiev's musical score (Figure 20). It is rather striking that this sequence, one that most fully contradicts the framework of the epic–heroic genre to which the film as a whole belongs, stood for Eisenstein as the most important formal achievement of *Alexander Nevsky.* As is well known, Eisenstein analyzes the sequence of anticipation at Lake Peipus as the representative example of his method of audiovisual or "vertical" montage.[70] But this fact relates to a broader principle concerning Eisenstein's work, namely, that almost all of Eisenstein's iconic

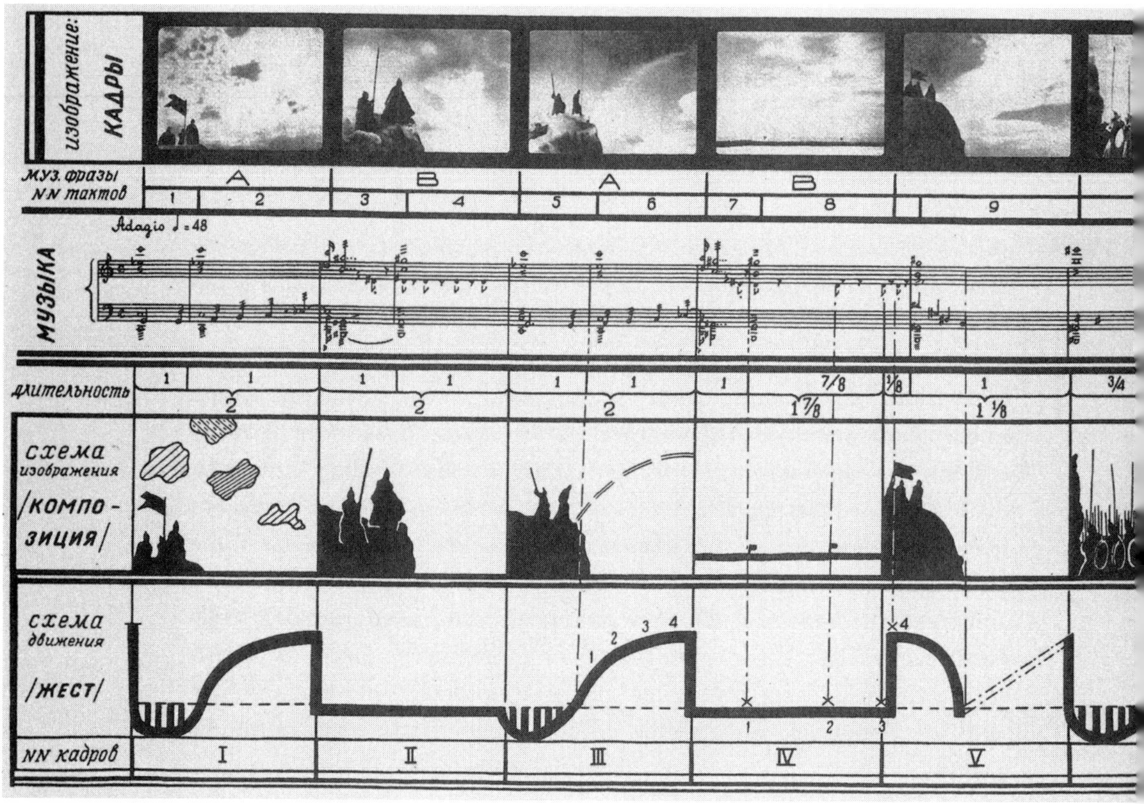

Figure 20. Eisenstein's analysis of the schema or the design of "vertical" (audiovisual) montage in the sequence of anticipation at Lake Peipus in *Alexander Nevsky* (1938).

sequences—those he extracts from the films to preserve in his analytical and theoretical writings—belong to the realm not of the epic–heroic but of the theatrical–grotesque. The example of vertical montage of the Lake Peipus sequence allows us to see the reason why this is the case. It is, namely, precisely because they suspend or withdraw the interest of "literal" movement, the "human" action in its epic and dramatic form, that these sequences, which are thereby transformed into something other than epic episodes, allow us to perceive the schemas of action that belong to the plasticity of movement itself, to movement radically distinct from the representation of human action and thus belonging properly to the work of montage construction.

While *Alexander Nevsky*'s inversion (or reversal) of the traditional epic binaries ultimately leaves the conventional terms of epic in place, Eisenstein's final film, *Ivan the Terrible,* operates differently, more subversively, not by inversion or reversal but through the operation of doubling. In inversion, a

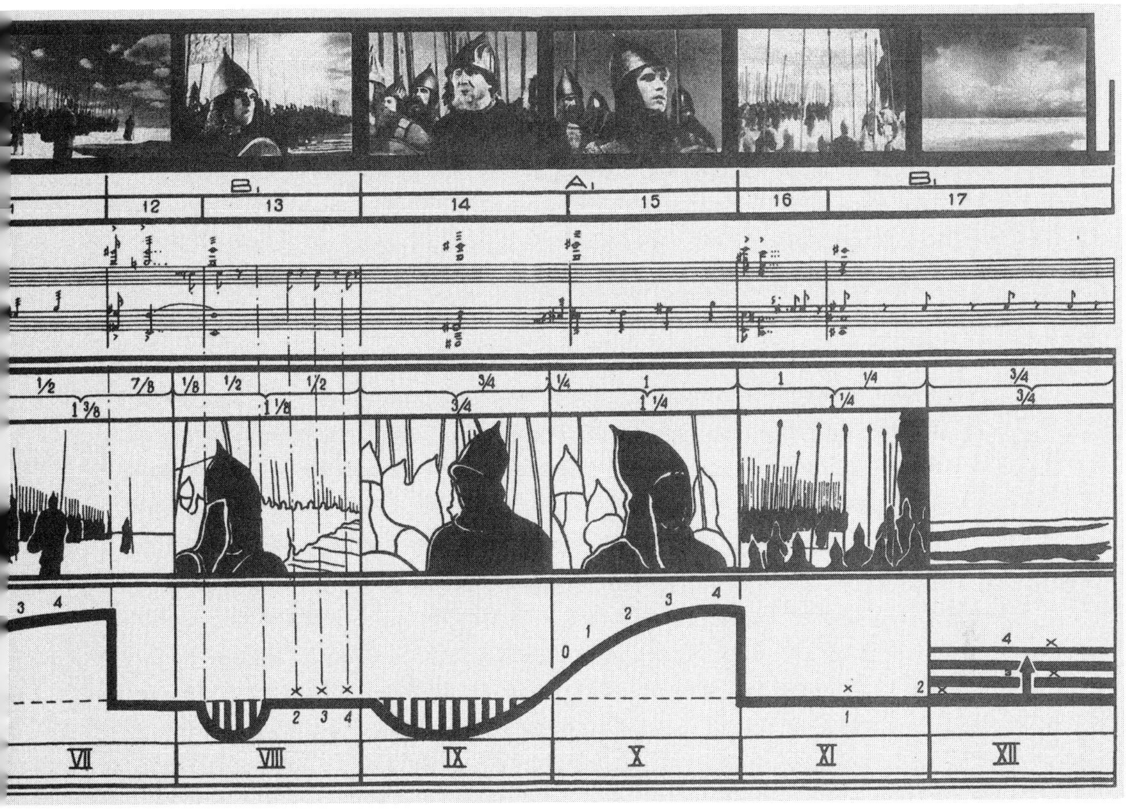

thing is turned on its head, yet the relations of its immanent structure—and thus the nature of the thing itself—are nevertheless maintained. In a moment of doubling, however, it is the very structure of the thing itself that redoubles and thus points to the faulty or insufficient nature of the thing. The case of inversion in *Alexander Nevsky* recodes some of the binary oppositions constitutive of the epic plot but leaves intact the binary structure itself and thus fails to radically threaten the ideological function of epic as the legitimating narrative of power. In the case of doubling in *Ivan the Terrible*—the film whose subject is precisely the question of absolute power—the epic narrative is not inverted, and its values are not reversed. Rather, they are estranged from themselves: the legitimating narrative of power is suddenly confronted with its own double, something that both *is* and *is not* itself, power's intimate likeness and the thing power is unable to openly avow. *Ivan the Terrible,* as has often been observed, especially about its second part, is at once a diagnosis and deconstruction of the Stalinist imaginary of power and specifically of the ideological operation of power that sought to legitimate itself through the figure of epic–heroic action and the genre of the historical film.[71]

The redoubling of the historical genre and its epic narrative within *Ivan* is supported by a series of various kinds of doubling, three of which are of particular importance for the analysis of Eisenstein's approach to the epic in this film.

First, there is Eisenstein's extensive use of shadows (Figure 21). The shadows, on one hand, double the human figures and their actions. But we must understand doubling here as more than merely repetitive imitation of human figures. In *Ivan the Terrible,* Eisenstein thinks shadows as doubles in precisely the dimension of the double that makes its phenomenon such a disturbing occurrence, namely, the double may appear to be my projection, yet it does not remain limited to an imitation of myself; in fact, the trouble with a double is that it looks like me and yet moves independently of my own movements. "The dual reading of the figure and its shadow [in *Ivan* must be seen as] an outgrowth [*als Auswuchs*] of the primal mental concept positing the *autonomy of each*."[72]

The shadow is an autonomous agent. It does not follow or repeat the movements and actions of human figures but might come in advance of them, enlarge them to monstrous proportions, and "metaphorize" the human figure, which then loses its literal ground.[73] With the discontinuity between the actions of human figures and the shadow-actions, we touch on the other aspect of doubling introduced by Eisenstein's use of shadows, namely, the autonomy of shadow-actions means that each movement and action becomes duplicated, folded in two, and must therefore be seen or read twice. Such a duplicitous sense of action goes against the clarity of the epic pageant, a fact that prompted Zhdanov to protest during Eisenstein's notorious meeting with him, Molotov, and Stalin.[74] For Eisenstein, the duplicity of action places on the viewer the responsibility of reading the images:

> *Overburdenedness* [English in original] with shadows? The film is crowded with too many images? [But they are "too many" only] for *those* who do not "*read*" films, but simply hurry on after its action. That is, for those who come to cinema looking for telegraphic syntax, and not for poetic writing with repetitions, visual analogies [*illiustratsii*] and music—for [those who come to the movies for the sake of] the anecdote alone.[75]

Beyond shadows, two other types of doubling take place at the level of the structuration of the film as a whole by supplementing what is otherwise a relatively simple plot structure in the film. Yuri Tsivian has identified the doubling or recurrence of certain visual and musical motifs (the motif of the "golden rain," for example) that bear a certain resemblance to Wagnerian *leitmotifs,* except that they defy this device's typical cinematic use. Rather than being tied to the appearance of individual characters or themes, Eisenstein's motifs occupy an autonomous formal level of their own. They belong to the

Figure 21. The autonomy of the shadow in *Ivan the Terrible*, part 1 (1944).

film, as Tsivian says.[76] Next to the doubling and recurrence of certain visual motifs, there also occurs, according to Tsivian, a mirroring and aping of certain dramatic and narrative situations, an operation of doubling that exists within, while at the same time going against the grain of, the development of the film's plot (such as the doubling of the coronation scene at the beginning of part 1 in the mock coronation scene during the carnivalesque banquet toward the end of part 2).[77]

Finally, what all these doublings (the use of shadows, the repetition of visual motifs, the recurrence of narrative and dramatic situations) suggest is that Eisenstein considers the formal operation of doubling—which we know from many romantic variations on the grotesque theme of the *Doppelgänger* is an operation of a radical and disturbing self-estrangement—is somehow indispensable for thinking the subject of his film: the constitution of absolute power. If the purpose of the Soviet historical film as a genre lay in the production of a certain epic narrative of heroic actions of the past that could serve to legitimize Stalinist state power in the present, what Eisenstein shows is the inherent doubling at work in this linear ideological operation of the epic.[78] By doing so, he points out the inherent inconsistency and immanent incongruity of the very figure of power the genre tries to produce. It is power—the subject of the film itself—that is to be grasped as redoubled and thus haunted from within by its own insufficiency. Eisenstein presents the disturbing doubling of the figure of power by relating Ivan's hesitation, his indecisiveness and inability to act, to an excess of action, which takes the shape of spectacular cruelty and obscene enjoyment of violence. We should here take seriously Stalin's own perceptive criticism of the film, where he compares Eisenstein's characterization of Ivan to Hamlet, the very figure of a call to action at once dwarfed by the enormity of the task at hand, while describing Ivan's *oprichniki*—the tsar's private army, whose wild orgy of violence Ivan stages in an attempt to combat his impotence—as the Ku Klux Klan (the figure of a secretive, unofficial, para-state excess of violence).[79] What Eisenstein stages in this marriage of the melancholy prince and the Ku Klux Klan—a grotesque combination if ever there was one!—is a figure of state power blocked by the demands of an act too great for its undertaking and a figure of power that, to overcome its own inability to act, resorts to the staging of an incredible spectacle of unjustified violence and cruelty, a sheer excess of action with which power seeks to overcome its fundamental impotence. The subject of *Ivan the Terrible* thus consists of the redoubling of the epic narrative of power with the revelation of its underside—the grotesque combination of impotence and excess.

In this way, the film negates not only the epic narrative of power that was, according to Kevin Platt and David Brandenberger, the preferred genre through which the official discourse of Soviet power imagined its own legitimacy. As well, *Ivan the Terrible* negates a certain tragic vision of power, which is how Platt and Brandenberger describe the film, noting that it was precisely history in its tragic mode that served as the preferred way in which Soviet artists imagined the state of things.[80] If, according to the vision of the epic, heroic action can be conceived as essentially continuous with state power, as it is heroic action that founds and legitimates power, then tragedy posits heroic action more clearly as something radically eccentric to state power and as something that state power is unable to assimilate or integrate (the paradigmatic figure of the tragic position would, of course, be Antigone).[81] Neither of these two possibilities, however, manages to fully account for *Ivan the Terrible.* Eisenstein clearly places action within the domain of state power: the film is an epic, not a tragedy. But at the same time, *Ivan* makes this "within" itself tumble and reveal itself as an impossibility: the film is thus also not an epic. The film does not present heroic action as constitutive of and fully internal to power; but neither does it present action as a force fully eccentric and thus external to power. Rather, the film diagnoses the *immanent eccentricity* of state power, the internal division of power undone from within in the attempt to constitute itself absolutely. *Ivan the Terrible,* especially in the second part, undermines the action of state power within its own proper (epic) genre. In some sense, the film makes superfluous the sublime, tragic staging of action as something externally opposed to state power (a favorite frame of reference for the Western liberal understanding of artistic dissidence under the various Stalinist regimes). The subject of the film thus concerns the action of state power (the unification of the country, territorial conquest, expansion to the sea) that is inherently decentered and redoubled from within by its own inability to act and by its own excessive attempt to overcome this inability in paroxysms of cruelty and destructive violence. In the film, the power of the Soviet state finds itself neither epically legitimated nor tragically opposed but grotesquely redoubled or intrinsically decentered, assuming the figure of its own failure (the failure to continue the revolution) and the figure of destructive overcompensation for failure (whose clearest expression one finds in the Stalinist show trials and purges).[82]

Figuring Revolution: Historical Action, More and Less Than Epic

According to Hegel, whose discussion of the epic in his *Aesthetics* is the starting point for practically all significant discussions of the genre over the course of the last two centuries (those of Lukács and Bakhtin, for example, but also more recently in Franco Moretti's *Modern Epic*), the object of the epic is "the occurrence of an action which in the whole breadth of its circumstances and relations must gain access to our contemplation as a rich event connected with the total world of a nation and epoch."[83] Epic representation of action is inseparable from the totality of the world-situation in which this action occurs and which it expresses. From this, it is clear why revolution would exert a tremendous pressure toward the epic, for a revolution is nothing if not an attempt on the part of human action to conquer a new historical situation in its totality, to exhaustively traverse a new historical reality. Conquest and traversal of the world must be understood broadly, not only in terms of territorial expansion but also as the seizing of political institutions and the means of society's economic reproduction, capturing cultural and ideological hegemony and finally mastering time itself—through the production of a new memory of the past and a progressive vision of the future.[84]

By representing action as a conquering movement across a rich and differentiated totality, epic creates the sense of a world-historical event: the entirety of a world-situation participating and transforming itself in action. Emerging from such universal transformation (revolution) is a new figure of human collectivity, a new people, whose emancipation Hegel ties specifically to the cultural revolution introduced by the appearance of epic poetry:

> Almost every people in its earliest beginnings has under its eyes a more or less foreign culture, a religious worship from abroad, and it lets these impose themselves on it; for it is precisely in this that the bondage, superstition, and barbarity of the spirit consists, namely not to have the Supreme Being as something indigenous, but to know it only as something alien not produced from its own national and individual consciousness.... Only when the poet, with freedom of spirit, flings off such a yoke, scrutinizes his own powers, has a worthy estimate of his own spirit, and therefore has got rid of a beclouded consciousness, can the period of epic proper dawn.[85]

These two relations—to the totality of a world-historical event and the founding of a new people, a new collective subject—make the action of the epic into something heroic. It is in epic heroism that individual human action becomes expressive of a world-historical meaning and a collective subject (a nation, a people).

Yet if Hegel allows us to point out the proximity between the epic and the figure of the revolution, he also allows us to remark on the limitations of the epic–heroic capturing of the revolutionary event, especially when it comes to the question of its modernity—the *presentness* of the revolution—which is a dimension of immediate concern for someone like Eisenstein. The epic might be suitable for registering the revolution's conquering movement, its heroic desire to represent action in the form of a developed historical totality and in relation to human collectivity. But it is also the case that the contour of such movement only occurs as a totality and as something collective (or recollected) once the action of movement has been accomplished, completed.

The sense of totality one attributes to action appears only once action has become a matter of the past. "The Greek *epos* . . . [means] 'word,' and what [it states] in general is what that thing is which has been transformed into the 'word.'"[86] In the epic, action has already passed over into language; the event of action itself has become a *narratable* event. An epic of the revolution that would be contemporary with the event itself, that would register the very modernity of revolutionary or historical action, is a contradiction in terms.

"The formally constitutive feature of the epic as a genre is rather the transferral of a represented world into the past," writes Mikhail Bakhtin in his "Epic and Novel."[87] And, as he almost immediately adds, this formal feature holds also for those works that are ostensibly about events in the present. An attempt to produce an epic of the present is only able to endow the present with an epic form if it at the same time transforms it into something that we essentially experience as belonging to the past:

> It is possible, of course, to conceive even "my time" as heroic, epic time, when it is seen as historically significant. . . . But in so doing we ignore the presentness of the present and the pastness of the past; we are removing ourselves from the zone of "my time," from the zone of familiar contact with time. . . . The epic world is constructed in the zone of an absolute distanced image, beyond the sphere of possible contact with the developing, incomplete and therefore re-thinking and reevaluating present.[88]

Epic places action inevitably in the medium of the past, where it may gain its expansive scope, but it then loses one of its fundamental characteristics: the openness, the inconclusiveness of its happening. In the epic, the present becomes presentless, an "object of memory" instead of a "living trial."[89]

Despite the fact that the epic offers a remarkably varied and developed representation of action, what counts in the epic is ultimately not action itself but the category of necessity or fate. In the epic, the experiences of the hero "occur as incidents in the journey without the hero's contributing anything to them."[90] This stunning statement is Hegel's version of the oft-remarked-on passivity of the epic hero—the fact that the epic hero always appears more as an instrument of his destiny, a spectator of his own actions, than as their subjective agent:

> What rules in epic, though not, as is commonly supposed, in drama, is fate. In drama, owing to the sort of aim which a character is determined to carry out in given and known circumstances, with all the resulting collisions, he creates his fate *himself*, whereas an epic character has his fate made for him, and this power of circumstances, which gives his

> deed the imprint of an individual form, allocates his lot to him, and determines the outcome of his actions, is the proper dominion of fate. What happens, happens; it is so; it happens of necessity.[91]

Action in the epic is not something presented for itself, in the event of its proper forms, but serves as the translating mechanism between fate (predeterminateness, necessity) and the completed event in which the fate has become realized. Action advances the accomplishment of the inevitable; it is what animates and helps realize the fateful predetermination already latently present in the world-situation. Epic action, expansive and totalizing in scope, is thus at the same time contained in advance and retroactively justified by the objective category of necessity.

Where may one look, then, for the sense of action in its revolutionary upheaval that would at the same time be able to present its happening as something modern, open in its form, still awaiting the seal of necessity? One such place is precisely the genre of the grotesque. In Charles Baudelaire's description of the "absolute comic" (his term for the grotesque), we find, for example, an explosion of movement that takes shape precisely as a form of action under which the ground of the past and of necessity has violently disappeared. Writing of a performance by an English pantomime troupe that he saw in Paris sometime in the early 1840s, Baudelaire introduces the comedic masks as "all but rational beings [who] do not differ much from the fine fellows in the audience." But then suddenly,

> a dizzy vertigo is abroad; vertigo swims in the air; we breathe vertigo; it is vertigo that fills the lungs and renews the blood in the arteries.
>
> What is this vertigo? It is the absolute comic, and it has taken charge of each of them. The extraordinary gestures executed by Leandre, Pierrot and Cassandre make it quite clear that they feel themselves forcibly projected into a new existence. They do not seem at all put out. They set about preparing for the great disasters and the tumultuous destiny which awaits them, like a man who spits on his hands and rubs them together before accomplishing some extraordinary feat [*action d'éclat*]. They flourish [*font le moulinet*] their arms, like windmills [*moulins*] lashed by the tempest. It must be to loosen their joints—and they will certainly need it. All this is carried out to great gusts of laughter [*éclats du rire*], full of huge contentment. . . . All their gestures, all their cries, all their expressions say: The fairy willed it, the destiny rushing us onward, I do not grieve; go! run! let us leap! And they rush through the fantastic work, which, strictly speaking, only begins there, that is to say, on the border of the marvelous.[92]

What is remarkable in Baudelaire's description of the scene of the *comique absolu* or the grotesque, which could be compared to the effect of some of Eisenstein's most iconic montage sequences, is the sense of a sudden intensification of action and movement, which is created by giving us only a slight sense of the kind of event we are supposed to be witnessing. "Extraordinary gestures"; a forcible projection "into a new existence"; acting *like* a "man who spits on his hands," but perhaps not quite; flourishing of arms *like* "windmills lashed by the tempest"—what does all this signify? Might there be a word for all this? But this is precisely the point. Baudelaire is attempting something paradoxical: to transform into language action that he at the same time attempts to describe in its absolute present and which is therefore something that must resist being named. He gives us in language action whose name might very well be the suspension of language. It is this dimension—the effect of the grotesque—that produces the vertiginous affect in the viewer. We are faced with a revolutionary event of action in the strange forms in which the action begins to take shape in the present, without yet having settled into something that might be simply told (as an epic event belonging to the past). What is thus "told" here are forms of action not preformed for telling, and what is "sung" are movements in which one would be hard-pressed to recognize the form of a poem.

Unlike what Baudelaire calls the "significative comic,"[93] a type of comic effect that makes us laugh by creating in us a sense of superiority over other (stumbling, falling) human creatures, the grotesque or the "absolute comic" is an experience of humanity's superiority over nature. Which is to say, in the grotesque, we experience our superiority over any substantial order of being in which we may wish to see ourselves embedded. From this there stem the unnatural, fantastic, and marvelous figures of the grotesque. But it is also in its suspension of nature—including human nature—that the absolute comic of the grotesque produces the vertiginous feeling of groundlessness. What distinguishes grotesque forms of action from the epic is that, in the epic, the subjectivity of heroic action, which appears as the expression of a recognizable human collectivity and the totality of the world-situation, is observed as it resettles this native, seemingly natural ground. Epic action is always already inscribed into the background of the objective situation (the necessity of fate), its subjectivity thereby canceling itself out in the very moment of its appearance. The theatrical–grotesque form of action appears, on the contrary, as though its subjectivity annihilated the objective and substantial background against which it appears. This is why it is rather impossible to measure the dimensions of the world-situation with the help of grotesque apparitions. These more often signal a vanishing of any kind of meaningful experience of a world. This is also why the appearance of grotesque figures—irreducibly subjective, monstrous and fantastic, arbitrary and always at the verge of nonsense—

usually leaves utterly unclear the question of human collectivity. At most, one could say that the grotesque presents figures of collectivity still dormant in the inhuman forms of movement performed by its actions. But it is also for this reason that grotesque may be the form in which the modernity of action, the very presentness of action itself, appears as something called forth by a destiny that is as forcefully willed as it is completely unknown—our future fate that may be revealed solely by the performance of a vertigo-inducing leap.

The idea of the revolution requires the epic, because it is in the epic and its heroic action that one may present the expansive conquest of a new historical totality as well as the vision of a new people and the historical forms of human collectivity in action. Yet at the same time, it is the setting of action in the form of the epic genre that strips the figures of revolutionary, historical movement of their modernity, of their subjective relation to the present as such. Insofar as the historical event of a revolution concerns us in our subjective relationship to the present, in the demand to be absolutely modern, the figuration of the revolutionary event and the explosion of historical action that accompanies such an event must by necessity exceed the possibilities of the epic. The subjectivity of modern revolutionary and historical action goes beyond the limit of epic heroism. (No modern revolutionary figure may be described simply and unequivocally as heroic. There is something else—both greater and baser—in the historical deeds of modern revolutionary action than may be contained by the classically composed heroic figures of the epic world.) Next to the pressure of the epic and the desire to see revolutionary action carried by the figure of heroism, the revolution requires that one experience the limits of the epic–heroic and that one give form to the desire to liberate historical action from its epic burden: to produce the sense of action in the subjective monstrosity it must possess in the absence of some properly representational relation to the objective world-situation and to describe actions of collective humanity in their nascent forms and designs, the still inhuman schemas from which a new sense of humanity may—or may not—appear.

The contradiction between the theatrical–grotesque and the epic is not merely a question of genre or of artistic construction of form; in some sense, it inheres in the event and the historical action of modern revolution itself. What we have been following in terms of the contradiction between the theatrical–grotesque and the epic–heroic in Eisenstein's handling of cinematic action allows us not only to locate Eisenstein in relation to the revolution that formed the most intimate subject of his films but to "locate" or to articulate the contradictory "place" in which the revolution itself, the problem of modern history, may be found. The phenomenon of the modern revolution is itself traversed by the contradiction and the impossible choice between the epic–heroic (the conquest of a new world-situation in its totality;

the founding of a new people) and the theatrical–grotesque (the liberation of action from fate and necessity; the absolutely immanent relationship of the remarkable forms of action to the present). Revolutionary and historical action that tries to be purely epic, that is, to see itself manifested in the substantive totality of the world-situation or in some identifiable figure of collective humanity, condemns itself immediately to the past and thus eliminates from action precisely the dimension that makes it modern: the excess of the subjective dimension of action over the substantial ground of its objective conditions (existing social order, tradition, etc.). If, however, one makes a wager on revolutionary action as purely this intense and excessive subjectivity, one will witness the sudden disappearance of the substantial background, causing the remarkable shapes that action appropriates for itself in the world to appear irreducibly theatrical and grotesque, intoxicating and vertiginously abysmal, thrilling and terrifying in their lack of meaning. One might, in other words, end up with a figure of historical action that is fully modern but not necessarily revolutionary.

This contradiction belongs to the revolution itself, and it would be possible to draw up a catalog of artistic and theoretical works in which the question of art is posed precisely as an attempt to imagine its possible "solution." Let us isolate here what may be called the most "classical" solution, which in a way registers the contradiction by attempting to deny its existence. Such is, for instance, the case of Goethe and Schiller's influential short text "On Epic and Dramatic Poetry," written in 1797, less than ten years after the French Revolution, which makes it rather difficult not to think of the text as an attempt to straighten out the contradictions of historical action so forcefully encountered in that momentous event.[94] According to Goethe and Schiller, "epic" and "drama" constitute two distinct and fully separate genres of representing action. They write famously that "the epic poet presents the event as completely past [*vollkommen vergangen*], and the dramatic poet presents it as completely present [*vollkommen gegenwärtig*]," suggesting an unbridgeable gap between the two. Despite the fact that epic and dramatic poets may "treat similar subjects," the completeness *(vollkommenheit)* of the temporal distance between the two genres does not allow them to register action as something that is split or divided inherently and might be immanently traversed by distinct and incompatible temporalities. In Goethe and Schiller's description, each of the two genres produces its own sense of action, which appears fully autonomous from the one presented in the other genre. "Epic" and "drama" thus constitute two distinct types of authorship (rhapsodist and mimic actor), two types of audience (the "quietly hearkening circle" for the epic and the "impatiently onlooking and listening circle" for the drama), two figures of humanity (man working outside himself in the epic; inwardly turned man in drama), two ways of imagining the effect of the work of art (disinterest in the case of the epic and "constant sensuous exertion" in the case of drama), and so on.

What we have attempted to describe in Eisenstein's work is the specific way in which he makes the contradiction between the "epic" and the "dramatic" (which in our case took the shape of the theatrical–grotesque) not into a classical opposition between two types of works but into something internal or immanent to his work as such. The two genres and spatiotemporalities of action—we can also say two types of audience (the concentrated community and the distracted masses); two kinds of authorship (Eisenstein as the rhapsodist of the revolution and as the revolutionary mime); two figures of humanity (humanity outside itself, conquering a new world, and humanity undergoing an "internal" revolution of human nature); two ways of envisioning the effect of the work of art on the spectator (the distance of an epic vista of history and the directness of the dramatic sensuous assault)—all of these battle it out inside the Eisensteinian work, providing the revolution in his films with its necessarily split figure as both a world-historical, epic event that may be recollected in its necessity and the theatrical event of action itself, the sudden appearance of unforeseen and free schemas of action that appropriate for themselves their place in advance of a world. Eisenstein's films give us the revolution as a phenomenon dynamically divided between the sense of an epic event, which offers something like the *truth* of historical action (the meaning of action from the perspective of collective memory, of historical necessity), and the grotesque *fabulation* of the event of action in the very forms or schemas of its own present. We will stress again that this is not a formal shortcoming of Eisenstein's project as much as it is a symptomatic registering, in the form of his work, of a basic contradiction, an impasse, that belongs to the very idea of the modern revolution as such: an idea that somehow contains without resolving—and this is the whole problem!—the desire for action monstrously freed from any substantive framework, which is at the same time a desire for action that could express the totality of a world.

THREE

The Event of the Image

BETWEEN SYMBOL AND SYMPTOM

(it is *readable* because it is an *image*)

■ Sergei Eisenstein, "Laocoön"

Obrez/Obnaruzhenie, Obraz/Izobrazhenie

The Russian term *obraz,* which we translate as "image," covers a large and complex semantic field. It means the external aspect, the outer form or the apparent shape of something or someone. It suggests a vivid and living representation of something, which ties the term to a sense of vitality, dynamism, and movement. *Obraz* also names the form of an artistic perception and presentation of a phenomenon, particularly as the latter takes place through some kind of concretization, for instance, when a phenomenon is made visible through another, more concrete one. It thus implies a certain indirectness of representation, use of comparisons, resemblance and likeness, synecdoche *(pars pro toto),* metaphor, and symbolization. But the term may also signify a general character or type produced by an artist (as when we say, for instance, "the character is the very image of a corrupt politician"). In addition, *obraz* is used when one wishes to speak of a way, a manner, or a mode of (doing) something ("a way of life" = *obraz zhizni*). And finally, *obraz* (this time with a different plural form) means "icon," which relates the term to a specific pictorial tradition of religious representation and ties it to the question of the sacred, incarnation and presence, mediation and intercession, and to the long history of ideological struggle over the political and social significance of image making.[1]

All of these meanings are in play in Eisenstein's concept of the image, and it is at least partly to the semantic richness and complexity of the term that we can ascribe the fact that, in Eisenstein's use, the concept remains relatively open, nonsystematized. Wolfgang Eismann writes, for instance, that "the concept of the image [*obraz*] plays an important role also in the aesthetic theory of S. M. Eisenstein. Unfortunately, as so many before and after him, he does not use the concept in a uniformly defined sense."[2] Anna Bohn similarly claims that it is impossible to provide a simple definition of Eisenstein's concept of the image, because the term's meaning is drawn from various discursive contexts. It comes from the study of literature and the tradition of Russian philology, where one feels a strong influence of Alexander Potebnia. But the understanding of the "image" is also significantly shaped by the discussions of art during the 1920s and 1930s, where it is particularly visible in the debate on the role of art as a "thinking in images"—a translation of Hegel's "picture thinking" introduced into Russian by the literary critic Vissarion Belinsky in the nineteenth century and later advanced within Marxist aesthetics by Georgi Plekhanov.[3] In Eisenstein's use, the term relies not only on the philological tradition and the canon of Marxist aesthetics but on several other discourses as well: that of Gestalt psychology, psychoanalysis, and ethnology, for instance. Rather than speaking of the *concept* of the image, Bohn refers to *obraz* as a "conceptuality" *(Begrifflichkeit)*, which we may translate also by saying that the term is meant to call into existence not so much a strict set of definitional meanings as a set of problems that are theoretical as well as practical in nature and around which Eisenstein builds his thinking of the cinematic form and of the nature of artistic work more generally.[4]

We should, however, not confuse this lack of a uniform definitional meaning for the absence of any determinate content carried by the concept of the image—by which Eisenstein almost always means an *artistic* image, an image produced by an artist and with artistic means. It is, namely, possible to quite precisely describe the problematic brought to light by the image as having to do with two related but distinct polarities.

The concept of the image *(obraz)* first appears in Eisenstein's writings in the mid-1920s. In a polemic against Béla Balázs in 1926, where he attacks the Hungarian theorist's privileging of the shot (and the corollary view of the filmmaker as "cameraman") over montage (and the filmmaker as "montageur"), Eisenstein writes, "Balázs always says 'picture,' 'shot,' but not once does he say *'sequence'*! The shot is merely an extension of selection. That is, a selection of one object rather than another, of an object from one particular angle, in one particular cut (or *Ausschnitt,* as the Germans say) and not another. The conditions of cinema create an 'image' [*obraz*] from the juxtaposition of these 'cuts' [*iz sopostavleniia etikh obrezov*]."[5] Image in cinema, which Eisenstein at a different point in the same essay calls a "poetic image" *(poeticheskii obraz),* does not belong simply to the pictorial dimension of individual shots. Each shot is framed and thus cut out of the continuum of reality. The cinematic image emerges when shots—and especially shots as they are constituted by cuts—are related to each other by the work of montage. Presented as an effect of montage (juxtaposition of cuts), the image is tied to the sense of negativity, of interruption and violence, and Eisenstein underscores this link by drawing our attention to the similarity of the two words: *obraz* and *obrez,* image and cut (or cutout).

The proximity of the image and the cut is then more fully fleshed out in another remarkable text, the 1929 essay titled "Perspectives," in which Eisenstein attempts to ground the intimate connection between the two terms through an explicit etymological exercise:

> You have only to look in a dictionary, not a Greek one but a Russian dictionary of "foreign words," and you will see that form in Russian is *obraz* or "image." "Image" [*obraz*] is itself a cross between the concepts of "cut" [*obrez*] and "disclosure" [*obnaruzhenie*]. These two terms brilliantly characterize form from both its aspects: from the *individually static (an und für sich)* standpoint as "cut" [*obrez*], the isolation of a particular phenomenon from its surroundings. . . . "Disclosure" characterizes image from a different, socially active standpoint: it "discloses," i.e. establishes the social link between a particular phenomenon and its surroundings.[6]

The concept of the image (as we see, Eisenstein here makes it synonymous with form) is thus determined as a double operation that combines the negative gesture of a cut and the positive gesture of disclosure.

This is the first polarity that belongs to the problematic of the image in Eisenstein's thinking: an image is a *cut,* because it always isolates a phenomenon by ripping it out of the continuity of its context; but it is also a *disclosure,* because this decontextualization of a phenomenon through a cut opens the possibility of relating cuts to each other and thus revealing a new set of relations, the previously unperceived context of the phenomenon in question. The negative gesture of cutting out the phenomenon from its "natural" context is the condition of the image's positive function, which is to make appear a phenomenon's relationship to its social context, to the context of historical struggles, and to endow it with a determinate ideological significance.

To this first polarity of the image (cut/disclosure), which Eisenstein formulates in the 1920s, we may then add a second one, a polarity that becomes central for Eisenstein's thought from the mid-1930s into the 1940s and that is most fully elaborated in his unfinished book on the theory of montage.[7] In the key texts that Eisenstein intended to include in this book ("Montage 1937," "Montage 1938," and "Vertical Montage" from 1940), the polarity that dominates now sets the image *(obraz)* against figurative representation (*izobrazhenie,* a term that has also been translated as "mere representation," "representation," or "figuration"). Between the 1920s and the late 1930s, there therefore occurs a certain shift in Eisenstein's conception, signaled by the transformation of a polarity *internal* to the image (cut/disclosure) into a polarity that appears to be an *external* one, an opposition between the image and figurative representation. The shift immediately evokes the more general and perplexing question about the periodization of Eisenstein's work: what is the relationship between the "late" and the "early" Eisenstein, the Eisenstein of the late 1930s to 1940s and the Eisenstein of the 1920s? Are there two Eisensteins or a single one?[8] The focus on the different polarities of the image would allow us to formulate the problem of periodization in a precise way. Namely, what is the relationship of the second polarity (image/figurative representation), in which both terms are positive, to the element of negativity (the gesture of the cut) that was so important for Eisenstein's montage-centered understanding of the image and form in the 1920s? Does the second, "late" polarity do away with the primacy of montage, the forceful sense of negativity and the cut, thus proving that there indeed existed two Eisensteins, or does it somehow preserve this element, albeit not signaling it as openly and heroically in the context of socialist realism and the culture of high Stalinism as it did during the avant-garde and experimental 1920s?

The purpose of the present chapter is to explore, though certainly not to exhaust, the ways and the strategies in Eisenstein's thinking of the image during his "late" period, particularly in his writings on montage from the late 1930s, in which the concept of the image plays a central role. What follows may also be understood as an argument that the dimension of the disclosing capacity of negativity and the cut, which Eisenstein explicitly formulated during the 1920s, is preserved in the polarity of the image and figurative representation that orients his thinking from the mid-1930s onward, but that it in some sense becomes dispersed, is less sharply in view, and must be constructed on the basis of Eisenstein's theory and his encounters with images.

Drawing a Barricade

As noted earlier, Eisenstein did not develop his concept of the image in a systematic way. His way of determining the meaning of the term *obraz* was to construct it step by step, through a series of examples, analyses, and readings of individual pictures, each of which at once confirms and transforms what has been established by those preceding it. Eisenstein builds his conception of the image not in a grand synthetic swoop but "by a succession of little touches, each one extending and modifying the other."[9] To understand what he means by the image, it is thus best to follow Eisenstein through his own encounters with images, to examine how he conceives of constructing and reading the image by focusing first on an individual case (or a few cases) and then extrapolating in the direction of a more general Eisensteinian conception of the image.

Our point of departure will be the drawing of a barricade in Eisenstein's text "Montage 1937."[10] This text, which Jacques Aumont has described as "probably the most purely theoretical text ever written by Eisenstein . . . the most foundational,"[11] was the first of the essays produced with the intention of being included in the larger theoretical work on montage that preoccupied Eisenstein toward the end of the 1930s. The drawing of the barricade, made by Eisenstein himself, appears in "Montage 1937" as a crucial demonstrative example. It is placed in a section dedicated to the question of single-shot composition ("montage in single-set-up cinema" or the "plastic composition of an individual montage fragment"), yet in its analysis, Eisenstein offers what is perhaps the most striking elaboration of the polarity—presented as a dialectical tension—between figurative representation *(izobrazhenie)* and the image *(obraz).* And because, according to him, this polarity characterizes the intimate dynamic at work at all levels of cinematic form (within shots, between shots, and in image–sound relations), it is not too difficult to see how the case of the barricade informs not only the analysis of the pictorial composition of a single ("static") shot but also Eisenstein's attempts to theorize multiple-shot composition ("montage in multiple-setup cinema") and audiovisual composition ("sound–film montage").[12]

Eisenstein's choice of the barricade as a central example in "Montage 1937" is hardly coincidental. As an object, the barricade fits all too perfectly the role of an iconic figure that somehow concentrates all the essential preoccupations of his cinema: violent historical conflict, revolution, the masses in movement. It would indeed be possible to insert the drawing of the barricade into a series of objects-become-attractions that in Eisenstein's work function as figures of a sudden reversal of historical fortune: the famous raising of the lion's head in *Potemkin,* the illogical bullet that suddenly assembles itself into a machine gun in *October,* the village co-op's ecstatic milk separator in *The General Line,* and so on. Yet it is primarily a different sort of reversal that the drawing of the barricade is meant to demonstrate for us in the text of "Montage 1937." It is, namely, supposed to show us precisely how one constructs an image *(obraz)* rather than a mere figurative representation *(izobrazhenie)* and how a drawing may suddenly be seized by the experience of imagicity *(obraznost'),* an experience that Eisenstein distinguishes from the more everyday and habitual forms of perception offered by merely figurative and representational pictures.

Putting things in these terms—sudden reversal, seizure of the picture by the image—already suggests to us something important about Eisenstein's conception of the image. An image is not something that is simply given with any picture. There in fact exist many pictures that could, in Eisenstein's terms, not be described as images. The image is not identical or continuous with the visual medium of the picture, and Eisenstein will indeed speak of the image in relation to sound and music as well as to the verbal media of literature and poetry. The image thus constitutes a more general, what today we would call a transmedial, aesthetic concept. It is not at all inherently visual or aural in nature but closer to the experience of a certain imagistic agency of form irreducible to individual media or the different registers of sensible experience. This means that Eisenstein treats the appearance of the image in the picture as the appearance of a qualitatively different experience, one that cannot be provided by the picture (or any individual medium) alone. One often gets the sense that an image, which is not simply immaterial but infects the picture with its own strange materiality, must be conceived as something that befalls the picture and thus occupies the status of an event.

But if an image is an event, something qualitatively new that happens to the picture, which may by itself be merely figurative and representational and not imagistic, then this means that all of Eisenstein's analyses of images must (at least implicitly) involve not one but two pictures, something like the "before-picture" and the "after-picture" separated precisely by the image-event: on one hand, a picture that is purely pictorial (figurative and representational; *izobrazhenie*), on the other, the picture as it is already seized and overturned, made unrecognizable, by the image *(obraz)* that has suddenly appeared in and through it. The sense of the image emerges from a montage of (at least) two pictures; it is immanently tied to the interval—the distance and the relation—that produces a change from one picture to the other. This implicit requirement that there be two pictures is made explicit in the example of the image of the barricade, which Eisenstein presents in "Montage 1937" with the help of two drawings, which we will now take up in succession.

In the first drawing (Figure 22), we see, according to Eisenstein, a representation of a barricade in terms of its purely naturalistic, everyday detail *(bytovaia detal')*.[13] The first drawing gives us a "mere representation," *izobrazhenie*, of a barricade.[14] We are dealing here with a depiction in which the work of the drawing traces the contours of its object, respecting its limits and imitating its shape, which it thereby contains as a figure within the disposition of the lines. The figurative depiction of the barricade appears in this first drawing as stable, eminently recognizable, and, for the same reason, Eisenstein adds, lacking in expressivity. The lack of expressivity in the drawing may be explained by the absence of any sense of happening and movement in the picture—as though the portrayed object and its surroundings

Figure 22. Eisenstein's drawing of the barricade as mere "figurative representation" in "Montage 1937."

were somehow indifferent to time. What predominates is the self-certainty of space. We do not perceive this first drawing as a depiction of a barricade awaiting battle, because any suggestion of some violent future occurrence seems to be missing from the picture. We are unable to perceive the picture as one of a barricade during battle, because the drawing includes no depiction of action. And we can also not say that this is a drawing of a barricade in the wake of battle, because both the barricade and its surrounding area are rather unperturbed, well composed, and well ordered.

The lack of expressivity and of a sense of happening already allow us to give more precision to the Eisensteinian term *izobrazhenie*—"figurative representation" ("mere representation," "representation," "figuration")—which he uses to describe the underwhelming effect of the first drawing. The first drawing gives us a representational figure of the barricade, a recognizable imitation of its phenomenal appearance. But, as Eisenstein adds, this spontaneously recognizable representation is also a depiction devoid of the barricade's essential idea; it gives us a representation of the object without the most elementary meaning and the affective charge of the barricade—the affect and meaning of violent confrontation, of conflict and battle, of struggle. It is precisely this essential dimension, the meaning of the barricade ("struggle"), which we find missing from the figurative depiction of the first drawing, that the second drawing of the barricade is meant to produce and make visible for us. And it is also with the appearance of the second drawing, which not only presents a figurative representation of the phenomenon but is able to give us both the figurative representation and the essential idea of the barricade (the meaning and affect of struggle), that a picture, according to Eisenstein, becomes transformed into an *image* of the barricade (Figure 23).

"The difference," Eisenstein writes, "is in the fact that one of the pictures (the second) as distinct from the other (the first) does not confine itself to mere representation [*izobrazhenie*] of a barricade, but is so constructed that in addition it also incorporates an image [*obraz*] of the essential significance of a barricade: struggle."[15] In the most general way, then, the appearance of the image in the picture will have to do with the ability to expand what a picture is showing us beyond the limit of mere figurative representation, beyond the "naturalist" imitation of a phenomenon or iconic resemblance, and to make appear in the picture something that does not properly belong to the level of appearances or their imitations, to make visible and sensible something that is in itself invisible and supersensible (the meaning, the affect or emotion, the idea associated with the depicted phenomenon).

The entirety of Eisenstein's discussion of the drawing of the barricade—informed by his quest to develop not only a theoretical aesthetics but an aesthetics that would be practical, "operational"—revolves around the explanation of how an artist may transform a mere figurative representation of a barricade into an image. What exactly happens between the first and the second drawing? Or, what must happen to the figurative imitation of the barricade in the first drawing so that it becomes invested by what Eisenstein calls the "essential significance" of the phenomenon of the barricade: the sense of "struggle," which is imparted in the second drawing not only as meaning but also as an expressive event meant to move and affect us? What happens between the two drawings that makes a barricade become a Barricade? But also, how might we, in the shift from the first to the second drawing—a juxtaposition in which we may recognize the presence of montage—perceive and describe the event of the image itself?

The answer to these questions lies in the establishment of the precise difference between the two drawings. For instance, we may oppose the general calm of the first picture to the sense of agitation that seems to animate the second: the disarticulated pieces of the barricade-figure that now appears as a series of triangular planes rather than as a depiction of a single coherent

Figure 23. An *image (obraz)* of the barricade in Eisenstein's drawing from "Montage 1937."

object; the almost dematerialized surface of the street, less carefully filled out, pointing to the hastiness of the sketch; the sidewalk, barely visible in the first drawing, but which seems to have metamorphosed into a railway track in the second. The general feeling produced by the second drawing is that of an explosion, of things moving centrifugally toward disorder, which endows the individual elements with a definition that is both more acute and stranger than the one they possess in the first drawing. It is as though the well-measured figurative representation of the first drawing suddenly found itself caught in a swirl of movement that threatens to destroy the calm composure of its space. In the second drawing, it is time, and specifically time in its irruptive quality, that prevails over the stability of space. Nowhere is this sense of a temporal emergency made clearer than in the pair of lines that, like a pair of tense wires, stretch from the barricade (a figure set within representational space) and wrap themselves around the upper right-hand corner of the drawing's frame, as though the limit, the very framing of figurative representation, were to be drawn into the space it was supposed to delimit, as the figure previously nested in this space suddenly becomes expelled from its position. The sense of representational objectivity or naturalistic depiction, which characterizes figurative representation in the first drawing, appears in the second to be taken over by a collapse of representational order, as though an earthquake or some other calamity has shaken the natural world of objects.[16] Unlike the first drawing, in which we were unable to perceive any expressivity and which was characterized by a lack of happening, the second drawing seems to be falling apart or breaking, which suggests the whole scene has suddenly been filled with time and that the space, folding on itself in the picture, must be understood as an effect of a more fundamental unfolding of a temporal event.

One, then, produces an image of a barricade—for, it bears repeating, only this second drawing is, for Eisenstein, also an image—by constructing the barricade not simply as an object of an imitative figurative representation but as a set of dynamic and rhythmic movements, as a play of forces that disturb the representational order and unity of the picture. What takes place in the second drawing is that the figurative representation of a barricade is submitted to a remarkable work of dynamization, in which the imitative figure emerges as one of the elements in a disordering movement performed by a series of expressive graphic and compositional gestures. In the second drawing,

> the plane of the barricade *cuts into* the wall of the houses . . . the line of the base of the barricade . . . *cuts into* the roadway . . . the line of the upper edge of the barricade . . . is shown as a jagged line.[17]

An image of the barricade appears in the drawing at first as a new type of dynamic unity, less a synthetic gestalt than a record of a temporal process, a composition of gestures and movements, an animation of the phenomenon that puts into crisis the calm unity of its representational figure.

It is worth opening a brief parenthesis here to note that *dynamization* is one of the central Eisensteinian terms. It is indispensable for his understanding of artistic form, which he does not grasp in opposition to force and dynamism but much more as an effect and a record of dynamic (and dialectical) processes and interactions.[18] François Albera has remarked on the similarity between Eisenstein's sense of dynamization as destruction of "the inertia of perception" and the formalist concept of estrangement (deautomatization of perception).[19] As Albera also points out, Eisenstein's use of *dynamization* bears a particular resemblance to the use of the term in Yuri Tynianov's *The Problem of Verse Language* (1924), to which we can add that Eisenstein's description of the expressive rendering of the barricade in the second drawing may be compared to Tynianov's description of the metamorphosis of objects—their *deformation*—in photography and cinema: "The picking out of material in a photograph leads to the unity of every photograph, to a peculiar *crowding of relationships* among all the objects or elements of a single object within the photograph. As a result of this inner unity the relationship between the objects[,] or between the elements within one object, is over-determined. The objects become deformed."[20]

The initial answer to the question of what an Eisensteinian image is may thus point to the image as a form of dynamization. By dynamizing the surface of the drawing, deforming and animating the figure and the composition of the picture, the image introduces into the latter, and thus also into our perception, an experience of rhythm. The first and the second drawings are distinguished by the fact that the first exhibits only the most mundane kind of rhythm, or perhaps it would be better to say that the first drawing fails to rhythmicize our perception in any effective way and rather stills and calms it by introducing a certain measure into our apprehension of the phenomenon. In Eisenstein's view, measure and rhythm should not be confused, and the first drawing indeed appears to be well measured rather than rhythmic in the disposition of its graphic form, while the second drawing subsumes representation and figurative measure (the predominance of space) under a forceful rhythmic movement (predominance of time).

The image brings about a divergence between figurative representation of an object (measure/space) and the dynamization of the graphic line (rhythm/time). The stronger the rhythm and the more forceful the dynamization of the phenomenon through a series of graphic and compositional gestures, the less coherently figurative and "objective" the picture will be. Dynamizing the surface of the drawing, in which we see the appearance of the image, thus in some sense tends toward the destruction of the figure and consequently the loss of the object the figure represents in the picture. The more a drawing tends toward realizing the barricade as a rhythmic play of forces or as a temporal process, the more "object-less" it will become, and the more it will lose the barricade as its content, becoming instead a remarkable exercise in the virtuosity of dynamic form without a clear relationship to an identifiable representational meaning (Figure 24).

Take the example of the "upper edge of the barricade" in the second drawing, which Eisenstein describes as "jagged" and which is, according to his description, supposed to give us the sensation of the rhythm of struggle, the ups and downs of conflict. This jagged line, which is part of the dynamic transformation and rhythmization of the figure of the barricade introduced into the picture by the image, can be revealingly compared to one of the examples in Paul Klee's *Pedagogical Sketchbook* (1925), in which the Swiss artist developed the possibility of plastic form on the basis of a purely nonfigurative and nonrepresentational conception of the graphic trace: "an active line on a walk, moving freely, without a goal. A walk for a walk's sake."[21] Which is to say, Klee develops the possibility of plastic composition by starting with a line that is self-moving or active on its own account and therefore does not relate,

Figure 24. The jagged upper edge of the barricade. Eisenstein writes the line "might be read as . . . *anything you like*" ("Montage 1937," 97).

through the figure, to an object or some content and meaning that it would have to represent in the picture (Figure 25).

The comparison between the two syncopated lines—Eisenstein's "jagged line" of the barricade and Klee's "active line, limited in its movement by fixed points"[22]—is instructive, for it illustrates the extent to which the image or imagicity (seen as a graphic and compositional dynamization and rhythmization of a phenomenon) in Eisenstein's case touches on the experience of the loss of the object in the picture. The Eisensteinian conception of the image includes the experience of nonobjectivity or "supra-objectivity" *(sverkhpredmetnost'),* of the dissolution of the body of the figure or "supra-corporeality" *(sverkhtelesnost'),* as he also calls it in *Nonindifferent Nature.*[23] The image, whose appearance puts the picture into a kind of shock, contains a tendency toward the collapse of imitative, figurative representation of an object and, as such, also the vanishing of (representational) meaning in the picture.

Yet it is also the case that, in his discussion of the second drawing of the barricade, Eisenstein registers the tendency of the image toward "supra-objectivity" mostly in a negative way, when he notes about the barricade's "jagged" line that a picture "from which the purely representational element

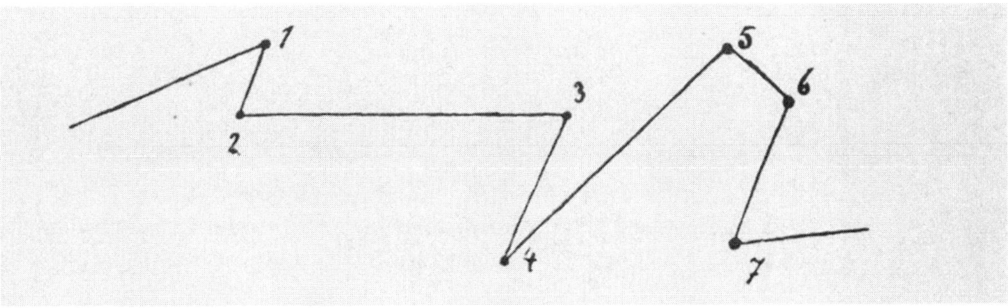

Figure 25. An "active line limited by points" from Paul Klee's *Pedagogical Sketchbook* (1925). Copyright 2017 Artists Rights Society (ARS), New York.

has been removed" and in which the dynamic and rhythmic force of the image took over completely "would be a bare, non-objective abstraction dangling in mid-air." It would be a picture "deprived not of the compositional outline . . . , but of the actual picture, and retaining only the 'image-expressing' zigzag line of its contour." In such a case, the picture might as well be called meaningless, because the pure rhythm of a syncopated line, the dynamic outline, the zigzag of the barricade taken by itself, "might not be read as a barricade but as . . . *anything you like*: as a graph of the rise and fall of prices, or as a seismographic trace of subterranean tremors, and so on and so forth."[24] The dynamic function of the image may thus lead us to the figure's disappearance, to the loss of the object, and finally to the negation of all content or "objective" meaning in the picture—a negation that is in Eisenstein's description identical to meaning's proliferation or, better, to a dissemination of meaning: a purely dynamic and rhythmic trace may mean "anything you like."

Now, unlike Klee, Eisenstein wishes to ward off this possibility of dissemination in the image. The image of the barricade (the second drawing) must, according to him, give us the phenomenon and its "essential significance," the barricade and the meaning of "struggle," not the phenomenon destroyed by the dynamism of a meaningless graphic line. As much as the image offers a kind of remarkable experience of the dynamism that seizes the pictorial surface, it will also have to involve a certain pulling back from this sensuous chaos-without-proper-measure into the realm of meaning. The dynamic and rhythmic tendency of the image will somehow have to be put to use in the name of representation. Eisenstein will insist on the irreducibility of figuration in the experience of the image, and we are thus obliged to note how the element of imitation and figurative representation *(izobrazhenie)*, which predominated in the first drawing of the barricade, is not simply absent from the second, from the image *(obraz)* of the barricade, but is rather maintained throughout its dynamic and rhythmic transformation of the picture. Eisenstein insists that the image should seize the picture in such a way that its dynamism and rhythm appear through and not at the expense of the representational figure.

What thus also belongs to the Eisensteinian image is something like a *return* to figuration and representation, which we must be careful to distinguish from any straightforward acceptance of the figurative function as something given or secured in advance. The insistence on the irreducibility of figurative representation is necessary only *because* one has passed through a moment in which a forceful tendency at work in the image revealed the threat of destroying the figure along with the meaning it produces in the picture. By being something one returns to rather than something one may take for granted from the start, the representational and figurative relationship of the picture has somehow been loosened up in the act of graphic and compositional animation (deformation) of its surface. By touching on the "supra-objective" and thus introducing a moment of discontinuity and loss in the continuous depiction of objective reality, the object can no longer be said simply to resemble itself in the figure. Indeed, if one takes a look at the second drawing, what one sees is a barricade that is equal parts figure and disfiguration. The second drawing, the image, offers us a picture of a barricade in which the iconic likeness of the figure is put under severe stress by the dynamic exercise of graphic form. In fact, it is quite possible that, had we initially not seen the first drawing, we would have had some difficulty recognizing what exactly the second drawing represents. Therefore one way of describing what happens in the second drawing would be to say that, with the appearance of the image, the picture's iconic function (likeness, resemblance) begins to collapse as the pictorial surface is turned into something like an index registering a play of forces, a set of dynamic and rhythmic gestures that inscribe themselves graphically in the picture. The attraction of the second drawing, that is, the attraction of the image, lies in the way the graphic lines here assert themselves as traces of movement against the iconic function that they to some extent continue to perform.

The Work of Symbolization

Yet this is only the first step. For this destabilization of the picture's iconic function by way of dynamism and rhythm (the graphic line as a trace of "supra-objective" movement) prepares the ground for a semantic expansion of the picture's representational relationship. The dynamic and rhythmic form, in which we first feel the seizure of the picture by the image, must in Eisenstein's view counter the picture's iconicity not on its own account but rather to open up the possibility for the picture to take on the function of symbolic representation. As Eisenstein writes, the purpose of the dynamism and rhythm that make the second drawing so attractive is to allow the picture not only to resemble the barricade but also to express its symbolic meaning, the "essential significance": struggle. The sensuous dynamism of the second drawing (and of any image) is thus motivated in the direction of symbolic meaning. Rhythm, Eisenstein asserts, must be conceived as the primary agent of "generalization": it interrupts, loosens up, syncopates the iconic relation of the picture (resemblance), so that the picture may receive and in a sense be amplified by the imprint of the "essence," the "meaning" of the phenomenon it depicts (expression).[25]

The movement of semantic expansion, which may also be called the process or the work of symbolization in the image, can, following Aumont's analysis, be broken up into three distinct and interrelated steps:[26]

1. The first step is that of the graphic *design.* For Eisenstein, the set of dynamic and rhythmic gestures that transforms the figure into a play of forces (the disfiguration of the barricade in the second drawing) is also what gives us a design, a formula, a schematic, a graphic outline of an interpretation of this object: the "jagged" upper line is a record of a dynamic process (which by itself may mean anything), but the shape of its rhythmic "supra-objectivity," when related to the figure of the barricade, evokes "the phases of a struggle: each peak of the spiky contour is a point of conflict in the changing fortunes of two opposing sides."[27] The composition of forces at play in the dynamic cut-up of the figure of the barricade is also an outlining, schematizing gesture through which the question of the phenomenon's meaning may begin to emerge. The dynamism of graphic traces (the cuts, the jagged line) that in the second drawing discombobulates the imitated figure of the barricade must at the same time be read as a "graphic projection" of the barricade's meaning, a "spatial calligraphy" or a "characteristic footprint" of its essential significance, "a seismographic trace" expressive of the phenomenon's content.[28]
2. The second step in the movement of symbolizing generalization is the discovery of the *metaphoricity* of the image. If the graphic design of the "jagged" line of the barricade evokes the meaning of struggle, it is because it may be read as a "'converted' metaphor" or a metaphor in reverse, which operates a kind of literalization of meaning and involves the passage not from something concrete toward something more abstract and indirect but, on the contrary, from something abstract (meaning) back toward its sensuous and kinetic shape. "It is well known—indeed the very meaning of the word 'metaphorical' (Greek: μετα-φορ = to carry over) constantly reminds us of it—that metaphorical connotations figured at an earlier

stage as simple, straightforward physical actions ('I am *drawn* to you,' 'I *grovel* before you,' etc., etc.)."[29] In this sense, the most clearly metaphorical detail in the second drawing of the barricade is, according to Eisenstein, the pretzel sign, which is displaced from the upper right-hand corner (in the first drawing) into the lower right-hand corner (in the second). It is through this displacement that the pretzel sign turns from something that, as Eisenstein writes, "cannot be interpreted on any other than a naturalistic level" into something that now bears a "subtextual meaning" and "reads not as 'a sign thrown down' but as 'an overthrow': that which was above is now below."[30]

3. The final step in this movement of symbolizing generalization performed by the image is what may be called *generalization* proper. Eisenstein will often speak of the "generalizing image" or the "global image," which he describes as a kind of sum of all the schematizing and metaphorical operations that combine in the image into an expression of an idea.[31] As a generalizing agent, the image is "responsible for expressing . . . the central *idea* that can be abstracted from the representation of a scene, and from this scene itself."[32] Eisenstein will describe this generalizing dimension of the image with different terms. As an agent of generalization, the image makes us perceive not only the phenomenon in its figurative particularity but also its "psychological content"; not only its particular appearance but also the sense of its "general conception"; not merely its individually explicit and obvious character but its essence, inner meaning, what is always "implied" by any appearance of a particular phenomenon. In an image, the particularity of a phenomenon appears as expressive of its inner form, or rather of the dynamic structure of relations that constitutes its general, universal significance.

Yet it is precisely at this point of the generalizing movement of the image that we should tread carefully. Aumont, for instance, reminds us how "Eisenstein emphasizes that *generalization* (the idea) *is not everything* and that there must be a final 'social' determination, which will allow the *global image* to be a *particular* generalization (a particular interpretation, one which takes sides)."[33] According to this crucial point, the idea of the barricade made visible by the image in the second drawing would not imply a neutral, disengaged, abstractly universal point of view. On the contrary, the idea or the essential interpretation of the phenomenon we reach through the image (the idea of "struggle" in our example) is, according to Eisenstein, always a manifestation of a particular—or, we may also say, partisan—attitude.

By generalizing from the particular depiction of a phenomenon (barricade), moving toward the symbolic expression of its essential idea ("struggle"), an image does not put to rest the tendentiousness and the need to take sides;

it is not a means of pacification of a phenomenon we could also somehow access in its universal meaning, above the particularity of its individual depictions, but on the contrary, it depends on the affirmation of a determinate standpoint, which always involves a series of individual and sociohistorical mediations:

> a *generalization about an object,* as distinct from the *object itself, "an und für sich,"* is a separate entity related to the artist's individual consciousness and is an expression of his attitudes towards judgments about the object in question: a self-expression mediated by the author's consciousness and reflecting the context of social relationships in which the artist's personality has been formed.[34]

If we say that the image in its generalizing function presents the idea or the universal essence of a phenomenon, we must immediately add that this universality is fully concrete and tied to a perspective that does not stand above other particular perspectives but takes place among and against them. "Struggle" as the idea of the barricade expressed by the image in the second drawing appears as such (as a universal essence of this particular phenomenon) only if one takes sides; for the enemy, the idea of the barricade may, for instance, be that of "disorder" or "crime," which would necessitate the production of a different image. In fact, it is "mere representation," the figurative imitation of a phenomenon, the seemingly "naturalist" depiction that we encountered in the first drawing of the barricade, that maintains itself in the illusion of a kind of universal neutrality, of an "objective," nonpartisan perspective on the world. The image as an expression of the idea, on the contrary, shakes us out of a contemplative attitude and commits us to a determinate subjective point of view—a partisan standpoint within a field of struggle. This is a crucial lesson of Eisenstein's dialectic of the particular phenomenon depicted and the universal idea expressed by the image: by producing or reading an image, that is, by making visible an idea, one always takes sides. "The characteristics of the barricade, read as concrete object, will, apart from this *general idea* of the barricade, always also include the particular *image of the idea* peculiar to the situation in which that barricade figures."[35]

The Symbol-Image

We have come to a point at which we can explain Eisenstein's conception of the image and his understanding of the experience of imagicity *(obraznost')* as a specific relation and interaction between three distinct functions. We began with the *iconic function,* which was the only one shared by the first and second drawings of the barricade. This function (imitative, figurative representation) establishes a relation of resemblance between the phenomenon and its depiction. It also presents the instance against which the agency of the image may be defined. For the appearance of the image may be recognized in the way the iconic function of the picture becomes destabilized, problematized, and ultimately motivated toward a different purpose. The primacy of the iconic function that we observed in the first drawing of the barricade is undone in the second drawing by the introduction of the *dynamic function* of the image, which transforms the depiction into a registering of a play of forces and which topples over the figurative space into the happening of a temporal event. The graphic lines become indices of a gestural and rhythmic process and are freed from the task of resemblance and the measure of likeness. This dynamic loosening of the hold exercised on the picture by the iconic function, the loosening of space by time, is then motivated in the direction of meaning, essential significance, the general idea of the depicted phenomenon that the image must express. Which is to say, the dynamization of appearances is turned into a vehicle for realizing in the image something beyond appearance, and time becomes in the sensible the agent of the supersensible idea. In the ability to present—with and through the dynamized depiction of the phenomenon—the phenomenon's essential meaning (barricade + "struggle"), we recognize the image's *symbolic function.*

All of these functions are in a sense irreducible and are always somehow triangulated in Eisenstein's conception of the image. Yet it is also clear that in the most general sense of Eisenstein's conception, a certain teleology is put in place that assures that the symbolic function will prevail and assume the role of organizing the relations between the triangulated functions into a unity. That is to say, if the image is to have a certain unity, if it is to be grasped as something more than merely an interplay of heterogeneous and possibly conflicting functions, it is because its *telos,* what it internally, organically tends toward, is the task of symbolization: the expression of symbolic meaning through the medium of the picture. The image is essentially a *symbol-image.* It certainly cannot do without the iconic and the dynamic functions, but the image does seek to dialectically sublate them or, at the very least, motivate them toward the aim of symbolic expression. The tendency of Eisenstein's general statements on the problematic of the image concerns itself primarily with the becoming-symbol of pictures: the possibility of transforming "preartistic" forms of iconic representation into artistic forms of symbolic expression. It is not difficult to see how the conception of the symbol-image relates to montage. For, according to Eisenstein, montage is precisely the operation that takes fragments of iconic representation and submits them to the process of dynamic and rhythmic articulation to produce the symbolic form of the cinematic discourse.

If we consider the function of the image as primarily a symbolic one, then we must understand the image as a form of organizing, unifying, and stabilizing the temporal force of our experience. Through the agency of the symbol-image, the dynamism and the rhythmic dimension are to some extent acknowledged, because they are needed as a kind of spurt toward formative activity, yet they are also articulated in such a way that they become expressive of something more stable, of a more permanent identity, which belongs to the dimension of meaning. It would appear that the Eisensteinian symbol-image introduces time, but only to the point where the temporal event may become separated from itself and turned into a means for representing a certain ideality of form in the picture. If we may once more refer to the example of the drawings of the barricade, we have said that the most immediate sense of the difference between the first and the second drawings has to do with the collapse of the primacy and the certainty of the figurative and iconic space, where a dynamic and rhythmic gesture of graphic form in the second drawing introduced an impression of a happening, of a chaotic and disordering temporal event. Under the perspective of the symbol-image, it appears, however, that the purpose of this introduction of time lies in the desire of the image to once again lead us toward an experience in which it is space that predominates. Yet at this point, space is no longer simply figurative, a space that iconically relates to our everyday experience, but becomes rather an *ideal* space expressive of an essence and meaning. If the image appeared at first as a disturbing event, seizing the surface of the picture dynamically and rhythmically, it appears in the end—that is, in its symbolic telos—as the opposite: a taming of the event, the stilling of the irruptive quality of time in the calming bath of form's ideality.

From the Symbol to the Dialectical Image

Does, however, this treatment of the Eisensteinian image as a symbol-image exhaust what might be said about the image's relationship to time in Eisenstein's thought? Is the relationship between image and time indeed governed so absolutely by the function of symbolism, according to which any temporal event must become expressive of some ideality, some meaning or "essential significance"? Is it so clear that the image acts to employ time solely in order to master its force? Do Eisenstein's constructions and readings of the image introduce the dimension of dynamism and rhythm (the force of time) only to deny it the status of an autonomous function of equal value as that of symbolization (the ideality of form)? Or may one find a more properly dialectical relationship between image and time, symbol and dynamism, form and force in Eisenstein's thought? Does the image, which in its symbolic function serves as the agent of meaning, not also serve time apart from symbolic expression? Does not the image, apart from symbolically ordering time, also suffer time, and specifically suffer time as that which topples the sovereignty of the symbol and thus puts into crisis the effectiveness of the symbolic function and the permanence of meaning the function guarantees?

The tendentiousness of the questioning will already suggest a conviction that there is indeed some other way, more dialectical and not exclusively symbolic, in which the image in Eisenstein's conception relates to time. A more complex relationship is, for instance, suggested already in the following remarkable description of the image (as a generalizing, symbolizing, idea-expressing agent) that Eisenstein offers in "Montage 1937," where the image is somehow seen as both a constituted unity and the flickering of a multiplicity, both symbolic expression of an idea or general meaning and a "swarm" of dynamic potentiality, an "end product" and a readiness to explode:

> Finally, the image, which in my view is constituted as a generalization, as an aggregation of separate metaphors into a single whole: this is again not a process of formation; it is an end-product, but an end-product which, as it were, contains a swarm of *potential* dynamic (metaphoric) features that are ready to explode. It is the sort of immobility that is not inaction but the acme of dynamism. It is potentially dynamic in the sense that its separate constituents flicker like summer lightning, each one capable of turning into a single lightning-flash of a metaphor.[36]

The problematic of the image is thus perhaps a bit more complex and ambiguous than might have been suggested so far by our focus on the image as an expressive form in the service of symbolization (the symbol-image). And to bring this complexity and ambiguity of the Eisensteinian image—its dialectical side—more firmly into view, let us, as we did with the initial introduction of the problematic, follow another of Eisenstein's own examples.

In his text "Montage 1938," Eisenstein introduces an example from Guy de Maupassant's novel *Bel Ami* (1885). He isolates from *Bel Ami* the scene in which the novel's protagonist, the irrepressible social climber Georges Duroy, sits in a cab waiting for Suzanne, the young daughter of the powerful financier and newspaper owner M. Walter. Duroy, who begins the novel as an unemployed provincial recently returned from military service in Algeria, plans to elope with Suzanne in order to force her wealthy parents to accept their marriage, thus securing for himself a place in the economic and political elite of the French Third Republic. Duroy's wait bears a fateful implication for him: if midnight strikes and Suzanne shows up, his remarkable rise up the rungs of Parisian society will be successfully completed; if she does not show up at midnight, all of his effort will have been for naught, and his rise will suddenly end in failure.

Eisenstein focuses in on Maupassant's construction of the "fateful hour" of midnight—at which point Suzanne indeed fails to appear. What interests Eisenstein is precisely how Maupassant creates not merely a simple depiction of midnight but an image of Midnight, that is to say, an expression that manages to present us both the time of midnight and the fateful, essential meaning—the *"emotional significance"*[37]—this particular hour has for the protagonist and for the story of the novel. He thus notices that Maupassant, to symbolize the meaning of the event (and of Suzanne's nonappearance), has not one but several clocks, arranged in spatial and temporal intervals of various dimensions, strike midnight:

> Somewhere far away a clock struck twelve, then again, nearer; then two other clocks struck at once, followed by another at a considerable distance. When the last stroke died away, he thought: "It's over. All is ruined. She's not coming."[38]

Eisenstein observes in the short passage Maupassant's precise method of producing the image of Midnight. There occurs, at first, a certain dynamization of the temporal event. Midnight is not depicted simply as a natural event, unique, occurring once in the sequential unfolding of time, an occurrence that could have been represented by a single striking of a single clock. Instead, Maupassant fragments the unity of the event. He multiplies and distributes the event's fragmented "depictions" in space and time. This way, what should in principle be a single natural event in the temporal continuum appears several times and at various distances. "Somewhere far away . . . then again, nearer; then . . . at once, followed by . . . at a distance." The writer thus turns a single moment into a dynamic multiplicity and introduces into it a rhythm by organizing the different measures of the same temporal event into a kind of intervallic structure. Yet, as is also clear from the passage, the operation of dynamization and rhythmization serves here primarily as a means of opening up the simple depiction of midnight to a specific symbolic meaning. Eisenstein writes,

> Twelve o'clock midnight. Here least of all is this a moment in astronomical time, but it is above all a time at which everything (or at least a great deal) has been gambled on one card. . . . We see from this example that when Maupassant needed to impress on his readers' minds the *emotional significance* of midnight, he did not limit himself to simply letting the clocks strike twelve and then one o'clock. He made us experience this perception of midnight by having twelve o'clock struck in various places by various clocks. Combined together in our minds, these distinct sets of twelve strokes have merged into a general impression of midnight. *The separate depictions have fused into an image.*[39]

Through the dynamization and rhythmization of the conventional measure of "astronomical time," the exceptional and essential significance of this hour is stressed, and we pass over to the unity of the symbol-image of "midnight, the hour of decision."[40] From a certain natural unity of a temporal event, we pass through a moment of disunity and multiplicity, through dynamism and rhythm, to the "perception" of time from the protagonist's perspective as a symbolic unity, expressive of a definite and total meaning (a moment in which the totality of Duroy's life appears to be decided).[41]

In Eisenstein's reading of the moment from *Bel Ami,* we thus get a clear example of the unifying role played by the symbol-image in relation to time. The image, in which the multiplicity of depictions fuses into one, presents itself as the agent of meaning and temporal unification: what matters ultimately is Midnight not in its multiplicity or the heterogeneity of its rhythm but as a symbolic expression of an event in which the entirety of the protagonist's life suddenly comes into view. We may say that the "astronomical time" of midnight becomes informed by existential time, which it suddenly expresses in its totality; the neutral and indifferent natural event is "spiritualized," and nature becomes "nonindifferent," as Eisenstein would say, transformed into a distinctly human, meaningful unity through the formative and symbolizing activity of the image.

This example, which is meant to show us how time may be transformed into an image, the force of its dynamic and rhythmic intervals turned into a symbolic form expressive of meaning, certainly succeeds in its purpose. It also reveals, however, something else, which throws the question of the symbol-image and its relationship to time into a different light. For what the little scene from *Bel Ami* brings into view is that the symbol-image, as much as it organizes the dynamic and rhythmic temporal multiplicity into a unity of expressive form, is also a response to a certain more fundamental division of time, or time *as* division, from which it gains its convincing power. Concretely, the effectiveness of Maupassant's construction of the symbol-image of Midnight relies on the fact that this image, the expression of the essential meaning of "Midnight," is a response and thus bears a trace of time as divided between two radically different possibilities: Suzanne will either appear or not appear; Duroy will either succeed or fail. It is the force of time as crisis, a confrontation of two irreducible trajectories faced by the subject, that endows the symbol-image of Midnight, which in some sense answers it, with its imagistic power. The meaningful unity of the temporal event that the symbolizing operation of Maupassant's image allows us to see must therefore be related to the moment of time's self-division; and we could even say that the symbol-image of Midnight and the meaning this image expresses would make no sense if they were not in some fundamental way first related to this crisis, the splitting that affects time in this particular moment of the novel.

In his brief discussion of the moment in *Bel Ami,* Eisenstein focuses on the tendency of time to become unified by the symbolic form at work in the artistic image and thus expressive of a determinate meaning. Yet his analysis does register ("everything has been gambled," "decision," "fateful hour") that this entire symbolic operation receives a sense of urgency not so much from itself as from the fact that it responds to a rather different tendency of time, which is that of time's self-division. To conceptualize this relation that the symbol-image, an image that expresses an intelligible meaning, maintains to the critical figure of time, we must look to Walter Benjamin and his theorization of the "dialectical image," particularly as this concept appears in the series of fragments that compose the famous convolute N, "On the Theory of Knowledge, Theory of Progress," in his *Arcades Project,* which served as the basis not only for Benjamin's writings on Charles Baudelaire and the Paris of the nineteenth century but also for his reinvention of the idea of historical intelligibility and the radical critique of progressive theories of history. What makes necessary that we take up a detour through Benjamin's theorization of the dialectical image (as he famously puts it, "image is dialectics at a standstill") is not that it more or less coincided with Eisenstein's own writing about the image in the second half of the 1930s but that Benjamin allows us to draw out a certain dimension of the image, which we have indicated in our discussion of the scene from *Bel Ami,* and which, while present in Eisenstein's thinking, is not fully and explicitly theorized by him as such.

For what is crucial in Benjamin's concept of the image, particularly as it relates to time and history, is that the legibility of the image, the fact that the image is readable or, as we would say, that it can function as a symbolic expression of a certain meaning, depends on the ability of the image first to bring to light the element of time that Benjamin calls "the perilous critical moment": "The image that is read . . . bears to the highest degree the imprint of the perilous critical moment on which all reading is founded."[42] Thus the image might make time or history intelligible, that is, it might be taken as a symbolic expression of time that bears a certain meaning for consciousness, yet this symbolic operation of reading is only possible because the appearance of the image happens in a moment in which a critical split or a discontinuity—indeed, a cut—is introduced into time itself. A moment charged with time is "blasted out of the continuum of historical succession," an explosion that Benjamin characterizes also as the "death of *intentio*"—the death of symbolic or symbolizing consciousness—and as the "birth of authentic historical time, the time of truth."[43]

With the appearance of the dialectical image, the past and the present no longer form a simple succession, but rather, as Benjamin famously puts it, "what-has-been comes together in a flash with the now to form a constellation."[44] In the example of Maupassant's Duroy, the present is a "critical moment," split between two possibilities. But in this moment it is also his entire past that is involved and that itself becomes transformed into a confrontation: will the past have led to failure, or will it have led to success? The past, which is suddenly opened up in this way, cannot be taken as identical to its own passing. It is in some sense still alive, still awaiting decision, still waiting to become a past, and as such it cannot form a continuous temporal sequence with the present. The two are rather suddenly brought together (or constellated) by a split that (in a flash) traverses them both. In a "critical moment," in which time itself divides, it is the fate of both the present and the past that is at stake in this division.

What is striking about Benjamin's formulation and what distinguishes his conception of the dialectical image from the symbol-image is that Benjamin makes the reading of images depend not on the meaning they express but on the contingency and the precarious nature of time itself. "What distinguishes images from the 'essences' of phenomenology," he writes, "is their historical index."[45] *Historical index* must here not be understood merely in a limited historicist sense, stating the commonsensical fact that images come to being and therefore bear traces of specific historical periods in reference to which their meaning may be read; that their "essence" is historically dependent, not absolute, and so on. Rather, the use of the term *historical index* wishes to foreground that images are made but that they also become readable only in certain critical moments: "above all, that [images] attain to legibility only at a particular time."[46] If images make time legible, that is, if they may be taken as instances of symbolic form, it is not because they manage to unify time from a perspective of its essence or meaning but because there is something in images, "in the movement at their interior,"[47] as Benjamin puts it, that allows them to register the irruption of a crisis in time itself. Only because the image is a trace of a critical dynamic of time, of time coming into conflict with itself, does it attain to a certain symbolic, legible status.

If the conception of the symbol-image relies on the conviction that, despite its dynamism and rhythm, time is ultimately subordinate to meaning (ideality of form, essence, stability, and permanence), the Benjaminian notion of the dialectical image suggests that this symbolic function of the image (the fact that an image has the ability to make time legible) is itself a function of a deeper crisis in time, of time's self-division, which imprints itself on any symbolic gesture that the image might perform. Time therefore does not appear in the image only as represented or expressed meaning but crucially also as the trace of its own disunity, which at once undercuts and provides the motivation for the function of symbolic unification, of ideality of form, permanence, and identity, of meaning or essence in the image.

The Symptom-Image

To extend our Benjaminian detour a bit further, we will now note that the French art historian and theorist Georges Didi-Huberman has linked the concept of the dialectical image, according to which any symbolic value of the image necessarily relates to the status of the image as the trace of a crisis in time, to the psychoanalytic notion of the symptom. The image introduces a dimension of "legibility which appears—a statement of key importance in Benjamin's conception—as a *critical point,* a symptom."[48] The comparison is pertinent, for it is precisely in the symptom that we most clearly encounter a phenomenon that appears to belong to the function of symbolism—it demands to be read, interpreted for its meaning—but that is carried by an imprint of time that refuses to organize itself into a meaningful totality or to represent something meaningful for consciousness. What manifests in the symptom is not time as the referent of a symbolic consciousness but a different kind of temporality, that of the unconscious drives, which Freud famously described as "timeless" *(zeitlos)*: "The processes of the system *Ucs.* are timeless; i.e. they are not ordered temporally, are not altered by the passage of time; they have no reference to time at all. Reference to time is bound up, once again, with the work of the system Cs."[49] What this means, as Didi-Huberman clarifies, is not that the unconscious (and with it any symptomatic manifestation, as well as psychoanalysis itself) stands simply outside of time or history: "In reality, Freud poses the *Zeitlosigkeit* of the unconscious as the dialectical condition—a fecund negativity—of the flow of time itself. For under the stream of time, one finds the riverbed: that is to say, the *other time of the flow.*"[50] Time is not one. And any act of symbolic construction or reading that seeks to discover in the flow of time a reference to a meaningfully ordered unity depends on but cannot exhaust this criticality, the division of time, which manifests in the form of a symptom. It is for this reason—namely, because symbolic consciousness may never fully turn the time of the subject into its proper referent—that a sense of timelessness attaches itself to the symptom, a manifestation that cannot be integrated into the meaningful sequence of one's conscious biography and that introduces its own kind of "temporality" (chronic repetition).

In Benjamin's conception as well, the "critical moment" of the dialectical image makes time appear not only as something that may be "temporally ordered" but as "what has been from time immemorial,"[51] which is to say, what is *zeitlos* or timeless. This means that the historian must take up not only the task of interpretation but "the task of dream interpretation," to read the images of the past not merely according to the principle of "what actually happened" (Leopold von Ranke's famous definition of history as "wie es eigentlich gewesen") but with attention precisely to the dimension of historical time that resists the account of history as a progressive unfolding of facts (as though some agency of consciousness were immanently at work in history, unifying and ordering time itself). As a reader of *dialectical* images, the historian becomes a dream interpreter in the Freudian sense, reading the manifest content of what actually happened to uncover a certain latency of time, the unconscious desire of history, the conflict of time with itself, which is no less part of our past than the set of actual events that took place, and which, according to Benjamin, flashes in critical and revolutionary moments that symptomatically interrupt time's progressive actualization.

The link Didi-Huberman establishes between the dialectical image and the symptom allows us to further elaborate the relationship of time and meaning in the image. What does it mean to say that this relationship is not symbolic but symptomatic? That there are symbol-images, but that there may also exist symptom-images? It means, first, that the image will bear an *imprint* of time that affects it beyond its symbolic, meaning-giving function (Benjamin's "historical index," the "death of *intentio*" signaled by the apparition of the dialectical image). This primacy of the imprint of time over the presence of meaning in the image is crucial, for it suggests that the ideal form of meaning achieved by the image is always a response to (perhaps even a defense against) the force of time and can never truly become permanent and stable. Second, lacking any symbolic stability, meaning will become subject to *displacement,* to condensation and figural transformation—what Didi-Huberman calls the "plastic intensity"[52] of the symptom-image. The imprint of time leads to the plastic dynamism of form, which is opposed to rather than merely subsumed under the form's symbolic ideality, because it has the capacity to suspend the sovereignty of the symbolic function in the image. And finally, the instability of the symbolic function and of meaning in the symptom-image might be brought to a certain limit point, at which the meaning may suffer a *reversal,* become antithetical in relation to itself, refer to both this and that, one thing and its opposite, in complete disregard of the principle of noncontradiction. In Didi-Huberman's words, this element of the structure of the symptom-image is called the image's "contradictory simultaneity"[53] and points to the resistance of the symptom-image to reading and interpretation, particularly when these are understood in terms of a symbolic deciphering.[54]

With its plastic intensity (displacement, condensation, figural transformation) and contradictory simultaneity (reversal or antithesis of meaning), the symptom-image relates interpretation to a point of incomprehensibility. "Etymologically, the symptom refers to what falls away, and not what signifies."[55] In Didi-Huberman's conception, the symptom-image refers what we see and what we may read in the image not to meaning but to the working of the unconscious fantasy:

> The symbol, ordinarily made to be understood, becomes symptom the moment it displaces itself and loses its primary identity, when its proliferation suffocates its signification, transgressing the limits of its proper semiotic field. . . . The symptom is a symbol that has become incomprehensible, endowed as it is with the powers of the *wirksamen unbewssten Phantasie* ("unconscious fantasy at work"): plastically intensified, capable of "contradictory simultaneity," of displacement, and therefore, of dissimulation.[56]

We must be careful here not to read the reference to the effectiveness of the unconscious fantasy in the image as a kind of return to meaning. The unconscious fantasy is not some secret, deeper content that we may read from the image if only we increase and make more subtle our interpretative effort. Rather than a kind of progressive symbolic interpretation of the image, the unconscious fantasy points to a movement of "*regression* of symbolic thought toward pure 'sensorial images' in which representation in some way returns to its 'primary matter.'"[57] These terms—*pure sensorial images* and *primary matter* of representation—which Didi-Huberman borrows from Freud, point to the dimension of the image, which may be considered as neither that of its active, formative, symbolic function (expression of meaning) nor simply its passive, receptive, material sensuousness (formless materiality) but precisely as a kind of imagistic matter that is formed immanently. What the symptom-image delineates is the possibility of a kind of material morphology of images, a morphology that does not have its destiny in a "symbology" of images but rather allows us to account precisely for that dimension of the image—the "purely sensorial" and "primitively material"—that might resist and in its resistance also motivate the acts of symbolic construction and interpretation. An image grasped in this sense becomes a site not of a symbology of meaning but of a "*symptomatology . . . of time.*"[58]

Toward a Symptomatology of Eisenstein's Images

What may a symptomatology of time accomplished with the help of the image and distinct from the image's symbolism look like? For some initial orientation, we can turn to a short, illuminating text by Slavoj Žižek titled "Hitchcockian *Sinthoms*," in which Žižek considers the status of certain visual "motifs" that repeat and form a set of series across the filmic work of Alfred Hitchcock. Žižek takes as his examples the "motif of 'the person who is suspended from another's hand,'" which appears in different guises in *Saboteur, To Catch a Thief, Vertigo,* and *North by Northwest,* and the motif of "unnaturally white milk," which we encounter in *Suspicion, Spellbound,* and *Notorious.* "How . . . are we to interpret such extended motifs?" Žižek asks, and his response, which is worth quoting at length, points precisely to what in Didi-Huberman's perspective appears as the symptom-image:

> If we search in them for a common core of meaning (reading the hand which pulls the subject up as a token of deliverance, of spiritual salvation, for example), we *say too much*: we enter the domain of Jungian archetypes which is utterly incompatible with Hitchcock's universe; if, on the other hand, we reduce them to an empty signifier's hull filled out in each of the films by a specific content, we *don't say enough*: the force which makes them persist from one film to another eludes us. The right balance is attained when we conceive them as *sinthoms* in the Lacanian sense: as a signifier's constellation (formula) which fixes a certain core of enjoyment, like mannerisms in painting—characteristic details which persist and repeat themselves without implying a common meaning (this insistence offers, perhaps, a clue to what Freud meant by the "compulsion to repeat").
>
> So, paradoxically, these repeated motifs, which serve as a support of the Hitchcockian interpretative delirium, designate the *limit of interpretation*: they are what resists interpretation, the inscription into the texture of a specific visual enjoyment. Such a riveting of our attention to *sinthoms* enables us to establish links connecting Hitchcock's films which, on the level of their "official" content, seem to have nothing whatsoever in common.[59]

Sinthom, the term that appears in Žižek's text, is the name Jacques Lacan gives in his late seminars to the symptom precisely insofar as the symptom insists in its repetition even after analysis seems to have successfully interpreted it.[60] The sinthom, which Lacan elaborates particularly in relation to the work of James Joyce, is a symptom that resists becoming deciphered for its (unconscious) meaning and thus integrated into the analysand's symbolic universe. What is striking in Žižek's formulation is the placement of the visual sinthoms or symptom-images precisely at the *limit* of interpretation, which is to say neither beyond interpretation, where they would be taken as simply meaningless, nor within interpretation, where their compulsive repetition and resistance could ultimately be formulated in some kind of meaningful statement. The limit of interpretation they designate is neither external nor fully internal; their relation to meaning and to the symbol is *extimate*: the bit of visual enjoyment they manage to configure is at once most intimate to meaning and external to it. The sinthom is "a certain signifying formation penetrated by enjoyment: it is a signifier as a bearer of *jouis-sense,* enjoyment-in-sense."[61] For this reason sinthoms might support, as Žižek says, a certain interpretative delirium, an attempt to capture what in meaning is at once more and less than meaning, and what constantly puts the interpreter in the position of saying too much (seeing the repetition of an image as an expression of some deep, meaningful archetype) and saying too little (seeing the images that repeat as simply dependent on their particular contexts).

We may here refer one more time to Benjamin and say that, in his conception of the image, too, this is precisely the double danger he wishes to avoid. The dialectical image is, on one hand, not a Jungian archetype. The difference between the two consists of the fact that while a dialectical image makes legible the historicity of phenomena, the archetype turns us away from history and back to nature: "The archaic form of primal history, which has been summoned up in every epoch and now once more by Jung, is that form which makes semblance in history still more delusive by mandating nature as its homeland."[62] But on the other hand, a dialectical image is also not to be interpreted in a purely historicist way, as though its meaning could be exhausted fully through the reference to its particular context. On the contrary, the dialectical image involves a manifestation, within and to a specific point in history, of a dimension of time that resists any simple historicist or contextual assignation: "In the dialectical image, what has been within a particular epoch is always, simultaneously, 'what has been from time immemorial.' As such, however, it is manifest, on each occasion, only to a quite specific epoch."[63]

The reader will at this point undoubtedly raise the question of what the symptom-image or the logic of the sinthom has to do with Eisenstein's conception of the image. Does not the fact that one needs to reach for different theoretical sources—Benjamin, Didi-Huberman and Freud, Žižek and Lacan—to arrive at the specific dimension of the symptom-image show that no such concept is conceivable from the perspective of Eisenstein's work? This would indeed seem to be the case. Is Eisenstein, namely, not the one filmmaker whose mission was not only to impose meaning but to make images speak a determinate ideological meaning, seen from a determinate standpoint? Is the Eisensteinian aesthetic not ultimately one that conjures the temporal powers of the image (the conflicts, the repetitions) only to give the image over to the function of symbolization, the ideality of form—an operation that is that much more effective (and suspicion worthy) given Eisenstein's considerable dynamic and rhythmic talent? It was not without reason that Roland Barthes, relating Eisenstein to Bertolt Brecht and Denis Diderot, spoke of his aesthetics as an essentially idealizing (idealist?) one, in which the aim is to produce the image as a *tableau*—an image that coincides with the ideal form of meaning realized in the visual medium of the picture:

> the tableau is intellectual, it has something to say (something moral, social) but it also says that it knows how this must be done; it is simultaneously significant and propaedeutical, impressive and reflexive, moving

> and conscious of the channels of emotion. The epic scene in Brecht, the shot in Eisenstein are so many tableaux; they are scenes which are *laid out* (in the sense in which one says *the table is laid*), which answer perfectly to that dramatic unity theorized by Diderot: firmly cut out . . . , erecting a meaning but manifesting the production of that meaning, they accomplish the coincidence of the visual and the ideal *découpages.*[64]

Without wishing to deny any of this, it is nevertheless possible to suggest the presence of the symptom-image or the sinthom in Eisenstein's work. The fact that, particularly from the mid-1930s onward, his theorization conceives of the image as almost exclusively a symbol-image—an imagistic form expressive of meaning, a form of essential interpretation of phenomena, and so on—cannot completely cover over the fact that the symbolic effectiveness of Eisenstein's images so often rests on the ability to produce in them a remarkable sense of "plastic intensity" and "contradictory simultaneity" (Didi-Huberman) or a configuration of "a specific visual enjoyment" (Žižek), which does not seem to be at all exhausted by the act of (symbolic) interpretation. Eisenstein's work has most often been read as an attempt to organize—to form—cinematic matter in such a way that its resistance to meaning, the limit the image sets to interpretation, could be overcome, the cinematic material becoming fully symbolized and thus interpretable without a remainder. Certainly Eisenstein's own writings have supported such an understanding, because they most often focus precisely on the (operational) question of how an effect of meaning may be calculated and produced by the formative capacity that takes possession of the material at hand. With Eisenstein, it seems, we never have to be in doubt about what he means or what he intends with his images.

What we wish to suggest, however, is that perhaps the time has come to reread Eisenstein's work, his remarkable symbolizing ability, the great effort of meaning in his cinema, from the perspective of the symptom; to pass in our reading from Eisenstein's symbol-images to what may be called the Eisensteinian sinthoms, the dimension of his images in which what comes to light is not meaning but the limit of interpretation itself. And if the passage from the symbol to the symptom-image required a detour, exiting Eisenstein's thought and returning to it with a little conceptual curiosity that might initially appear foreign to it, it is because such is the path of the symptom itself. The symptom, namely, never arrives as a product of an organic and immanent development, but always as an intrusion that must, at first, be encountered as something inassimilable, as though it came from the outside and can only then be slowly assumed as something intimate, very much belonging to the interior, which it, however, necessarily disturbs and divides.

Take as an example the famous shot from the end of *Ivan the Terrible,* part 1, in which the close-up of Ivan's head in profile, occupying the upper right quadrant of the frame, is juxtaposed with the snakelike procession of the people we see in the background in the frame's lower left quadrant. The shot produces a striking effect, which may be ascribed to the "plastic intensity" achieved by the violent juxtaposition of the enlarged detail of the head and the distant, "miniaturized" figure of the people in the depth of the image. The conflict of planes produces in our perception of the shot a distinct dynamic and rhythmic shock, which opens up the shot to its symbolic meaning that once again unifies the picture: Eisenstein says, for instance, that both the enlargement of a part (the close-up of the head) and the "miniaturization" of a figure (the distancing of the masses) may serve as means for expressing a totality of meaning.[65] What the shot depicts is not merely the anecdotal event: the mass of ordinary people has come to plead with Ivan for his return to Moscow, thus confirming him as the tsar of the popular masses and legitimizing his attempt to assume the unified and absolute power of the state against the fragmented feudal aristocracy of the boyars. The shot is also an image (a symbol-image) expressive of the meaning of this event; it is an exercise in imagistic form that renders the event along with its essential interpretation (the idea of the unity of the leader and his people): the tsar does not merely bear over the masses but must "condescend" to their desires as the father might condescend to the wishes of a child (Eisenstein has Cherkassov lower his head into the frame as we hear the masses sing "Come Back, Beloved Father!"); the tsar must first listen to the people before he may see the nature of his historic mission (Cherkassov's eyes are first closed and only then open); and the head of the state may in this sense occupy a space in which he is simultaneously joined and separated from the masses, at once responding to and distancing himself from them, in sync with their movement (horizontal, a winding curve) and different from it (vertical, up and down, as though punctuating and articulating the continuous figure of the mass of people that resembles the stream of a river). What we find here—in this remarkable mise-en-scène of the Stalinist imagination of power—is perhaps a symbol-image expressive of the symbolic function itself: a symbolic instance of the tsar condescending to the sensuous flux of the masses, which thereby come to represent unity, stability, historical meaning, for the figure of the leader, the consciousness or the head of state.

But the conception of the symptom-image and the suggestion that, as there exist "Hitchcockian sinthoms," one may also be able to find Eisensteinian ones now allow us to take this highly significant shot from *Ivan the Terrible* and replace it within a series of shots gathered from Eisenstein's other films, which we will here present in reverse chronological order: *Ivan the Terrible*, two stills from *Bezhin Meadow, Que Viva Mexico!, The General Line*, and *Strike* (Figure 26).

Figure 26. The symptom-image or the image-in-series. *Ivan the Terrible,* part 1; two shots from *Bezhin Meadow;* and one shot from each of *Que Viva Mexico!, The General Line,* and *Strike.*

What is the effect of such a displacement of the image from its more obvious and immediate context (from the montage sequence in which it is embedded and the narrative and dramatic fiction of the particular film in which it is used) into such a series? Perhaps we could say that the effect lies in the foregrounding of the image's "plastic intensity" and the weakening of its determinate symbolic value. The image-in-series brings to light the "pure sensorial image" (Freud), which does not refer symbolically to some unified field of meaning. Each of the individual shots in the series repeats in its own guise the gesture of a violent juxtaposition of two incongruous elements within a single frame. We could say that what makes the series is the presence of a montage-like construction within the frame and that the series thus makes visible the moment of the cut or of diremption as in some sense constitutive for the production of the image. At the same time, however, the effect of the image-in-series also seems to prevent us from referring this moment of diremption and the plastic intensity it produces to an instance of meaning that would once again inform it, motivate it, and symbolically unify it. On the contrary, while there may be a certain sensorial exactness at work in the plastic intensity of these individual shots that allows us to place them in a series, there is no exactness of symbolic meaning that would at the same time ground or justify our operation. At the level of meaning, the plastic intensity of the image-in-series would here have to be tied not to the unity of a symbol but to the sense of a "contradictory simultaneity" (a set of reversals, antitheses).

We have thus established for ourselves a series of formal resemblances without any firm iconographic basis. This is perhaps a good way to describe precisely why the image-in-series, the image that assumes the form of a certain compulsion to repeat throughout the work, is related to the symptom and the experience of the limit of interpretation. It is precisely the formal resemblance at work through the series—the fact that a certain configuration, a certain plastic intensity, repeats itself—that produces the desire and the necessity to interpret. Yet, at the same time, this element of formal resemblance finds no guarantee in the symbolism of meaning: the insistence of a certain plastic configuration that repeats throughout the series is not supported by the ideal form of meaning, which makes any conclusive gesture of interpretation impossible. The symptomal image-in-series thus at least momentarily opens up the experience of form as eccentric with regard to its own ideality, introducing the task of reading as something that occupies the limit of interpretation, touching both on its necessity and its impossibility, what is at the same time most intimate to and beyond the reach of meaning.

From this point, it is not too difficult to see how we may be tempted to say too much about the image-in-series, explaining it in terms of an archetypal ur-image, which would at once unify the series and give the images within it the status of mere copies, secondary manifestations of some deeper, transcendent reality. But we may also be tempted to say too little, referring the individual shots back to their obvious and more immediate contexts, the individual films, thus denying and dissolving the consistency of the series itself. Both options (deeper, archetypal unity of meaning; dissolution in particular, contextual meanings) solve the problem posed by the image-in-series by referring the symptomatic occurrence of the image to a clearer instance of meaning and by situating our reading firmly within (rather than at the limit of) interpretation. At the same time, it is also not difficult to see how the analytical and theoretical gesture of producing the image-in-series might bring about a veritable "delirium of interpretation." It is, namely, always possible to transform the repetition and insistence of a certain plastic configuration or visual enjoyment that occurs symptomatically into a set of symbolic correspondences that enlarge and multiply the meanings of individual shots. Thus, for instance, developing the symbolic correspondence between the shot from *Ivan the Terrible* and that from *The General Line* (of Marfa threatened by one of the kulaks) might suddenly enrich the interpretation of the former, into which we may now be able to read the meaning of the peasant mass terrorized by the violence of an overbearing and historically regressive figure—a reading that would subvert our initial (and perhaps too naive) interpretation of the shot from *Ivan* as a symbolic expression of the mise-en-scène of Stalinist state power.

Archetypal interpretation, contextual interpretation, delirious interpretation: it would perhaps be possible to describe other ways in which the occurrence of the series of the symptom-image prompts us to seek refuge in the symbolism of meaning and produces in us a desire to integrate it under the sovereignty of the symbolic function. This is in some way inevitable. For, as we know, it is rather difficult to sustain oneself in the face of the symptom. The symptomatic series of an image that repeats compulsively creates a tear in the very texture of the work as something meaningfully organized. The series of the symptom-image is inevitably fragile and under constant threat of losing the specificity of its own dimension. If it is not simply dismissed as a nonevent or a nonentity, the symptomatic occurrence is turned into an event of a symbolic nature and taken as a configuration of elements that in its appearance expresses a determinate (biographical, historical, cultural) meaning that may be deciphered through the work of interpretation.

Someone who takes a look at the image-in-series, which seems to us the most effective way of drawing attention to the presence of the symptom in Eisenstein's work with images, may always say, "This is nothing! What you are presenting has no actual reality in Eisenstein's work and should thus not make a claim on our knowledge of his work either." To which we can reply that, while such a claim is in a sense correct, it is also the case that the necessity and the reality of any work always articulate themselves not around something positive but precisely around absences, around that which, strictly speaking, is not. According to Žižek,

> Symptom, conceived as *sinthome,* is literally our only substance, the only positive support of our being, the only point that gives consistency to the subject. In other words, symptom is the way we—the subjects—"avoid madness," the way we "choose something (the symptom-formation) instead of nothing (radical psychotic autism, the destruction of the symbolic universe)" through the binding of our enjoyment to a certain signifying, symbolic formation which assures a minimum of consistency to our being-in-the-world. If the symptom in this radical dimension is unbound, it means literally "the end of the world"—the only alternative to the symptom is nothing: pure autism, a psychic suicide, surrender to the death drive even to the total destruction of the symbolic universe.[66]

What gives consistency to the subject, according to this account, is not meaning but a particular or singular binding of enjoyment and the signifier, which produces a symptom that, in turn, allows the subject to sustain itself in the face of negativity—in the face of the fact that, as a subject, it has no positive being at all. It is the symptom (signifier permeated with enjoyment; a concretion of *jouis-sense* or enjoy-meant) that grounds or that serves as the condition of the symbol and the symbolic (signifier as a vehicle of meaning), rather than the other way around.

In the same way, the actuality of a filmic work, whose symbol-images we may interpret for their meaning, is built on the work's sinthoms or symptom-images. The status of an artistic work as a symbolically meaningful unity depends on an element that is extimate, neither simply internal nor simply external, to the work's meaning. It is the sinthoms or the symptom-images—concretions of *jouissance* bound to some formal disposition of artistic material—that first allow the work, which in itself has no positive or substantial being, to sustain itself in the face of nothingness. Any "symbology" of artistic images—their iconographic interpretation, for instance, which seeks to explain their reality by elaborating their symbolic meaning—is thus impossible to conceive without a prior symptomatology. The individuality of the symbol-image is impossible to grasp without the image-in-series that gives body to the work's symptom. The question of symbolic interpretation, which organizes the progressive temporality of a work into a meaningful unity, makes little sense—quite literally, the work does not produce sense—unless one first admits the "reality" of the symptom and its compulsive temporality, its insistent repetition within a work.

In the end, we want to ask (and leave the question for the future) what some fuller reading of Eisensteinian images from the perspective of the symptom might look like. Would the construction of the symptomatic images-in-series that traverse his work manage to confront our interpretation of Eisenstein's remarkable symbolic achievement with its limit, its proper extimacy? Could his cinema, which he himself taught us how to read, and which we have most often understood as a powerful symbolic machine for making meaning, be used to make visible not the symbol or the symbolic mastery of time but time's conflict with itself? What would the great Eisensteinian symbolism of history appear like if it were possible to see it from the perspective of the formal disorder of its symptoms—the "plastic intensities" and "contradictory simultaneities," the "visual enjoyment," without the "ideal form" of historical time?

The present chapter has, hopefully, managed to indicate the possibility of a constructive rereading of Eisensteinian images, a practice of reading that might, with the help of the concept of the symptom-image and the methodological vehicle of the image-in-series, be able to take up Eisenstein's work from those points at which it does not touch on clear symbolic meaning but rather encounters a certain weakening of symbolic expression, an evanescence of meaning, and thus makes appear a crisis in time (the Benjaminian "critical moment" or the symptom). Thus, proposed here is an idea of reading whose goal is not merely interpretative but explicitly diagnostic and constructive, involving an active transformation of Eisenstein's images and their relations within his work. As with any encounter with a symptom, such a task of reading belongs to the future, yet it belongs to the future precisely insofar as the latter serves as the place for the invention of a new past. The lesson of psychoanalysis, which we have followed here, is that in the end (in the achievement of analytical treatment), the patient stops believing in her symptom, which is to say, stops believing that the symptom may ultimately reveal its meaning, some final significance, and instead begins to *identify* with the symptom (to identify with the symptom precisely as sinthom, beyond interpretation). In the end, one ceases interpreting and becomes—in some sense, invents—one's symptom.[67] *Wo Es war, soll Ich werden.* Should not the same lesson apply to us, the patients of Eisenstein's images? Does not the future of these images depend on our refusal to continue believing in them (the refusal of interpretation) and on our ability simply to identify with them, to become them, which is to say, to invent them? Where they were, we must come to be.

■ ■ ■ ■ FOUR

Montage of Forms

CONCEPT AND *WITZ*, ORGANICISM AND THE COMIC

I felt a Cleaving in my Mind—
As if my Brain had split—
I tried to match it—Seam by Seam—
But could not make it fit.
The thought behind, I strove to join
Unto the thought before—
But Sequence ravelled out of Sound
Like Balls—upon a Floor.

■ Emily Dickinson

Eisensteinian Concepts as Montages

If there exists such a thing as a *concept* of montage in Eisenstein's thought, it is first necessary to distinguish it from the other concepts discussed so far in the present book. Montage, namely, participates in other concepts much more intimately than is the case the other way around. In the preceding chapters, the concepts of movement, action, and image have been presented as dialectical unities (unities of opposites) that required not one term but a juxtaposition of two terms to bring to light the nature of their dynamism. Thus, for instance, the Eisensteinian concept of *movement* must be thought as a dialectical unity of the movement that belongs to the visibility of the figure (kinematographic movement) and "another movement" that puts the visibility of the figure into crisis and, through this, constitutes the cinematic gesture as such. The concept of *action* is itself a split and problematic unity made up of two genres of action, grotesque and epic, whose relation is dialectical, because each of the two genres is not merely externally opposed to the other but somehow works the other from within as well. And finally, the previous chapter argued for a division traversing Eisenstein's concept of the *image*, which has to be grasped as both a symbol (how Eisenstein predominantly theorizes it) and a symptom-image (without which the symbolic power of Eisenstein's work with images cannot be adequately explained).

Eisenstein's concepts themselves function as montages. None of the concepts is a simple unity, but we are, in each case, also not simply dealing with two distinct concepts. Rather, each concept is a unity that depends on splitting and division—an instance of a cut—as its constitutive moment. In this sense, the concept is one precisely insofar as it is also not a unity. Or put differently, what makes an Eisensteinian concept thinkable as a unity is that it is not one. An analogy may be drawn between this logic of Eisensteinian concepts and the logic of montage. Is not montage itself also characterized by the fact that it presents us with something that is neither one, because any montage involves at least two heterogeneous elements, nor simply two (or more), because montage also presupposes some kind of unitary effect (regardless of the question of whether such an effect is actually delivered by a concrete instance of montage)? Just as the Eisensteinian concepts, then, a montage configuration presents us with a unity that is not one. Or we may talk of one montage, *a* montage, precisely to the extent that it is not a unity.

The relationship between montage and other Eisensteinian concepts can, however, be determined in a more precise way. For montage does not simply resemble but rather explains the very necessity of division, the moment of dis-unity, which we find constitutive of the Eisensteinian concept. To take again the example of *movement,* what operates the discontinuation and the disturbance of the kinematographic figure—what, in other words, puts into crisis the figurative visibility of movement as such—is nothing other than montage. Montage introduces "another" movement, which interrupts and displaces the movement of the kinematographic figure and thereby forces us to think the concept of movement itself as something divided. In the case of *action,* it is clear that what divides it and turns it into a formal problem is also the intervention of montage. For it is precisely the latter's pretension that it may produce the sense of action through a break with its representation that splits Eisenstein's conception of action from inside. Montage here produces a presentation of action (grotesque and theatrical in its schematic design) that contradicts its own representation (heroic and epic in its totality).

And finally, the division of the *image* between its symbolic function and its symptomatic force depends on the idea of montage as the primacy of the cut and negativity. If, as Eisenstein writes in the 1920s, an image is a cut that discloses, then the image is essentially dependent on the operation of montage. This primacy of montage introduces a profound undecidability into the concept of the image. On one hand, the cut, which installs the image as an interruption of our perception, a break or an event that seizes our experience, may be motivated toward symbolic production. The cut of the image is, in other words, necessary to liberate the picture from the straitjacket of iconic resemblance and turn it into a symbolic sign, a vehicle for the realization of meaning. On the other hand, however, the negativity of the cut opens up the possibility of a very different relationship to time than the one offered by symbolic representation. A cut may not be exhausted by the work of symbolization and the stable, permanent figure of time offered by the symbol-image. The negativity of the cut might, on the contrary, point to a conflict in time itself, the fact that time may not be fully subsumed by the symbolism of the image but instead produce configurations in which it appears as though it were lost to itself—a dimension of the image as a symptomatic occurrence. If montage, which is unthinkable without the cut—because it is nothing but the production of relations between cuts—may be considered as the constitutive moment of the Eisensteinian conception of the image, it is precisely because it is both a remarkable means for organizing time from the perspective of meaning (the symbol-image) and a vehicle for disorganizing meaning from the perspective of time (the symptom-image).

All of this suggests that we must conceive montage as intimately tied to the dialectic of division, which we have traced across his key concepts, and which is characteristic of Eisenstein's thought as such. With this in mind, it is clear that montage cannot be counted merely as one Eisensteinian concept among others. Far more, montage is something like the necessary moment at work in the constitution of all Eisensteinian concepts. That is to say, montage has to do with the very "conceptuality" of these concepts; it is the condition of all Eisensteinian concepts.

Yet the relationship between this condition and the concepts is not without its problems, and it seems that it would not be wrong to describe it with the help of the deconstructive formula, according to which the condition of possibility of something is at the same time the condition of its impossibility. On one hand, it is clear, for instance, that what makes the question of movement in cinema worthy of conceptual elaboration, what turns cinematic movement into what needs to be thought, is precisely its relationship to montage. Only because of the presence of montage is it possible to speak of cinematic movement as something that opens up the gap (and thus the possibility of a constructed relationship) between its own proper gesture and the kinematographic (re)production of movement. On the other hand, however, it is also clear how montage comes to trouble any simple or unproblematic sense of cinematic movement, which as such is nothing natural but is, in fact, discontinuous with the movement of reality and does not possess the coherence and unity of an "object." The very "objectivity" of cinematic movement always bears the stain of the "subjective" moment of montage—of a decision, an intervention, of commitment to discontinuity. Which means that the concept of cinematic movement will always remain tied to a certain irreducible dimension of negativity or of the cut, of heterogeneity and division, of the juxtaposition of incommensurables supported by its montage-condition, which thus troubles the concept's validity as much as it helps establish it.

Is There an Eisensteinian Concept of Montage?

The sense that the concepts of cinema are conditioned by something (montage) that is at once proximate and distant to them, intimate and seemingly foreign to the very status of the concept, is confirmed in Eisenstein's case by any attempt to produce from his work such a thing as the *concept of montage.* Is it, for instance, possible to speak of one, single concept of montage in Eisenstein's thought? An answer to this question has to first remember that the introduction of the term *montage* into the field of art aims precisely at dividing and thus problematizing the field's uniqueness and conceptual unity. The "beautiful word,"[1] as Eisenstein calls it, not only is a transplant from a foreign language, coming into Russian from French, but enters art and aesthetics from the heterogeneous technical field of engineering.[2] Eisenstein's appropriation of the word, as the term around which to orient his entire project, is thus meant to estrange the very notion of *artistic* work, to disidentify the artist from the traditional or classical view of his function, and, by provocatively calling montage *beautiful,* to split or put into crisis the concept of aesthetics as such.[3]

The word is thus not merely a technical one, because it has been appropriated or "detourned" from the technical field, refunctioned for a different purpose, but neither is it fully artistic, because it always—and quite proudly—flaunts the mark of its technical provenance. If this is the case and the primary purpose of montage is indeed to mark off a space of technical and artistic nonidentity, in relation to which the work of cinema must find its orientation, then we may also wonder if it is at all appropriate to speak of montage as subsumable under a concept—one, single concept—in possession of its own unity and an unambiguous field of application.

Eisenstein most often does not speak of montage in general but of determinate types of montage: montage of attractions, intellectual montage, overtonal montage, interior monologue, vertical montage. These are not merely individual species indicating a zoological variety within a stable genus but stand in a more dialectical relationship with the latter. Each of these terms, namely, presents a reevaluation of montage as such, a veritable monstrosity that puts into doubt the very genre of montage, which thereby loses the status of a stable category and instead assumes the shape of a series of divergences.

In his *Montage Eisenstein,* Jacques Aumont refers to the "extreme diversity" of Eisenstein's work and the "ceaseless transformation of his conceptual system: in short, everything that might lead (and has often led) to the legitimate conclusion that there are *several Eisensteins.*"[4] This conclusion finds its most decisive support in the "recognition that there is no unitary 'concept of montage' that comes to theoretical fruition over the course of [Eisenstein's] career—at least, not in the limited, rationally defined, and constant form by which one could characterize a true concept."[5] If it is the case, as we claimed earlier, that montage is intimately connected to the Eisensteinian concepts of cinema, that it in some sense informs the very "conceptuality" of these concepts, then we would now have to say, following Aumont, that the "conceptuality" of cinematic concepts depends on montage as an improper concept. From this, one could in turn draw an important point about the very nature of Eisenstein's film-theoretical enterprise (and perhaps any film-theoretical project at all), namely, that the latter must always remain vigilant in admitting that the consistency of its concepts takes shape in relation to an element that is not properly conceptual and does not offer the support of a "true" unity of the concept.

Aumont affirms the disunity of the Eisensteinian conception of montage and asserts with it also the plurality of Eisenstein's thought. Yet, if we are unable to arrive at some unitary *concept* of montage, it is at the same time difficult to deny that montage does in some way constitute the unifying thread of Eisenstein's multiple efforts. Aumont signals this unifying function of montage by calling it a principle, even the principle of a philosophical and aesthetic system: "the *principle* of montage plays a crucial part in his writing as well as in his films, and occupies a central place in his philosophical and aesthetic system."[6] Eisenstein's

> theoretical accounts [of montage] are neither rationalizations, however incomplete, of empirical givens and cumulative practices of filmmaking, nor are they simple, formal variations of any one, basic conceptual model—but . . . from one version of the theory to another, a project is being worked through, a theoretical space is being marked out. Or to put it another way, what is at stake in Eisenstein's work is not the elaboration of *methods* of montage, nor the formulation of one single concept of montage, but a kind of ongoing and even somewhat systematic study of the principle of montage (or the phenomenon of montage).[7]

In Aumont's characterization, montage thus assumes the peculiar status of a false or improper concept that is at the same time a systematic principle of Eisenstein's thinking. Montage is denied proper conceptual coherence and unity to assume the unifying function at the level of the principle itself, from which any conceptual and theoretical development within Eisenstein's work flows—a ground that opens up the theoretical space for the unfolding of the Eisensteinian concepts.[8]

Montage as Nonrelation

We typically consider montage a form that relates—and thereby contains—two incommensurable elements. Montage signals a type of form that installs the provision of a common measure between elements that are otherwise not commensurate in any obvious way. According to Aumont, the "historical problem of montage" in cinema very early on became that of "overcoming the potential contradiction between a (visual or imaginary) break and a (mental) continuity; to organize a dialectic of editing"[9]—that is to say, to organize an incommensurability at the level of the visible as a form of mental commensurability. It is worth stressing, however, that montage poses a *problem* precisely because it assumes that the break, the discontinuity, the incommensurable, is primary—a fact that threatens to put the very sense of a common measure (or the measure of a common sense) into a profound crisis. Through the operation of montage, the relation that is produced between two incommensurable elements itself becomes affected by the incommensurability. Montage is thus not merely a juxtapositional relation of two (visual) incommensurable elements productive of a (mental) continuity but primarily a division or a discontinuation within the (mental) relation or the measure of continuity itself. Montage might therefore name the loss of any common measure in form—the loss of form as common measure—capable of organizing a set of discrete elements of a work around the work's "nexus of meaning."[10]

In montage, we encounter not only a relationship that links two elements but also a relationship that becomes juxtaposed or comes into conflict with itself. The relation itself begins to relate to what it is not, what is heterogeneous to it—nonrelation. Montage is in this sense a negation of form, if we understand form as that which guarantees the unity of a set of relations in a work. If montage is an event in the history of form, it is because it points to the fact that form itself may not (may no longer) be conceived positively as a relation of relations but must instead be grasped as what refers any relation to an irreducible moment of nonrelationality. It is in this sense that we may read Theodor Adorno's statement in his *Aesthetic Theory*, according to which montage signals a moment in which "negation of synthesis becomes a principle of form."[11] Montage means that there is no metarelational unity that could—as form—support the construction of relations or the creation of juxtapositions between elements that make up the work of art.

It becomes clear why it is wrong to think of montage as an operation that informs heterogeneous elements with a degree of common measure. Montage always and more fundamentally reveals the very relation linking the elements as something in itself incommensurable or nonrelational. It is in this sense that montage cannot simply be considered a form, or a uni-form, of thinking. It, namely, always involves a juxtaposition of different, heterogeneous forms, which as such point to thought's incommensurability with itself. Or put slightly differently, montage is never merely a form of juxtaposition but always also a juxtaposition of form against itself—it brings about the possibility of form conceived as a confrontation of (at least) two distinct and incommensurable types of relation, two distinct and incommensurable forms.

What we are describing here is something like the ideal type of montage, montage in its bare structure, which does not yet by itself explain the full effect of the phenomenon of montage. By shifting the focus from montage conceived as a form that unites incommensurable elements to montage as the incommensurability of form with itself, there appears the dimension of montage as a fundamental threat to the very possibility of form. Montage in its purity (nonrelation) always signals the danger of the destruction of form (a relation of relations), of a separation of elements into a state of pure nonrelationality in which they may become impervious to any kind of relational continuity among them. "The principle of montage was conceived as an act against a surreptitiously achieved organic unity; it was meant to shock. Once this shock is neutralized, the assemblage once more becomes merely indifferent material."[12] Montage, which may be associated with a certain malignancy of form—it openly exposes any given relation between the elements to the force of a nonrelation; it disintegrates bodies—may therefore also end up turning its disintegrative powers against form itself. To this threat of inorganic indifference, the form will respond by strengthening its immunity and developing certain prophylactic measures that seek at once to harness the remarkable force of montage while declining it away from its destructive path. No phenomenon of montage can therefore appear without at the same time triggering a certain "countertendency" in the very body of form, which now seeks to motivate the malignant indifference (back) in the direction of form, to present the aimless and potentially endless disintegration with an aim or some vision of an end to which it may be directed. No phenomenon of montage, it seems, can be fully comprehended without taking into account also a desire to be done with montage, whose aim is to rescue some sense of formal unity from the perspective of its collapse.

Logically, the countertendency comes after the disintegrating tendency of montage, yet it would be wrong to conceive of it as simply secondary. Rather, the countertendency of a new formal unity is inscribed into the very phenomenon of montage as such and is necessarily invoked as an essential qualification whenever the disintegrative tendency of montage makes its presence felt. The phenomenon of montage must therefore be understood as an impurity of conflicting tendencies: it is itself a montage. But this means that the other way around also obtains. There is no countertendency of montage (no desire to be done with montage, no new unity of form) that does not at the same time confirm the irreducible fact of any montage phenomenon, which is that montage not only relates nonrelated elements but primarily turns any relation itself—any form—into something nonrelational. The nonrelational kernel of montage opens up the desire of its countertendency toward the discovery of a new unity of form, a new type of relationality capable of both admitting the disintegrative force and motivating it toward some kind of overcoming. Yet the more this countertendency (to be done with montage, to construct a new unity of form) asserts itself, the more the nonrelational tendency makes itself felt as the truth of any relation; the kernel of disintegration and division manifests itself as the truth of any (formal) unity.

The significance of Eisenstein's thinking on the question of montage lies in its ability to clarify the phenomenon of montage precisely as something constituted by a tension between two opposing tendencies. The Eisensteinian dialectic of montage is, in other words, characterized not merely by an historically original recognition of the disintegrative force of nonrelation and negativity (Eisenstein's insistence on the primacy of the cut and conflict), the corrosive and critical power montage carries into the domain of form, but also by the constant attempts to invent the countertendency of a new type of form invoked by the disintegrative tendency of montage. Eisenstein is as much a filmmaker of montage as he is a thinker of new ways to be done with montage, as much an experimenter with the potentially endless disintegration of form as he is an inventor of new ends for montage's corrosive force. Yet, again, the case must be put the other way around as well. Wherever Eisenstein posits a new type of unity of form achieved by the specific motivation of the work of montage, this unity quickly begins to register the disintegrative tendency of montage and itself becomes divided: the new form that was to be achieved by the harnessing of montage toward a new kind of unity reveals itself as a *montage of forms.*

Intellectual Montage as Montage of Forms (the Gods of *October*)

Perhaps the clearest example of such a montage of forms may be found in Eisenstein's idea of intellectual cinema or intellectual montage, elaborated in a series of famous texts from 1928 and 1929 that followed his work on *October* ("Our *October*. Beyond the Played and Non-played"; "An Unexpected Juncture"; "Beyond the Shot"; "Perspectives"; "The Dramaturgy of Film Form"; "The Fourth Dimension in Cinema").[13] In the idea of intellectual cinema, the disintegrative tendency of montage is made particularly visible. Montage, namely, aims violently at the dissolution of the representational function of form and seeks to free the composition of cinematic images from any analogy with reality. According to Eisenstein's idea of intellectual montage, form may no longer be justified in relation to a preexisting reality. It has instead become "genuine pure cinema"[14]—form as an absolute of sorts, which sustains itself precisely in the dissolution of all representational relations (within images, between images, and between images and reality). The purity of intellectual montage lies in its ability to pulverize all representational links, whose resistance must be broken, in order that the composition of cinematic movement may become a bearer of some genuinely intellectual matter, the materiality of thought itself:

> The property of this montage is to submit the analogical representation to a work of construction, and to propose the real as the result of a search and not as a *given*: it is in the production of meaning that we grasp the world, not in the reproduction of its appearances; to *representation* as figurative imitation of reality, Eisenstein therefore opposes *the image* as an abstract element produced through montage in a perfect independence with regard to the elements represented.[15]

We see how, in relation to the disintegrating, pulverizing tendency of montage, the corrosion of any representational relation by the force of nonrelation, there immediately emerges the countertendency that motivates montage in the direction of a new type of unity of form. The new form no longer aims to represent, but rather to create, the sense of reality. Eisenstein thinks the new unity produced by the work of intellectual montage not as a representational but as a *discursive* form—cinema "trying to seek out *speech*"[16]—where "discourse" has to be understood not simply as a set of symbolic operations mirroring reality but as constitutive and productive of the latter. The becoming-discursive of cinematic form means not only abstracting the form from its representational relation to the world but also the ability of formal articulation to become capable of intervening in the world, of ordering reality, taking command of it, and giving it a new meaning. For this reason, Eisenstein conceives of the cinema of intellectual montage as the production of form assuming its unity *"under the aegis of a slogan."*[17] For a slogan is precisely the kind of discursive form, a type of discursive unity, that does not seek to represent the world but to mobilize it and transform it; it is a form of symbolic articulation that does not mirror material reality but rather itself produces a set of material effects.

Intellectual montage thus means both the destruction of form's representational unity (the disintegrative tendency) and the production of a new unity of form, which is the unity of a discourse or a slogan (the countertendency of montage). Only when we take into account both tendencies are we able to describe "the general movement of the Eisensteinian inquiry, which finds the elimination of realism—and of its ideological burden—in the return to a reality conceived as a product not as a given: the product of a history, but also, and first, the product of a discourse."[18]

It is through a breathtaking analysis of the famous sequence of the gods in Eisenstein's *October*—the sequence that Eisenstein himself held as the perhaps sole fully successful realization of his idea of intellectual cinema—that Marie-Claire Ropars has probed the project and the discursive revolution proposed in Eisenstein's idea of intellectual montage. In "Polonaise of the Gods," she writes, "Eisenstein had pushed farthest his research into the discursive power of montage and its role in the elaboration of a cine-discourse independent of visual denotation."[19] The sequence in question is thus the privileged moment in Eisenstein's cinema, "a model for the filming of abstract concepts,"[20] in which montage manages most fully to dissolve the representational (denotative) function of cinematic form and replace it with a new type of formal unity, which belongs to the order of discourse.

What interests us in Ropars's analysis of the intricacy of Eisenstein's "cine-discourse" is that her text forcefully demonstrates how this new, discursive unity of form itself exists only as divided; or how, in order to work, intellectual montage must assume a form that has to be grasped as a montage of two different forms. Ropars writes, for instance, of the "duality of discourse" produced by the intellectual montage in this particular sequence. This duality has to do with the fact that Eisenstein wishes to develop a critique of divinity—to show the emptiness of the notion of god, the cultural and geographical relativity of religious and ideological dogma—which can, however, be accomplished only if he at the same time "builds up" the concept of god. The discourse of the montage sequence is thus constituted as a "double movement, of contradictory suggestion."[21] And what is crucial, according to Ropars, is that the "contradictory nature of the movement is more important here than signification."[22] That is to say, a certain duality at work within the discursive form of the sequence, what we call a montage of forms, takes precedence over the unity of discourse, particularly insofar as this unity may manifest as unity of meaning.

What, then, does this double movement, which turns the discursive form of intellectual montage into a contradictory unity or a montage of forms, consist of? On one hand, the sequence of the gods realizes a movement through which the discourse of montage builds a concept of God with the help of an associative series of images of divinity (the baroque Christ; the Hindu god

Shiva; the sitting Buddha; Chinese, Japanese, and African statues and masks; and at the very end, a Nivkh idol). The discursive movement assumes here a form that may be called empiricist, according to which abstract ideas or concepts, such as divinity, have to be understood as universalizations or generalizations created on the basis of associations among concrete sense impressions or images.[23] The principle that governs this first movement is similarity, which obtains both between the individual images themselves and between the images and the idea ("god") they symbolize.

Yet, on the other hand, as Ropars states, "it is not only a matter of building the concept, demonstrating the discursive power of the cinema, but also and especially of deconstructing it, thus proving the dialectical impact unique to such a discourse."[24] The aim of the sequence is not merely to produce the abstract universality of "god" but to deconstruct, to empty this idea and its universal status. This movement of evacuating meaning, which forms a kind of counterdiscourse within the discursive construction of intellectual montage, may, however, only take place if similarity is not the sole principle governing the logic of associations between the individual images in the sequence. And indeed, alongside similarity, the sequence realizes a process of transformation or dissimilarity: from the baroque Christ to the Nivkh idol, from the "developed" to the "primitive," from what is culturally near to what is culturally distant, and from the recognizable to the unrecognizable. Ropars describes this dissimilating movement of transformations as the movement of "impoverishing reduction."[25] Thus, to the empiricist form of "universalizing abstraction," which leads us from (concrete) images of divinities toward the (abstract) concept of god, we must add also the presence of a radically different form, that of "impoverishing reduction," which seeks on the contrary to confront the concept of god with an image this concept itself cannot assimilate and which, consequently, manages to estrange the concept from itself. It is the presence of this second movement, the movement of reduction, that leads Eisenstein to declare that the effect of the sequence on the spectator has to be understood in the form of the following judgment: "God is a block of wood [*Bog—churban*]."[26]

The sequence thus at once builds and deconstructs the concept of God; it assumes the form of constructing similarities, which support the notion of god as a "universalizing abstraction," and the transformative form of dissimilation, which produces an effect of god's "impoverishing reduction" to a log or a block of wood (we may also say, from the godhead to a blockhead). The form of the discursive whole produced by montage is thus itself contradictory and divided: "Through this contradictory system, different representations are taken into the same whole, and the concept is built; the whole locates the difference in the meaning of a transformation, and the concept is deconstructed."[27] It is in this sense that we wish to understand the form of intellectual montage as a montage of (two) forms. Montage construction, namely, gives us a form that is at once associative—constructing the (abstract) concept out of a series of similar, commensurable (concrete) images—and the opposite of associative: transformative and dissociative, impoverishing and reductive, deconstructing the concept (God) by confronting it with an incommensurable piece of maximally reduced concreteness (the block of wood), which the concept is unable to integrate without itself falling apart.

In this second impoverishing and reductive form ("God is a block of wood"), montage is no longer associative in its logic but rather seeks to assume the speculative form of infinite judgment—Hegel's "spirit is a bone" from the phrenology chapter of his *Phenomenology of Spirit* serves here as the paradigmatic example—in which it is precisely the associationist-empiricist logic of montage that stumbles into an impasse it is unable to traverse. Unlike the associative form, which assumes a fundamental commensurability (similarity) among the images that compose the concept, the form of infinite judgment ("God is a block of wood") juxtaposes the concept of god with a predicate that results from a process of reductive transformation and is as such radically incommensurable. According to Hegel, this lack of commensurability, which is precisely what the form of judgment is meant to secure, means that infinite judgment can be viewed as a form in which the very form of judgment as the guarantee of meaningful discourse becomes destabilized. Infinite judgment is "a judgment in which even the form of judgment is set aside. But this is a *nonsensical judgment*. It is supposed to be a *judgment*, and consequently to contain a relation of subject and predicate; yet *at the same time* such a relation is supposed *not to be in it*."[28]

The form assumed by the discourse of intellectual montage is a montage of two forms. One of these forms follows the path of the genesis of conceptual meaning. It is associative and additive, relies on similarity and the operation of universalizing abstraction, and is ultimately expressive of a belief in the commensurability of relations. In the other form, the conceptual meaning encounters form as the bearer of nonsense, form (infinite judgment) within which it is precisely the existence of a meaningful relation (of relation *as* meaning) that becomes suspended. This second path is speculative and reductive. It is based on transformation and dissimilation and realized through an operation of impoverishment. As such, it assumes form as incommensurability or nonrelation. We could also say that the form of montage in the sequence of the gods in *October* functions as a montage of the form of the *concept* (built from the associative articulation of images) and the self-negating form of judgment that we would be hard-pressed to distinguish from the operation of *Witz* and what Freud called the latter's "liberation of nonsense"—an effect that depends on the possibility of bringing together a set of incommensurable elements.[29] Intellectual montage is a montage of the *conjunctive synthesis of the concept,* which we can represent as Christ AND Vishnu AND Buddha AND . . . = "God"; and the *disjunctive synthesis of infinite judgment* or *Witz,* which relies on a kind of unbearable copula or an impossible IS, through which God relates to (is, in fact, identified with) a block of wood. Intellectual montage is in this case to be grasped not merely as cinema's striving toward the concept—a desire that must, according to most interpreters, remain a frustrated one because the images of cinema can only pretend to the discursivity that would be on par with the philosophical use of language—but also as cinema possessing a certain lesson it is able to impart on conceptual thought itself. This is, namely, the lesson of an intimate link that exists between the synthetic capacity of the concept and the disjunctive operation of *Witz.* Rather than distance, there exists a proximity between thought's ability to construct a distinctly conceptual sense of things and the "play of images" through which wit confronts us with nonsense as the genetic element of all sense.

A further twist may be added to our discussion here, which would lead us in a slightly different direction than the one offered by Ropars's interpretation. In Hegel's *Logic,* the nonsensical moment of infinite judgment, in which the very form of judgment collapses, is also the condition for the emergence of a genuinely philosophical, speculative concept. Hegel considers "infinite judgment" as the moment of the *"reflection of individuality* into itself, whereby it is posited for the first time as a *determinate determinateness."*[30] Infinite judgment, in which God is identified with something absolutely incommensurable—a block of wood—is a moment of negativity, the moment of God's loss of all its meaningful predicates, but also a moment of God's reflection of the loss, of negativity, into itself. Following Slavoj Žižek, we could say that the (speculative, philosophical) identity of God is nothing other than the reflection into the concept of God itself of the radical gap, *"this unbearable discord,"* that separates God from any positive predicate (be it man, animal, or a block of wood).[31] In Hegel's deduction, it is thus only at this point, at which it begins to reflect negativity within itself, that the concept of God attains determinate philosophical content and requires the passage into a different form of judgment (no longer judgment of existence but judgment of reflection). Only by passing through the moment of infinite judgment—the speculative moment of *Witz*—in which the form of judgment itself stops making sense, may the identity of God begin to appear in the form of a self-relating negativity; and only in this way does the concept of God leave the sphere of indeterminateness and abstract immediacy and begin to move toward genuine universality. The contradictory, dual movement of the discursive montage sequence of gods in *October* could, following all this, be interpreted also as staging not merely the contradiction between the concept of God and its witty deconstruction but more precisely the contradiction between the formal genesis of an empiricist concept of God and the subversion of the form of judgment that leads to the threshold of a genuinely speculative, nonempirical concept of God (possible only through an initial deconstruction of the empirical concept).[32]

Deleuze's Eisenstein: Montage and Organicism

While the moment of the late 1920s, when Eisenstein develops his theory of intellectual montage, was rather brief and stood for a kind of utopia of montage as the means toward the achievement of a pure cinematic discursivity, the most sustained and all-encompassing attempt on Eisenstein's part to motivate montage in the direction of a new unity of form belongs to the so-called late period of his career, during which he develops a conception of form as organic unity. It is in Eisenstein's late writing, particularly in *Nonindifferent Nature,* that we discover an attempt to turn the disintegrative and antiorganic tendency of montage toward the construction of a new type of organic form, a new conception of organicity.

In the most general sense, Eisenstein understands with "organic unity" a form regulated by the "principle of *the unity and inseparability of the whole and of all its parts.*"[33] In the organic unity of form, individual parts and their relations express the whole, while the whole itself does not have an independent, separate existence but must be grasped precisely as expressing itself exhaustively through the parts and their relationships. Eisenstein figures his conception of such an organic unity in the form of the logarithmic spiral (Figure 27), which he describes as *"the most perfect linear image of the expression of the principle of proportional evolution in general."*[34]

There are two important aspects of the logarithmic or organic spiral. First, the expanding curving movement of the spiral brings into focus growth as the "typical sign" of any organic phenomenon. If form is an organism, it must follow the evolutionary movement of growth characteristic of all living and natural phenomena.[35] Second, this process of growth does not behave randomly but obeys on its path a precise "formula." The growth of an organic unity of form (or of form as organic unity) is governed by a fundamental proportionality and maintains throughout its movement the same ratio that determines the relations of the whole and the segments. This ratio—the "'formula' of growth"—is the golden ratio or the golden section. The golden section divides the movement of the spiral in such a way that, at any point on the spiral, the ratio between the whole and the larger segment of its movement is the same as the ratio between the spiral's larger and smaller segments of movement:

$$\frac{oA}{oB} = \frac{oB}{oC} = \frac{oC}{oD} = \cdots = m.$$

Under the organic formula of the golden section, the same ratio governs the whole–part relation and the relations between the parts. The movement of

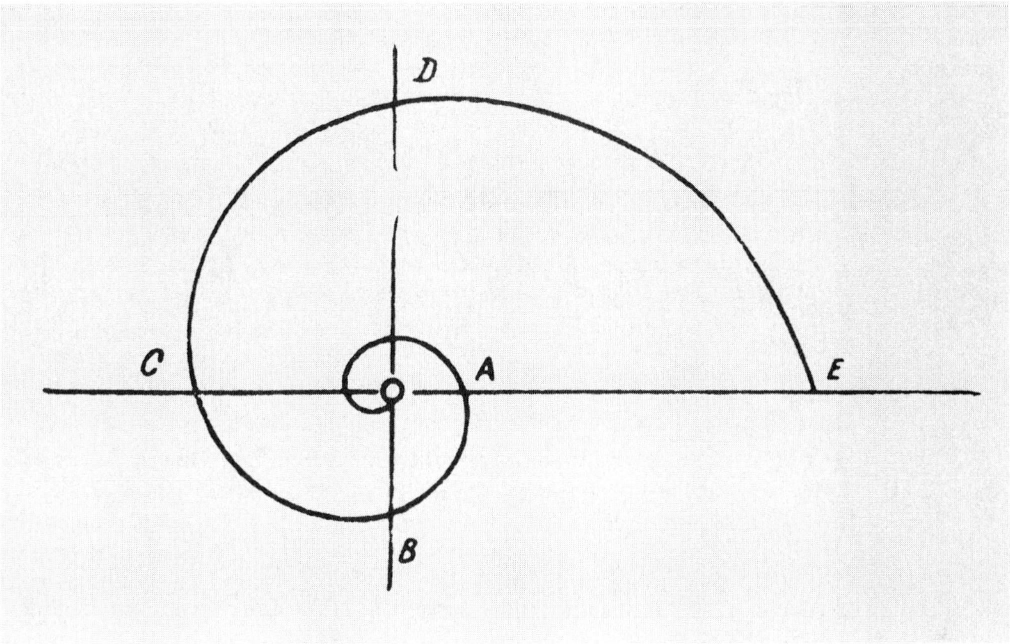

Figure 27. The logarithmic spiral with which Eisenstein illustrates his organic conception of montage in *Nonindifferent Nature.*

the logarithmic spiral, the movement of form conceived as a growing organic totality, maintains itself at all levels of its process by the rule of the same proportion. And what is particularly striking about this, of course, is that the golden ratio, which regulates and secures the ultimate rationality of the form's organic growth, is itself an irrational number.

According to Gilles Deleuze, who in his *Cinema 1: The Movement-Image* identifies Eisenstein fully with this organicist vision of montage-form, the Soviet filmmaker in this way develops a new conception of the organic. The conception is new particularly in relation to what Deleuze sees as the organicism of Eisenstein's predecessor, D. W. Griffith. In Griffith, the vision of organic unity is still empirical. That is to say, the whole is understood as merely a collection of distinct lines of movement describing a parallelism. In Eisenstein, on the contrary, the organic movement of form expresses itself in a single line—the line of the expanding, growing logarithmic spiral—which is given not an empirical but a mathematical, "scientific" definition (the golden section as the mathematical formula of organic growth). The moments of difference or division in the case of Eisenstein therefore do not exist between separate, externally related lines of movement but are instead explained through the genetic law of the dialectical process that Eisenstein applies to his organicist conception of cinematic form: "the movement of the One, which divides itself in two and recreates a new unity."[36]

The organic spiral, apart from presenting us with a proportional movement of a form's growth, is thus also a figure of a unitary and dialectical movement that proceeds through a series of divisions—oppositions and contradictions—that, however, remain internal to this movement itself. In Eisenstein, Deleuze writes, "*Montage of opposition* takes the place of parallel montage,"[37] which was the key formula of Griffith's films. In the case of Griffith, the different lines of action or movement run in parallel. They are not grasped as belonging to a genuine unity, whereas in Eisenstein, the difference between movements is conceived as an opposition formed within a unity, within a uniform dialectical movement that constantly divides and re-creates itself: as an opposition or contradiction emerges in the division of the One, so it is overcome in the next step in the form of a new and "higher unity."[38] As Deleuze describes it, in Eisenstein's vision of form as dialectical–organic totality, montage progresses through a series of oppositions or contradictions, but what is expressed in this way is always the movement of the One, constantly dividing itself and recomposing itself from its own divisions.

It is within this dialectical–organic conception of the totality of form that Deleuze then places the moments of *pathos,* the "remarkable points or privileged instants" that, according to him, "belong fully to the regular construction of the organic spiral."[39] In *Nonindifferent Nature,* Eisenstein himself defines moments of pathos as leaps in quality, instants of qualitative transformation in the unity of form. At the level of the *whole,* the movement of form is determined as an immense, growing spiral, progressing through a series of oppositions that divide the unity of the whole and from which unity is re-created at ever-higher stages of its movement. But at the level of the smallest *intervals* of movement, out of which the movement of the whole is composed, the same form is determined as pathos, as a moment of sudden qualitative leap or transformation. It is in this sense that Deleuze can describe Eisenstein's conception of montage as organic (determination of the whole) and pathetic (determination of the interval of movement), or as composing an "organic–pathetic set."

What is crucial in Deleuze's stunning description of Eisenstein's conception of montage in *Cinema 1* is his claim that pathos or the "pathetic should not be confused with the organic." While the organic concerns the evolution of the unity of form at the level of the whole through a series of oppositions, the pathetic refers to

> the transition from one opposite to the other, or rather into the other, along the spans [of the spiral]: the leap into the opposite. There is not simply the opposition of earth and water, of the one and the many; there

> is the transition of the one into the other, and the sudden upsurge of the other out of the one. There is not simply the organic unity of opposites, but the pathetic passage of the opposite into its contrary. There is not simply an organic link between two instants, but a pathetic jump, in which the second instant gains a new power, since the first has passed into it. From sadness to anger, from doubt to certainty, from resignation to revolt. . . . The pathetic, for its part, involves the two aspects: it is simultaneously the transition from one term to the other, from one quality to the other, and the sudden upsurge of the new quality which is born from the transition which has been accomplished. It is both "compression" and "explosion."[40]

The organic movement of the whole, the growth or evolution of the form following the logic of the organic spiral, is thus dynamized by these concentrated and explosive moments of pathos, in which what suddenly occurs is not merely the continuous organic division and re-creation of unity but leaps from one quality into another, from one term into its opposite, and vice versa.

As an example of this type of organic–pathetic montage, one may take the famous sequence of the milk separator in *The General Line,* an example that Eisenstein himself in *Nonindifferent Nature* isolates as a singularly successful achievement of organic–pathetic montage. Just as the sequence of gods from *October* served to embody the work of intellectual montage, so the sequence of the milk separator represents the canonical example of organic–pathetic construction. The sequence follows the principle of organic growth, "from the general situation to the transformed situation, through the development and transcendence of the opposition."[41] In this case, we begin with the situation in which the farm cooperative is to try for the first time its newly received milk separator. This general situation divides itself into an opposition, presented by Eisenstein mostly through a juxtaposition of close-ups and "group shots," between the large number of suspicious and doubtful villagers and the confident and aspiring yet small group of cooperative members who operate the machine (Marfa Lapkina, the Lenin-like agronomist, and the young Communist Leaguer Vasia).

Through an accelerating montage of oppositions expressive of a precarious moment of political conflict—"a play of doubts and aspirations, suspicion and confidence, plain curiosity and unconcealed anxiety"[42]—Eisenstein builds tension and anticipation, until the suspense suddenly breaks as the separator begins to work and the milk condenses and begins to flow from the muzzles of the separator pipes. It is through this success of the small group of cooperative members in demonstrating the miraculous effectiveness of the machine that the opposition is overcome and a new higher unity is created. Just as the processed milk pours from the separator, new members begin to flow into the cooperative, which thereby records its first victory in the form of a newfound collective joy.

It is within this "large form" of organic growth of the whole (which Deleuze would formalize as S–A–S': from the general situation through action or Eisensteinian opposition to a new situation) that Eisenstein organizes a series of pathetic intervals, through which the images composing the whole undergo a series of leaps or qualitative transformations. The pathetic leaps may be understood as what dynamize and organize the movement through a series of binaries: the leap from figurative representation into metaphor, from black and white into color (Eisenstein intended to use a series of color images in the sequence), from this new chromaticism into achromaticism (as something distinct from the monochromaticism of the initial black and white), from representation into nonrepresentational abstraction, from picture to sign (number), from image to concept, from consciousness to affect, and so on:

> Within the very method of show and tell, there is a similar leap from dimension to dimension: from an exposition by subject to an exposition by metaphor ("fountains of milk").
>
> But montage does not stop there, it makes a new leap, into a new image—the image of "blazing fireworks."
>
> Seizing upon the shimmer of the water fountain, . . . montage elevates the level of this shimmer to a new heightened class of intensity . . . —color. . . .
>
> But even this did not exhaust the montage "fury" of the scene.
>
> Flashing dizzyingly on the screen for a time, these color cuts would again swing over into cuts that are . . . colorless.
>
> Because for *chromatic* cuts, the leap into *achromatic* ones is a new leap, again, into a new quality! . . .
>
> Simultaneously, the structural system itself skipped over from the sphere of *representational* to its opposite sphere of *nonrepresentational*: white zigzags over a black background.[43]

The example of the milk separator sequence in *The General Line* thus demonstrates the remarkable power of Eisensteinian organic–pathetic montage. The power of the organicist conception of montage can be observed in the ability of Eisenstein's montage composition to begin with a mundane object, such as the separator, and to progressively raise it to a veritably cosmic dimension. The everyday time of the separator and farm labor, with which we begin, undergoes the process of evolutionary growth. It is as though the everyday situation falls into the movement of the immense organic spiral and reaches the temporality of the cosmos itself. The new collectivity, which emerges through this remarkable evolution, is no longer the everyday peasant community, nor does it signify simply the existence of a new historical group. Rather, it draws the appearance of a new historical collective into a dimension of cosmic joy or exaltation.

Now, this remarkable transformation is only possible because of the construction of pathos. Only because he makes pathetic leaps (qualitative changes) occupy the intervals of movement is Eisenstein able to compose a sequence of such astonishing evolutionary growth of the whole. In Deleuze's terms, the qualitative leaps of pathos realized as a series of formal transformations and intensifications of the image (from figurative to abstract, from black and white into color, from abstract patterns to numbers, etc.) add themselves to and perfect the movement of the organic spiral, and it is through their addition and perfection that the movement of the organic whole manages to pass so rapidly between the initial situation of the everyday and its cosmic destination—two dimensions that would otherwise (in the case of a nondialectical, empirical construction, for instance) stand irreconcilably apart, but which Eisenstein is able to present within a singular movement of the dialectical–organic whole.[44]

The cosmic dimension that is reached through a series of pathetic leaps in Eisenstein's organic construction may be considered as the moment of a properly transcendental, sublime experience. Indeed, in the second volume of his *Cinema,* Deleuze will reintroduce Eisenstein as the representative filmmaker of the "*sublime* conception of cinema":

> what constitutes the sublime is that the imagination suffers a shock [in the case of Eisenstein, the shock is administered by the leaps of pathos] which pushes it to the limit and forces thought to think the whole as intellectual totality which goes beyond the imagination [what we have called the cosmic evolution of the whole].[45]

Yet the fact remains that, even though Deleuze crucially distinguishes pathos from the organic and describes the specificity of their respective functions within Eisenstein's conception of montage-form, he conceives the sublimity of pathos in the case of Eisenstein as fully internal to the movement of the organic whole. The interval of movement—the shocks produced by pathetic leaps of qualitative transformation—might, in other words, lead us to a moment of transcendental joy, but this sublime moment remains fully overdetermined by the organism or the organic totality of form. The pathetic leap, a moment of the sudden emergence of a new quality, functions as the dynamic element that does not deviate from but instead supports the organic growth of the whole. Rather than breaking with it, the interval of pathos helps secure the construction of the whole as an organic, growing, evolving totality. Thus, even in moments when qualitative change appears to be formally absolute (for instance, in the leap from black and white to the red of the flag raised in *Battleship Potemkin*), this formal absoluteness is, in fact, made relative to the self-differentiating and reunifying movement—the organicity—of the great spiral. Formal breaks, qualitative leaps of pathos that occupy the privileged intervals of movement in Eisenstein's montage construction, are subordinated to a deeper organic unity, which maintains itself as growing, constantly evolving through instants of formal division and recomposition.

This "dialectical" conception of the sublime also means that any transcendental moment, any moment of the sublime, which Deleuze elsewhere in *Cinema 1* defines in opposition to the organic, does not possess in Eisenstein's conception a degree of sufficient autonomy. Unlike German expressionist cinema, for instance, which thinks the *"non-organic life of things,* a frightful life, which is oblivious to the wisdom and limits of the organism,"[46] in Eisenstein, as he is described by Deleuze, the dialectical operation draws everything into the evolving limit of an organic totality. Or put differently, if, in the mechanical sublime of the French and the dynamic sublime of the German schools of prewar cinema, montage reaches a sublime, cosmic level that breaks any "sensible attachment" to the organism, then in Eisenstein's dialectical organicism, the cosmic expansion takes place *within* the limits of the organism or of organic nature, which it nevertheless raises to a higher unity.[47]

Pathos and Ex Stasis

It is precisely Eisenstein's insistence on overdetermining the montage construction of movement with the principle of organic unity that requires that the pathetic leap be defined exclusively as a moment of *qualitative* transformation. Both in Eisenstein's canonical theorization in *Nonindifferent Nature* and in Deleuze's description of it, the pathetic interval of movement that marks a qualitative transformation allows for both the expression of difference (unity divides itself in pathos) and the recuperation of unity (which is reexpressed as a new, qualitatively different unity reconstituted on the basis of the interval or the pathetic leap). The organic–pathetic form of montage construction signifies a type of form simultaneously capable of realizing a great degree of difference, from which the affective force of pathos is ultimately derived, while at the same time maintaining unity as the condition for this difference and the affective experience it produces. In fact, the organic nature of Eisenstein's conception of form assumes that the integrity and the unity of a work are seen as the very condition, and not the opposite, of the experience of difference, of the affect and the shock of pathos.

In subsuming pathos under the organic, Deleuze closely follows Eisenstein's own central elaboration of the link between the two in *Nonindifferent Nature.* There, in a brief footnote, Eisenstein excludes from the "definite law of structuring" an organic work of form precisely those types of intervals of movement that may not be understood according to the principle of growth (the organic spiral) and the logic of qualitative transformation between opposing terms (the pathetic leap). There are three kinds of intervals of movement that Eisenstein excludes, and from which he wishes to distinguish the properly pathetic interval of qualitative transformation:[48]

1. First, he excludes from consideration the interval that juxtaposes and relates two identical terms (oB = oA), that is to say, an interval in which no new quality emerges between the two terms. Rather than a qualitative leap between two opposing or contradictory terms, the interval here describes the movement of *repetition*. In the interval of repetition, nothing grows or develops, no qualitative leap happens, and no new, higher unity is made to emerge. This means that the movement of the whole can no longer be figured as an organic, evolving spiral but instead turns into a blindly revolving circle.
2. The second interval of movement excluded by Eisenstein juxtaposes and relates one term (oA) to nothing (oB = 0). That is, the interval robs the first term of its positive opposite, in which case the very dimension of the interval is negated, and one can imagine the organic spiral suddenly straightening itself out into a line. Without the dynamic concentration of opposing terms and the explosion of a qualitative change between them, montage movement becomes linear, in which case, again, it becomes impossible to speak of an organic evolution in the movement of form.
3. Finally, there is the possibility that the interval of montage juxtaposes and relates one of the terms (oA) neither to its opposite, nor to a term identical to it, nor to nothingness, but to the infinite (oB = ∞). In this case, the case of an infinite interval, the spiral of the organic whole becomes reduced to a point. And what we get with this possibility is a construction of montage that is neither pathetic (qualitative change), nor repetitive (sameness), nor linear (single straight line), but purely punctual.

What Eisenstein excludes from the organic–pathetic conception of montage are thus repetition (or pure circularity), linearity, and punctuality. These three possible determinations of the interval of movement deviate from what he calls the "idea of uniform evolution,"[49] which is expressed by the organic (or logarithmic) spiral and its pathetic dynamism.

Why does Eisenstein feel the need to both register and dismiss these alternative possibilities of determining the interval of movement, the exceptions to the uniform evolution of an organic whole that observes the rule of the golden ratio? The reason these alternatives appear as possibilities requiring a dismissal lies in a tension within Eisenstein's concept of pathos and of the pathetic interval of movement. For, before pathos signifies an organic–dialectical transition of one opposite into another, before the interval of movement is determined as the operator of a specifically qualitative transformation, Eisenstein ties it to the notion of ecstasy, or *ex stasis,* which is not reducible to the organic–dialectical determination of pathos as qualitative change, because in itself it signals only a being's passage outside itself. To be in ecstasy is to be outside or beside oneself—without necessarily passing into one's opposite or a new determinate quality. In the first chapter of the present book, we have described ex stasis as the limit case of pathos. Now, however, it seems necessary to stress the difference between the two, between pathos as qualitative leap into an opposite term and ex stasis as leaping outside oneself. Or rather, the introduction of ecstasy at this point allows us to notice in Eisenstein's writing not one but two determinations of pathos—the organic–dialectical pathos that assumes the form of sudden qualitative transformation and the ecstatic definition of pathos that stresses not the attainment of a new quality but a being's being outside itself.

The two kinds of pathos—organic–dialectical and ecstatic—may certainly be related, but they are not identical: the organic–dialectical determination of pathos presupposes two separate terms that mark the qualitative change produced by montage in the interval of movement, while ecstasy only requires a single term, yet a single term that is split, beside itself and not necessarily transformed into its opposite. Eisenstein's dialectical–organic conception of montage thus involves a specific determination of the (pathetic) interval of movement, which may at first be merely an ex static self-othering and only subsequently become interpreted or motivated as the movement of qualitative change. In the following passage from *Nonindifferent Nature,* we note how Eisenstein both acknowledges the difference between the organic–dialectical meaning of pathos and ex stasis and strives to subsume the latter, which appears as primary, under the former:

> Putting it more elegantly, we might say that the effect of the pathos of a work consists in bringing the viewer to the point of ecstasy. Such a formula adds nothing new, for three lines above we said exactly the same thing, since *ex stasis* (out of state) means literally the same thing as "being beside oneself" or "going out of a normal state" does. . . . But this is not sufficient: "To be beside oneself" is not "to go into nothing." To be beside oneself is unavoidably also a transition to something else, to something different in quality, to something opposite to what preceded it. . . . Thus, just from the most superficial description of the ecstatic effect, which produces a construction of *pathos,* we can see what basic feature the construction must have in a composition of *pathos.* In this structure the condition of "being beside oneself" must be observed in all of its features, as well as the constant transition to a different quality.[50]

In the interval of movement, a thing may come to stand outside itself, but this does not necessarily mean that the thing has become qualitatively different or that it has assumed a new quality. The definition of ex stasis in terms of qualitative transformation therefore requires a secondary motivation—a motivation that is not necessarily inherent in the ex static nature of the interval of movement itself but which rather is supplied by the organic–dialectical schema that overdetermines the interval. Eisenstein seeks to elide the difference between organic–dialectical pathos and ex stasis, between qualitative transformation and being beside oneself; and yet, the difference is there in his text, particularly in the final sentence of the passage quoted earlier, in which he claims the importance of examining *all the features* of the ecstatic interval ("being beside oneself") "as well as"—marking this dimension of the interval as distinct from ex stasis—"the constant transition to a different quality."

Before closing off the question of pathos by linking it exclusively with the organic–dialectical or evolutionary meaning of qualitative transformation, Eisenstein thus opens up the interval of movement constructed by montage to a different possibility, offering perhaps other, nonorganicist paths for what he calls "*pathos* composition" or "construction of *pathos*." We will explore here one such different possibility of an expanded notion of pathos that does not have to do with the organic and the pathos of qualitative metamorphosis but with repetition (an element of the inorganic) and the comedy of finding difference in sameness. The significance of this possibility is that it leads us out of organicism and reveals the presence of another form, suddenly appearing in—and against—Eisenstein's development of his conception of organic–pathetic montage.

Repetition: From the Cosmic to the Comic

To begin our exploration, we may note that at several points in *Nonindifferent Nature,* where Eisenstein discusses the experience of pathos and ecstasy, he turns for illustration to examples that are comic or humorous in nature. The first image of ecstasy in the section of *Nonindifferent Nature* titled "On the Question of Suprahistory," which follows a discussion of the technique of religious ecstasy in the writing of Ignatius of Loyola, is a scene Eisenstein borrows from the *Adventures of Baron Münchausen,* in which Münchausen beats a bear so intensely that the animal ecstatically leaps out of its own fur coat.[51] The second, more significant example, which Eisenstein discusses at some length and which gives the name to the section in which the laws and the method of the construction of pathos are discussed, is that of a comic image of a series of kangaroos jumping out of each other's pouches:

> Not one after another!
> But one out of another!

> Out of the "pouch" of the biggest arc flies out the second in size. Out of the pouch of the second—the somewhat smaller third.
> Out of the third—the fourth!
> Out of the fourth—the fifth!
> And it seems that it won't end until the sixth, until the twelfth!
> What is going on?
> What is the source of this chain of kangaroos, scared to death, ejected "rocketlike" from each other?![52]

Eisenstein first encountered this image in an illustrated humorous story by the French writer Edouard Osmont published in the 1916 issue of the British *Strand* magazine (Figures 28 and 29).[53] The author of the drawing that struck Eisenstein so forcefully is W. Heath Robinson, the well-known British cartoonist most famous for drawing pictures of exceedingly complex contraptions used to accomplish the simplest of tasks—a genre that would be popularized slightly later in the United States by Rube Goldberg.[54] Eisenstein relates part of the story that the drawing of the kangaroos accompanies on the pages of *Strand*: a certain Professor de Tournemolle (*tourne,* "turn"; *molle,* "flaccid, soft, weak, limp, flabby"), who is "touring the world's music halls with a troupe of a dozen kangaroos," arrives at the Romanian border. He finds out that the Romanian government has recently imposed a prohibitive customs tax on the import of cattle. And though he is convinced that it would be unfair to consider his all-female troupe of kangaroos cattle, he nevertheless wishes to protect himself from paying the exorbitant duty that the customs officials might demand from him. And thus he proceeds to stuff the kangaroos, one by one, from smallest to largest, into each other's pouches. At the end of this operation, only one kangaroo is left standing, containing all the others. Her name is Adela, and Osmont's story describes her as a "beast of really gigantic proportions."

So it now appears that Professor Tournemolle is traveling with only a single kangaroo. As they cross the border, at first everything appears to be going smoothly. Yet the Romanian customs officials are troublesome and take too long to inspect the professor's documents, which causes all of the eleven kangaroos hiding in Adela's pouch to become restless and start kicking. Adela is in stress and begins to undergo an "intolerable shake-up." And just as the customs officers are returning to let the professor and his beast of a kangaroo through,

> suddenly something seemed to snap. Like a jack-in-the-box, the eleventh kangaroo shot up into the air, and came down a few paces further on. The Customs' officials stood motionless as though petrified. From the crowd came cries of stupefaction. Scarcely had the animal touched the ground before the tenth kangaroo appeared in its turn, then the ninth,

gigantic proportions. Moreover, she was a most devoted creature, and did everything in her power to carry her unaccustomed burden. Taking advantage of her good will I assisted her to clamber into the caravan, and lost no time in driving to the Roumanian Custom-house. To all appearance I was accompanied by a single kangaroo.

insupportable — this strain alone would have been more than enough, in all conscience—but the eleventh kangaroo, which was almost stifling inside the pouch, was evincing growing restlessness. Even so, Adela might still have borne with her troubles a little longer had not the whole series, in their respective pouches, begun to kick and wriggle in turn.

The net result for Adela was an intolerable shake-up. It was pitiful to look at her.

"A goodish number of people had collected round us — quite a crowd, in fact, of idle sightseers, anxious to examine this strange quadruped at close quarters. Adela got the impression that she was in the presence of one of her usual audiences. I fixed upon her the severe look I reserved for special occasions,

Figure 28. W. Heath Robinson's drawing of the kangaroos illustrating the short story by Edouard Osmont, "Nothing to What I Once Saw!" in *Strand* 52 (July–December 1916).

> the eighth, and so down the line, until finally little number one rolled out like a ball.[55]

It is this moment of kangaroos leaping out of each other's pouches and forming a kind of ecstatic series that is captured by two of Heath Robinson's drawings that accompany the text.

In recounting the story—in which, as it must have become clear at this point, the embarrassment or fear of premature ejaculation (the kangaroos spill out too soon and cause a problem for Professor "Turned-flaccid") is transposed onto or mixes with a fantasy of birth, generation, productivity—Eisenstein invents a detail that cannot be found in the Osmont story but that now attributes the explosion of the series of leaping kangaroos to a sneeze that has suddenly seized the first kangaroo containing all the others: "But then at the critical moment the largest of the kangaroos . . . sneezes! And . . . what happens is that they run like black spots across the white margins bordering the story. Like a catapult, all twelve kangaroos shoot out of each other!"[56]

stood motionless as though petrified. From the crowd came cries of stupefaction. Scarcely had the animal touched the ground before the tenth kangaroo appeared in its turn, then the ninth, the eighth, and so down the line, until finally little number one rolled out like a ball.

" In less than five seconds, all told, there were my twelve kangaroos, in a row, squatting on their haunches, delightedly inhaling the pure air and making joyful movements with their front paws.

" Half the people in the crowd had taken to their heels, terror-stricken. The rest remained rooted to the spot, eyes and mouth wide open, evidently in doubt whether they were the victims of some illusion, or whether they were witnessing a specially clever bit of juggling. As for me, whistling to my little troupe, I skedaddled for all I was worth, without waiting for developments."

The Vice-Consul had been exhibiting for some moments growing symptoms of uneasiness. When the narrative came to a close he put forth an observation :—

" You have wonderful imagination, Professor."

" Not at all, not at all. I am merely recalling old memories."

" You don't mean to say that you expect

of the hotel where I put up with my little troupe ? "

" No. I give it up."

Figure 29. W. Heath Robinson's second drawing of the kangaroos illustrating the short story by Edouard Osmont, "Nothing to What I Once Saw!"

This comic image of kangaroos leaping out of each other's pouches, says Eisenstein, presents us with a kind of literalization of the principle of ecstasy and of the dynamic and pathetic conception of form. The kangaroos give us the formula of ecstatic–pathetic leaps, of a state of things being beside themselves by rendering this formula in a literal representation. "It is difficult to conceive of a more 'literal' interpretation (i.e., a reverse transposition from a metaphoric concept to a nonmetaphoric) of the formula 'being beside oneself' than a kangaroo jumping out of the 'pouch' of another kangaroo."[57] Eisenstein's statement suggests something remarkable: the example of the kangaroos, as well as Eisenstein's discussion of this example, not only repeats the old insight, according to which a comic interpretation of a phenomenon is most easily produced by rendering it in an unexpected literal form, but also posits that pathos, while perhaps spiritually closer to the serious and elevated experience of the cosmic sublime, is *literally*, according to its letter, comic or humorous.

The image of kangaroos indeed turns out to be a bit more than a marginal example of pathetic–ecstatic composition, because Eisenstein, who seems himself to be surprised that this comic picture would insert itself among his more serious examples of ecstatic–pathetic form (Piranesi's architectural drawings and El Greco's paintings, for instance), also suggests that it was the kangaroos, whom he calls "friends of childhood" and his "contemporaries,"[58] that first brought to light, even if he was not conscious of it at the time, the formula of ex stasis. So the image appears not only as a comic illustration of the method of ecstatic construction but also possibly as a trace of the latter's initial discovery. In fact, it is worth stressing that it is rather unclear how what Eisenstein calls a "comic interpretation" or a literal rendering of the construction of pathos differs from the structure of pathos as such, particularly because, for Eisenstein, any construction of form or any structural principle of formal construction concerns not only spirit or the spiritual meaning of a work but also crucially how such spiritual meaning becomes embodied, incarnated in the material or literal aspect of the form of the work.

Regarding the status of his comical example of the kangaroos, Eisenstein begins to equivocate. He suggests that it is possible to draw a distinction between the structure of pathos proper, a kind of serious and sublime vision of ecstasy one may find in El Greco or in the meditations of Ignatius of Loyola, and the comic interpretation of the ecstatic structure as it can be found in the example of the kangaroos. The difference would lie in the fact that in a genuinely pathetic construction, the formula of ex stasis occupies the place of the dynamic principle of form, whereas comic interpretations of ecstatic construction present this formula "concretely," literalize it, and render it directly in figurative depiction. Yet this distinction, too, is difficult to sustain, because Eisenstein's "serious" and "sublime" examples of pathos and ecstasy possess exactly the same quality that he ascribes to the "comic interpretation" of these phenomena. What is shared, for instance, by Piranesi's *Carceri* and El Greco's *The Resurrection*, two of Eisenstein's key examples of ecstatic construction in *Nonindifferent Nature*, is precisely that they, too, render ex static movement, the leap of pathos, concretely in the disposition and the shape of their architectural and human figures.

Eisenstein must therefore acknowledge that the serious–sublime pathos or ecstasy and its humorous–comic "interpretation" not only appear to be similar but might indeed be identical at some more profound level: "through a comic structure there operates the same basic generalization of the law that underlies serious structures (partly also at the basis of structures of *pathos*, where they are presented and act in the most complete form), thus ensuring the efficiency of the construction."[59] In this light, the comic is not a fundamentally different phenomenon but an "accent" of pathetic construction. The experience of laughter, which belongs to the humorous and comic example of the kangaroos, is just as much of a powerful discharge of affect as the more serious and elevated affective experience of the sublime. Which leads Eisenstein to write the following: "without plunging into the most essential aspect of this question—the problem of the main compositional difference in an identical external appearance between structures of *pathos* and comedy (this is a problem for a separate work)—let us only point out the remarkable similarity (identity!) of the method of constructing one and the other."[60]

Eisenstein's equivocation in this specific instance is related to a larger problem he has with integrating the comic and the humorous into his vision of organic–pathetic construction of montage. On one hand, he gives the comic a prominent place as one of the pillars of his "building to be built," with which he illustrated his idea and method of cinema. On the other hand, however, he simultaneously claims that the comic follows the dialectical principle of organic–pathetic construction only in appearance—that is to say, not in a decisive, essential way:

> A construction becomes comical when it violates the dialectic in its essence, while it, in its form, lays claim to all the signs and elements characteristic of a true and fully established dialectical process. . . . The condition of comic construction is an essential a-dialecticism which formally observes the features of the dialectic.[61]

The comic is something substantially a-dialectical that conforms only to the formal appearance of the dialectic (it appears as a unity of opposites). It is a kind of dialectical formalism lacking any genuine dialectical content—a form dialectical in its letter, but not in its spirit. Or, as Eisenstein also puts it, the comic gives us a static glimpse of the dialectic without any genuine dialectical—which, in Eisenstein's case, is also evolutionary and organic—movement. Thus, a comic effect may be produced by "forcibly fusing two epochs that are otherwise separated by centuries," an operation that "forces the normal course of the basic law of nature—the unity of opposites—to serve as a device, sign, and method of comic construction,"[62] but that, at the same time, does not describe the genuine dialectical–organic or evolutionary movement that passes between the opposing terms. The comic is thus a misuse of the dialectical form or a use of the formal appearance of the dialectic ("the comical as formally-dialectical"[63]) against the proper dialectical essence, the essential dialectical movement of reality.

The distinction between the two kinds of dialectic serves Eisenstein, once again, to draw the line between the pathetic and the comic, thus separating pathos as the genuinely dialectical interval of movement—"the moment of a dynamic fulfillment (becoming) of the dialectic of a phenomenon"—from the comic, which stands for the "formal application of the dialectical source to a static case."[64] The comic thus signifies an interval of movement that is falsely dialectical—which is to say, above all, that it is not genuinely movement. An example of such a purely formal application of the dialectical principle of movement (unity of opposites) that produces a comic effect but is not genuinely dialectical in its nature may be found, according to Eisenstein, in the Marx Brothers' film *Animal Crackers,* which contains Eisenstein's

> favorite *gag.* They throw themselves at one door—snowstorm, blizzard, rain, and wind. They don't like it. They rush to the other door. There—the sun shines, birds are singing, the balmiest of climates. . . . The purest appearance of the unity of opposites—contrary to understanding and against the logic of natural elements.[65]

The comic gag of the Marx Brothers (Figure 30) creates an interval of movement that links (creates a montage of) two incommensurable situations—it creates a unity of opposites out of two kinds of weather—without overdetermining this interval with the effectiveness of the organic whole or the growth and development of a natural organism, which would allow us to observe the meteorological change as a process or an evolutionary becoming. The juxtaposition of two meteorological states ("snowstorm" and "perfect seasonal weather") is, in other words, not organically, naturally justified, and it is the lack of this type of justification of the interval of movement that Eisenstein considers both comical and a-dialectical.

What Eisenstein finds a-dialectical or improperly, only apparently dialectical is what Ernst Bloch would have called the form of "abrupt mediation" *(jähe Vermittlung).* Bloch opposes abrupt mediation, which he associates with montage, to "broad-calm mediation," which is characteristic of the classical form and concept of reality.[66] Unlike the broad and calm mediation of classical form, montage as abrupt mediation does not "open . . . in the breadth of the context"[67] but rather opens up an interval of movement for which a broad, extensive, and unified context is missing. Abrupt mediation or the comic montage juxtaposition creates the sense of an interval of movement that points to the nonexistence of the whole as an organic totality: the unity of the meteorological system in the scene in *Animal Crackers* does not evolve

Figure 30. Eisenstein's favorite gag from the Marx Brothers' film *Animal Crackers*: "A pure appearance of the unity of opposites—contrary to understanding and against the logic of natural elements."

organically as a whole but is rather presented as one big contradiction, at once blizzard and shining sun.

In relation to Eisenstein's description of the comic as only "formally-dialectical" or as "a-dialecticism" appearing in the guise of a dialectical form, it is possible to raise at least two significant objections. First, it is clear that in his vision, which is strongly influenced by the conception of the dialectics of nature characteristic of the dialectical materialism predominant in the Marxist Orthodoxy at the time, Eisenstein presupposes an isomorphism between the evolutionary movement of natural and the dialectic of human or historical phenomena. But it is worth remembering that in a different conception of the dialectic—that of Hegel, for instance—the dialectic of the spirit comes into being and develops precisely through the violation of what Eisenstein calls the "logic of natural elements." Any genuine dialectical thought must be able to think the seemingly impossible unity of opposites presented in the gag in *Animal Crackers* precisely because such a juxtaposition points to the loss of thought's or spirit's natural ground. It is through the abnormal violation of natural normality, rather than the observance of the organic schema, that genuine dialectical thought proceeds. A literally or formally comical moment, in which there occurs a sudden, "unnatural" juxtaposition of two mutually exclusive meteorological states, is not external to dialectical thought but rather serves as the very moment in which (dialectical, speculative) thought abandons the situation of its subservience to nature and reveals itself as independent from, indeed as breaking with, any organic or evolutionary continuity.

But second, we may also note that Eisenstein's demarcation of the comic (as mere form, appearance, letter) from pathos (as nature, essence, the genuine spirit of dialectical movement) itself rests on a thoroughly nondialectical treatment of such conceptual oppositions. For does not dialectical thought suppose also a different way of thinking the relationship between essence and appearance, between content and form, spirit and letter, in which the latter term functions not merely as the falsification of the former but also as an instance necessary for the uncovering of its truth? That is to say, if we may use another, oft-recited joke by the Marx Brothers, if the "unnatural" and "abnormal" logic of the comic *appears* dialectical, if the comic unity of opposites *appears* to follow the same form as dialectics, and if it *appears* to behave in a way identical to dialectical movement, we should not be fooled by this: for the comic *is* part of genuine dialectical movement. If there is a difference between a properly pathetic interval and the comic interval of movement, it should not be described as one between genuine dialectical movement (organic–pathetic) and false, merely apparent dialectical movement (inorganic–comic). The difference, the contradiction of the organic and the inorganic, should rather be conceived as inherent in the dialectical movement itself—in fact, it might be the very contradiction between organic–pathetic and inorganic–comic that propels the dialectical movement forward.

Eisenstein himself confirms the difficulty of separating some genuine organic montage construction of pathos from the comic use of montage when, only a few pages following his discussion of the kangaroos, he notes how one could point to several examples in which "the 'formula of the kangaroos,' taken not really figuratively but as a structural principle, is employed in the interest of . . . effects of pathos."[68] This is a remarkable statement, for it reverses the distinction that made the comic (the kangaroos) a merely apparent version of the essential, structural principle (genuine pathos), suggesting now that pathos, in its serious, noncomic effect, might ultimately be structurally comic. Eisenstein confirms this by showing us how even such a remarkable work as Leonardo da Vinci's painting *The Virgin and Child with Saint Anne* (circa 1503) follows "the formula of the kangaroos," with each of the figures in the painting appearing as though ecstatically leaping out of the older figure behind it (Figure 31). So that, following Eisenstein, it would be possible to imagine St. Anne sneezing, like the first in the series of kangaroos, and thereby producing ecstatically, out of her "pouch," the series of figures—Virgin Mary, infant Jesus, and the lamb—in Leonardo's painting.[69]

According to his account in *Nonindifferent Nature,* the image that triggers for Eisenstein the memory of the picture of the kangaroos first encountered in *Strand* during his teenage years is one of Saul Steinberg's cartoons from the *New Yorker* (Figure 32). In this cartoon (published in the February 3, 1945, issue), a hand with a pen draws a figure of a man, who then draws a figure of a man, who draws a figure of a man, who draws a figure of a man, and so forth. Eisenstein writes, "Here that same thing that was represented in our kangaroos is depicted in black and white. Here step by step a man comes out of a man, comes out of a man, comes out of a man. But each person is identical to the other, and thus the man continuously—is being beside himself!"[70]

The series of human figures in Steinberg's drawing follows the ecstatic principle we saw at work in the series of kangaroos. There is, however, one crucial difference between the two examples, which Eisenstein also stresses. In the case of the Steinberg drawing, the "attraction" the series exercises on the spectator—Eisenstein calls it a "hypnotic effect" produced by the "automatism" of the drawing—has to do with the sameness of the figures. In the case of the kangaroos, the question of the size of each individual kangaroo was crucial for the effect of the drawing (as well as for the story the drawing illustrated): just as smaller kangaroos were put into larger kangaroos' pouches, the ecstatic effect of the "explosion" had to do with the series subsequently trailing off as ever-smaller kangaroos leaped out of the other in reverse order. In the case of Steinberg's drawing, Eisenstein writes, "The difference in size is not even distracting."[71] That is to say, the leaps in this cartoon are clearly

Figure 31. Leonardo da Vinci, *The Virgin and Child with St. Anne,* circa 1503. Oil on wood, 66 × 44 in. (168 × 112 cm). The Louvre, Paris.

accompanied neither by a pathetic leap into a new qualitative dimension nor by a quantitative change or a significant modification in size. In Steinberg's drawing, "a person is beside himself, is beside himself, is beside himself . . . , but he does not leap into a new quality, but remain themselves, themselves, themselves."[72] In other words, what the Steinberg drawing points to is the possibility of ecstatic construction, of a pathetic conception of form, that is not predicated on the sharp experience of qualitative change but is accomplished by an interval of movement that has become purely repetitive. We find here precisely a series of intervals (oA = oB = oC = . . .) that Eisenstein had excluded from his initial definition of organic–pathetic construction. What the Steinberg drawing makes appear is the possibility of ex stasis and pathos divorced from the "concentration" and "explosion" of qualitative difference and consequently standing apart from the evolutionary or organic conception of the movement of the whole. Or, as Eisenstein also puts it, one finds in Steinberg's drawing an organism for which the crucial rule of organic development, the leap into new quality, does not obtain: the "chain-reaction force of organic prescription" remains in effect, but the qualitative, developmental leap is missing. The effect of this is, according to Eisenstein, comparable to that of a three-dimensional knot "straightening into a chain of a mono planar ornament" or a harmonic chord dissolving into a sequence of notes. Which is to say that, in Steinberg's drawing, the force of seriality breaks the "three-dimensional" and "harmonic" organic unity, about which we may now begin to wonder whether it could ever still "be psychologically collected into one."[73]

Rather than organic movement, the logarithmic spiral dividing and recreating the movement of the Whole, what Eisenstein finds in Steinberg's drawing is "constant monotonous repetition."[74] Strikingly, he describes this element of repetition as "an extreme version of the formally observed condition of ecstatic construction"[75]—ecstatic construction taken to its formal limit, so to speak. We are thus led to suggest that Eisenstein here discovers something like the form of differentiation and repetition beyond the limits of the organicist schema that otherwise overdetermines his thinking of pathos and ex stasis. For, if one takes a look at the Steinberg drawing in the same manner as Eisenstein does, stressing its monotony and the sense of automatic repetition, one can say that, because in the drawing the experience of difference is not related to the criterion of qualitative change and development, difference becomes related solely to itself. What one gets is the experience of the minimal, *pure difference,* a difference between the same and same—a difference that is, in this case, not the opposite of but rather constitutive of the experience of sameness. Anyone familiar with Steinberg's work will recognize in the treatment of this minimal, pure difference, which does not depend on any determination of qualitative change, one of the fundamental characteristics of the cartoonist's work. Similarly, the experience of repetition in the

Figure 32. Saul Steinberg, *Untitled,* 1945. Ink on paper, 19.5 × 14.5 in. Beinecke Rare Book and Manuscript Library, Yale University. Copyright The Saul Steinberg Foundation/Artists Rights Society (ARS), New York.

drawing is not that of repetition unfolding through a set of ever-higher stages within the (re)productive teleology of the whole or the spiral. Repetition, in Steinberg's case, does not support the process of growth. We are dealing with *un(re)productive or sterile repetition,* repetition whose sole purpose appears to be the repetition of the minimal difference ("man is beside himself") constitutive of sameness ("themselves, themselves, themselves").

In Steinberg's drawing, and more specifically in the way Eisenstein analyzes it, one gets, if we may for a moment borrow a couple of concepts from Gilles Deleuze, the experience of "difference in itself" and the experience of "repetition for itself."[76] These are, perhaps it is needless to add, concepts of difference and repetition that Deleuze would himself certainly deny to Eisenstein's conception of montage, because he identifies the latter exclusively with the dialectic of the organic–pathetic schema, in which difference and repetition are made to serve the (re)productive purpose of evolutionary growth and qualitative development of the whole. But it seems indisputable that Eisenstein, in the very last pages of the section of *Nonindifferent Nature* explicitly dedicated to the question of pathos, touches on the possibility of a pathetic, ecstatic interval of movement that breaks and reaches beyond the organicist dialectical schema within which he otherwise wishes to canonize it.

The point here is not to suggest that this makes Eisenstein into a kind of Deleuzian avant la lettre. Saying so would be to deny the side of dialectical organicism in his conception of montage and form, a dimension that Deleuze's philosophy breaks with completely. What we are trying to suggest instead is that, in his discussion of the comic in *Nonindifferent Nature,* Eisenstein glimpses a different image of difference as well as an anomalous repetition of the theme of repetition with respect to the way these two notions are typically presented (by Eisenstein himself as well as his interpreters) in the discussions of his late turn toward organicism. This in turn suggests that organicism, the conception of montage-form as organic unity, does not and cannot exhaust the question of montage in the late Eisenstein. And it is indeed possible to reread *Nonindifferent Nature* and Eisenstein's theory of the organic unity as a battle waged *within* his conception of form between two visions of the vitality of form. On one hand, there is the fully fledged (re)productive organicism, which understands pathos as a qualitative, developmental difference leading to the evolution of the whole. On the other is a vitality of form that is the organicism's other, its immanent subversion: an inorganic life, a sort of sterile or monotonously productive vitality, in which montage maintains the interval of movement open to a different possibility than the one offered by the organicist, evolutionist idea. Neither of the two possibilities can assume primacy without being either overcome, as when repetition and the comic are motivated toward the reproduction of form as an organism, or undermined, as when the organic whole of the form and its pathetic development are subverted by becoming practically indistinguishable from the inorganic logic of repetition and the comic. We can understand Eisenstein's late writings as an attempt to invent a new vitality of form, using montage to return form to life after its crisis, which was to a large extent provoked by his earlier work. Yet it is also clear that a straightforward resuscitation, which would maintain form as some kind of vital unity, is not possible. What, namely, comes first when we speak of montage-form is the negativity of the cut, in relation to which any vitality of form must assume a necessarily split, divided existence. It is precisely in a montage of forms, incompatible and conflictual, that we must look for the fundamental characteristic of any genuine form of montage-work.

Conclusion

EISENSTEIN, OURSELVES

Concepts and Crisis

We have sought throughout this study to elaborate the key concepts of Eisenstein's idea of cinema by treating each concept as a dialectical unity of opposites. The Eisensteinian dialectic of division, which grasps concepts as unities held together by nothing but sets of opposing determinations, describes also the critical value of these concepts, where this term—*critical*—must be understood in two distinct ways. On one hand, concepts are critical in the sense that they help us describe cinema's *conditions of possibility*. Indeed, we cannot grasp any idea of cinema without taking into account the specific determinations of movement, action, image, and montage upon which such an idea depends. If cinema is to be thought, some articulation of these concepts is fundamental. And this applies also to those conceptions of the cinematic idea that seek to negate one or more of the concepts as essential for cinema, such as the attempts to exclude from cinema any mimesis of (human) action or, for instance, the desire to construct the idea of cinema on the interdiction of montage. Any negation of the conditions that make possible and determine the idea of cinema is itself a type of determination and as such belongs to the same conceptual field.

On the other hand, the critical status of the concepts needs also to be understood in the sense of *crisis*, which in Eisenstein's case is attributable to the dialectical moment of division essential to the dynamic of the concept itself. Each concept stages a crisis by figuring its own division: a concept is thus a critical unity—a unity that emerges only through negativity and disunity and that we know only through the antagonism that splits it. Concepts thus not only lead us to cinema's conditions of possibility but also show us how these conditions do not belong exclusively to the order of the positive and thus cannot provide for cinema anything resembling a stable ground for its identity. On the contrary, the criticality of the concepts reveals that the possibility of cinema depends on a series of crises. This is the fundamental lesson of Eisenstein's thought: the idea of cinema emerges when we are able to grasp the determinate shape of the crises that traverse the set of its conceptual conditions.

Movement. To make cinema intelligible, it is insufficient to claim movement as the distinctive condition that separates cinema from other arts. Indeed, one has expressed only a part of what cinema is if one merely points to the production of movement and the kinesthetic sensation as the conditions of the specifically cinematic effect that impresses itself on the spectator.[1] It is, namely, necessary to see also how the thinking of cinematic movement introduces a crisis into the production of movement and kinesthetic perception, that is, how the fact of movement and its perception become interrupted, disturbed, and disorganized by the thought of movement. Eisenstein's conception of movement depends precisely on bringing into crisis the visible movement of the kinematographic figure and on the troubling of the impression of the mobile figure's sensorial effect. There is "another movement," a movement that must not only be seen or perceived but also read, that we must be able to think in dialectical tension with the fact of kinematographic movement if we are to come up with a full account of the properly cinematic gesture of movement.

According to the powerful diagnosis by Gilles Deleuze in his *Cinema* books, the postclassical situation of cinema is characterized by an exhaustion of movement, which for Deleuze began with the violent break of World War II. In its affirmative aspect, the exhaustion of the cinema of movement has led to the creation of a new type of image (the time-image), found first in Italian neorealism, which signaled the emergence of a new kind of cinema defined by Deleuze as a "beyond of movement."[2] Today it does not seem too controversial to suggest that this "beyond of movement"—Deleuze's cinema of the time-image—has itself become exhausted or transformed into a cliché, which has prompted film theorists to follow a set of Deleuze's own rather cryptic remarks in *Cinema 2* in exploring the possibility of new types of cinematic images (digital image, neuro-image), thus attempting to mark off the dimension of a "beyond of time."[3] Contrary to the "Deleuzian" search for novelty, the Eisensteinian critical perspective offers in this context a seemingly more modest possibility, which is that of a renewed examination of the question of movement. A certain exhaustion or a crisis of movement is, for Eisenstein, inscribed already in the concept of movement, which means that, from an Eisensteinian perspective, what lies "beyond of movement" is precisely cinematic movement itself.

Action. In a similar way, one must illuminate the idea of cinema as mimesis of action only by grasping the concept of action as, in fact, an articulation of the crisis of action. In this context, the formal problem of Eisenstein's filmic work can be presented as a contradiction between the detotalized presentation of the theatrical–grotesque event of action and the epic–heroic desire to represent action as a narratable event within a totality. The question of historical and revolutionary action appears in the form of a problematic gap between the evental appearance of new (grotesque and theatrical) schemas of action and the (epic and heroic) desire to inscribe action into a larger context of a fully developed historical totality.

With his notion of the "aesthetics of cognitive mapping," Fredric Jameson has offered an articulation of the same formal problem for our own contemporary situation.[4] Jameson uses cognitive mapping as a way to think the gap between the always-local situatedness of individual experience and the global totality of the capitalist world-system—a gap that relates closely to the question of action. For the inability to represent or figure a global totality from the perspective of locally situated individual experience—that is, the inability to produce from our particular perspective a cognitive map of the capitalist world-system as a whole—induces in us a sense of paralysis, an overwhelming feeling that we are somehow unable to act or that the reality of our actions lies far beyond our grasp and control. The task of any political or politically pedagogical art of today thus lies, according to Jameson, in an essentially epic project: to make emerge within the dimension of individual experience a representation of totality or History as such. Yet, because History today assumes the shape of a virtually unrepresentable global system of relations, it is not so much successful representations of it as the failures to represent it, the distance that separates us from some genuinely epic grasp of History, that become particularly instructive, pointing, albeit negatively, to the possibility of some fuller grasp of the world and our place within it. Eisenstein's formal problem, as we have seen, adds to this the following shift of accent: what Eisenstein's filmic work makes visible is that History, in the sense of historical, revolutionary action, does not appear simply as an unrepresentable totality, the sublime Other, from which our always partial experience is separated by an unbridgeable gap and which some fuller epic capacity will perhaps one day make accessible. Rather, History is the gap itself, the moment of crisis that separates the global and the local, the collective and the individual, the sense of action that tends toward a total context and action in its detotalized or partial appearance, the epic–heroic quest and the grotesquery and theatricality of events. The task of political art is not so much to overcome this crisis as it is to invent new ways of making visible its gap or separatedness, which is also the locus of any genuinely political and historical desire.

Image. Eisenstein's concept of the image introduces the problematic of time: the symbolic capture of time versus the symptomatic *Zeitlosigkeit,* or timelessness of time, as it manifests in the form of the symptom. In the context of such an understanding, an Eisensteinian formulation of the question of the image has the capacity to free us from the predominant and seemingly exhausted "Bazinian" attempts to address its fate in our own moment. To many, the crisis of the cinematic image appears today as primarily a question of the digital break with the photographic image's analogical relationship to reality.[5] The introduction of digital technology has had the retroactive effect of defining the cinematic image as almost exclusively photographic in nature (at the expense of ideas of cinema not based on the photographic medium). Following this identification of the image with the photographic basis, it has become difficult to claim that such a thing as the cinematic image continues to exist in any coherent way in the conditions of digital (re)production. One consequence of such a stance is, for instance, the denial of time in the new, digital image. According to the argument of the photographic medium-specificity of cinema, it is only the photographic–cinematic image, consubstantial and isomorphic with reality itself, that is capable of registering the reality of duration (Bazin's "change mummified"), which somehow eludes the digital image.[6] Such an understanding denies the image the status of agency independent from the technical properties of the medium. The "Bazinian" tendency of contemporary film and media studies does not so much think the image—what the image does or what the image wants—as it thinks the dissolution of the image within what is perceived as the truly determining instance of our experience of "imageness," namely, the technical medium itself.

In Eisenstein's formulation, on the contrary, the image remains irreducible to the technical properties of the medium. The question posed by Eisenstein is close to the one recently advanced by Jacques Rancière in his *The Future of the Image*: "Does not the term 'image' contain several functions whose problematic alignment precisely constitutes the labor of art?"[7] For Rancière, it is necessary not to confuse the aesthetic effects of the image with the technical properties of the medium that carries these effects:

> The technical properties of the cathode tube are one thing and the aesthetic properties of the images we see on the screen are another. The screen precisely lends itself to accommodating the results both of *Questions pour un champion* [a French game show] and of Bresson's camera [in *Au hasard Balthazar*]. It is therefore clear that it is these results which are inherently different. The nature of the amusement television

> offers us, and of the affects it produces in us, is independent of the fact that the light derives from the apparatus. And the intrinsic nature of Bresson's images remains unchanged, whether we see the reels projected in a cinema, or through a cassette or disc on our television screen, or a video projector.[8]

According to Rancière (and Eisenstein), the image constitutes a series of effects intrinsic to themselves and not dependent on the technical medium as their cause. The image is an independent function or a set of operations that have to be explained according to their own logic and that we miss when we attempt to equate them exclusively with the technical properties of the medium carrying the image. If one thus raises the question of the image as a relation of time, the crucial distinction might not be between the photographic image of cinema (supposedly the guarantee of the presence of time as real duration) and the digital "image" (from which time is supposedly absent) but a possible conflict of time intrinsic to the independent effects of the image itself. The crucial question and the more fundamental temporal crisis of the image belong not to the break between the photographic and the digital but to the fact that the image is always, as Rancière would put it, a "problematic alignment" of opposing functions. The Eisensteinian problematic of the image, as we have seen, revolves around the split between the image's symbolic function, which stabilizes time and transforms it into a representation of meaning, and the "function" of the symptom/sinthom, which makes time in the image appear as a limit to any symbolization. The image in this sense is a crisis of time, which finds itself confronted with its own timelessness *(Zeitlosigkeit).*

Montage. The concept of montage is intimately tied to the internal dynamic of other Eisensteinian concepts. In Eisenstein's thought, the concepts of movement, action, and image are unthinkable without montage. When discussing montage for itself, however, we have described it as having to do with the crisis of form. Montage makes form appear as something critical, in the sense that any montage-form must, above all, itself be understood as a montage—a conflictual juxtaposition—of forms. Here form no longer functions as a meta-relation governing relations between the individual elements that make up a work and guarantee the work's status as an instance of an embodied unity of thought. Rather, montage implies a work—as well as the sense of the work's formal construction—as a division of thought, the presence of (at least two) contradictory forms of thought (associative and disjunctive; concept and *Witz*; the thought of the organism and the thought of the inorganic automatism). Montage-form consists of nothing other than a conflict of forms, a conflict of thought with itself.

Cinema as "Historical Form"

In his *Drei Studien zu Hegel,* Theodor Adorno dismisses the attitude of historicist "appreciation," the condescending approach of those in the present who think themselves superior and thus able to judge the past, selecting from the past what is "still living" and rejecting what is "already dead" (as was proposed by Benedetto Croce in the title of his 1906 book on Hegel). Contrary to the judgment of historicist appreciation, Adorno dismisses the present's claim of superiority, which is based on little more than our "dubious good fortune to live later." Indeed, why should we assume that the present does not at least in certain aspects bring a regression in relation to the past? Why should we not assume that artistic and intellectual work in the past was able to formulate problems and questions that possess more force than anything being accomplished by our present moment? Thus Adorno suggests that the right question to ask ourselves is not what a figure such as Hegel means in the light of our own present moment but rather "what the present means in the face of Hegel."[9]

Adorno's correction of historicist smugness may easily be extended to Eisenstein as well (the "cinematographic Hegel," as Deleuze called him).[10] The aim of the present study has not been to put Eisenstein in his proper historical place and to decide between the living and the dead aspects of his thought but to attempt to take up his cinema in its contradictory entirety and to open up the possibility of the Eisensteinian idea as a critical perspective on our own present moment—not, in other words, what Eisenstein means for us but what we (our cinema, our attempts to think it) mean in the face of Eisenstein. How does *our* present fare when confronted with Eisenstein's critical idea of cinema, the remarkable achievement of his filmic and theoretical work—not what is living and what is dead in Eisenstein but how alive (or dead) are we if we measure ourselves up to the vitality of Eisenstein's project?

If we can, at least for a moment, drop our historicist guard and expose ourselves to the anachronism of these questions, we will most likely admit to a feeling of embarrassment. Our current situation is characterized precisely by a certain dislocation between the critical idea of cinema and the sense of the present. Today, on one hand, much of the discourse in the heterogeneous field that calls itself the discipline of film studies paints a picture in which cinema has essentially become a matter of the past, an object of nostalgic and melancholic longing—an object often referred to, seemingly without any irony, as lost: "I once thought that one of the most rewarding tasks of a film teacher was to restore for students the historical and phenomenological experience of watching silent films. But I have recently come to realize, with some personal alarm, that during the past twenty years we have all lost in some degree the capacity to involve ourselves deeply and sensually in the 35mm image, well projected in a movie theater. . . . Theatrical cinema is, no doubt, the ancient land."[11] In this perspective, a critical idea of cinema, along with a complex elaboration of its concepts, persists but is divorced from the present. The fact that, in our moment, cinema is produced, advertised, and consumed—but also studied and taught (that is, academically legitimized)—on an unprecedented global scale contributes little to prevent an overwhelming sense of its disappearance: "It is quite likely that film is no longer modern or constitutive of our modernity."[12] The privileged place of cinema is the archive, while its "virtual life" (a life rather difficult to distinguish from death) continues in the form of "information and as art."[13]

On the other hand, opposed to the turning of cinema's critical idea toward the past, there exists another option, which is that of an enthusiastic embrace of the remarkable proliferation of the moving, "cinematic" images that suffuse our everyday experience. The development of new digital technologies has not condemned cinema to the past and the archive. Rather, it has contributed to cinema's rapid expansion ("expanded cinema"[14]), extension ("extended cinema"[15]), and relocation or displacement[16]—all processes leading to the point at which our social reality and its mode of reproduction themselves begin to appear as essentially cinematic.[17] According to this view, the place of cinema is potentially everywhere. The becoming-cinematic of our consciousness and our reality—the assertion that they have in some sense become commensurate with cinema (a variation of Guy Debord's thesis on the society of the spectacle)—is envisioned in this perspective as a kind of vast, delirious present, lived in its affective intensities, which, however, do not seem to carry in themselves any radical possibility of crisis. What characterizes the present, according to these accounts, is precisely that cinema spills "uncritically" and infectiously beyond all limits, forming a purely positive feedback loop with our self-awareness and our reality, in which no room for the critical gesture of negativity and division remains possible.

We are thus faced with something like the choice between a critical idea of cinema without the present or the "cinematic" intensity of the present without the idea. If the first option insists on the critical significance of the idea of cinema and pays the price of ultimately losing its claim on the present, the second option, in which cinema's "center no longer exists,"[18] manages to address the present cinematically only by giving up any serious claims to the criticality of the idea and its concepts. In the split between the weight of the growing critical archive contemplated by an essentially melancholic consciousness (critical idea without the present) and the giddy presentism of what announces itself as the horizon of "expanded cinema" (cinematic present without the critical idea), there emerges the shape of our failure to grasp the genuine historicity of the cinema characteristic of our own situation. For the sense of historicity can rest neither simply in critical perception (without the present) nor merely in the act of giving oneself over to the intensities of the present (without criticality) but precisely in the ability to articulate the two together: to approach criticality as a matter of the present or to perceive the present itself critically—something that neither a melancholic nostalgia for cinema nor the intoxication with the expanded intensities of the present is able to do.

What perhaps embarrasses us about Eisenstein and what tempts us into assuming the historicist attitude of "appreciation" and selective judgment is that his work succeeded precisely where our own moment fails. What is, namely, most remarkable and in some sense strangest for us in Eisenstein's films and writings is that they offer a model of bringing together the critical idea of cinema and the satisfaction of the need for orientation in the historical present (which for Eisenstein was, of course, the October Revolution and its world-historical consequences).[19] Eisenstein's work is characterized by its unwavering conviction in cinema's critical ability to orient people in relation to the time they inhabit, what the French film historian Antoine de Baecque calls "historical form." Historical form names for de Baecque a form that assumes the capacity of offering people access to the sense of their time:

> Cinema gives our time its form in the same way as the novel had done for the nineteenth century, theater for the seventeenth century, the encyclopedic dictionary for the Enlightenment, and the lampoon for the French Revolution. In a given historical moment a historical form becomes both most revealing of what is at stake, the tensions and sensibilities, and also the most adapted to enabling people to satisfy their sense of living in their times.[20]

It is important to read de Baecque's definition of historical form in the strongest way possible. What he says is not merely that the sense of a time deposits itself in the works of a certain form or that a historical reality, which exists independently of form, expresses itself through form. His claim is a different one: the historicity of our reality, the very sense of time we inhabit as historical, emerges only with the intervention of form. As de Baecque puts it, films "develop a cinematographic form that itself produces history."[21] There is, in other words, no historical reality—no time and no present—to be had without the intervening gesture on the part of the historical form.

Eisenstein's cinema is undoubtedly one of the first instances—the first instance?—in which cinema as such became aware of its capacity to shape time and orient people historically in relation to their present. According to Eisenstein's numerous statements, it does not suffice to say that cinema offers us a way to contemplate or passively know the time in which we live. Rather, cinema plays an active role in constructing our time, which thus enables us also to know, contemplate, and reflect on it. "Cognition is construction. The cognition of life is inseparable from the construction of life, from its *re-creation.*"[22] "Art has always appeared in the form of 'one of the means of violence'—as a tool (a weapon) of transforming the world by processing the consciousness of the spectators."[23] Eisenstein's cinematic work is from its very beginning set into movement by the belief that one must not show an event simply in the mode of its "static reflection," as though the event were simply given to us as something already completed that we can look at from without. The decisive ability of cinema lies, on the contrary, in the production of an event from the perspective of the event's own coming into being. Cinematic form places us on the inside of an event and constructs its immanent temporal sense through the composition of effects that are not available to external reflection but are, rather, "logically implicit in that event" itself.[24]

Yet if cinema in Eisenstein's case undoubtedly assumes the role of a historical form—if cinema must, according to his idea, place us on the inside of events rather than help us contemplate them from outside—how exactly does this work of orienting us in time take place? In his 1929 essay "Perspectives," in a passage we have already discussed in chapter 3, Eisenstein proposes his definition of the image. The term for the image, as we will remember, is *obraz,* which may also be made synonymous with form itself. Eisenstein's definition says that image or form is to be understood as "a cross between the concept of 'cut' [*obrez*]" and "disclosure [*obnaruzhenie*]." Cinematic form in Eisenstein's conception thus contains a double operation: a cut that isolates a particular phenomenon from the continuum in which the phenomenon had previously been embedded, while simultaneously disclosing a new link between this "particular phenomenon and its surroundings."[25] *Form is a cut that discloses.* One finds here the most rudimentary idea of montage, on which Eisenstein builds his critical idea of cinema: whatever the cinematic form might ultimately disclose, its existence is not predicated on some fundamental continuity with the surrounding reality but rather on the negativity, the criticality, of the cut that brings form into existence as something separate from reality and as essentially discontinuous. And it is precisely for this reason of discontinuity that form is also capable of "disclosure," of producing a new visibility of the "surroundings."

Eisenstein's definition of form also contains a certain figure of time. The passage may be used, for instance, to show how cinema's formal operation produces a sense of time, makes time intelligible, first, as a break, a radical separation of a moment from its temporal context (from the context of tradition or some classical ground), and second, following from the break or the cut, as a sudden disclosure of an unprecedented link between two or more incommensurable realities (a new context). Cinematic form orients us in time by allowing us to sustain not one but two seemingly incompatible experiences: one negative and destructive (the cut), the other relational and constructive (disclosure). In the light of cinematic form, our existence in time is experienced as being ripped out of any continuum and, at the same time—due to the fact of discontinuity itself—as part of a new configuration with what surrounds it (the opening of a new relationship to the past, for instance). The intervention of cinematic form divides time—in fact, divides the present itself—into something discontinuous (break, cut) and something continuous (disclosure, new context). It is the ability to maintain such a discontinuous–continuous figure of the present (a figure that Ernst Bloch called the "tension-shape" or "tendency-figure") that is missing today, when we are seemingly forced to choose between cinematic form as pure discontinuity (cinema as the "ancient land" of the past) or as pure continuity (the present as a continuous expansion of cinematic intensities). Neither of these two possibilities, which end up giving us a far too simple and far too homogenous perception of the unities of time, lends itself to the elaboration of the idea of cinema as historical form, whose effectiveness relies on the articulation of the unity of time as the division of the discontinuous and the continuous.

POLEMOS

Unlike Eisenstein's time, which is that of unities produced in division, our situation appears to be that of differences predicated on the act of keeping the more radical moment of division at bay. What carries the power of disclosure today does not appear in the guise of the cut but rather as a gesture of positive identification within a differentiated but essentially consensual milieu. Nowhere is this clearer than in the discourses and the differential identities that make up the contemporary field of film studies. From the perspective of Eisenstein's film-theoretical discourse, our situation appears above all as antipolemical in its spirit, a discursive field established on the foreclosure of the dissensual dimension of theoretical claims, in which difference appears primarily as a difference of opinion rather than as a contestation of truths (or contestation of truths against untruths). How different the nature of our discourse from that of Eisenstein's, whose consistency and intelligibility are so closely tied to the exercise of *polemos*! As he put it in a 1930 lecture at the Sorbonne, just before being expelled from France, "it is always interesting to understand and evaluate things on diametrically opposed grounds."[26] In the case of Eisenstein, polemic is essential to thought, which requires a moment of divisive confrontation on the path of establishing its own position. *Polemos* is, in other words, not merely accidental, an outer, rhetorical form of some more essential thought-content; rather, a polemical discursive strategy is the very element within which this content develops and without which the Eisensteinian idea of cinema would itself disappear from view.

Throughout, Eisenstein's discourse is a discourse of combat. Only the tactics change. The appearance of his first great conception of montage, "montage of attractions," is unthinkable without the polemical confrontation, in the mid-1920s, with both Hollywood (Griffith) and Dziga Vertov.[27] And the concept of intellectual montage (montage of intellectual attractions) developed in the "Dramaturgy of Film Form" of 1929 depends on a quarrel with Kuleshov and Pudovkin.[28] The question of sound, before the technological and economic conditions even allowed it to become a matter of filmmaking practice, took shape in 1928 through a polemical defense of "the culture of montage," which was to be protected from the dangerous trend of the "unimaginative use [of sound] for 'dramas of high culture.'"[29] The conception of montage as "interior monologue," another important moment in Eisenstein's "montage theory," would certainly not have been worked out as concretely by Eisenstein had he not chosen to dispute the producers at Paramount who put an end to his adaptation of Dreiser's *The American Tragedy.*[30] Eisenstein's insistence on the prelogical, the regressive, the unconscious in art, which became particularly pronounced from the end of the 1920s onward, owes much to an engagement with scholarly authorities (Levy-Bruhl, Frazer, Cushing, etc.). But the essence of these ideas emerges when Eisenstein deploys them as weapons through a series of polemics with French surrealism (in 1930)[31] and later with Soviet socialist realism (from 1935 onward).[32]

The status of Eisenstein's *polemos* with respect to the socialist realist period, the period of Stalin's intense clampdown on all artistic experimentation, is certainly complex and might require its own separate study. For now, suffice it to say that one of the first things to suffer during this time was the militant virtuosity of the polemic, a fact most visible in the exercises of "self-criticism" that the various dissenting intellectuals were forced to perform to humiliate themselves and repent in the wake of their "deviations." The genre of Stalinist self-denunciation is essentially a polemic against the polemic as such, a discourse whose goal lies not only in the direct humiliation of the person made to undergo this nasty ritual but perhaps even more in turning the practice of polemic itself into something indistinguishable from mere farce. The exercise aims to discredit polemic by its own means and to thereby usher it, mockingly, out of existence. After seeing Eisenstein polemicize against his own *Bezhin Meadow*—"Where lay the original error in my world view that flawed the work, so that despite the sincerity of my feelings and my dedication, it turned out to be patently groundless politically; and anti-artistic in consequence?"[33]—after such cheap pathos, who would ever again want to take him seriously as a polemicist?

Eisenstein's discourse and rhetoric change during this period, becoming, on one hand, more conciliatory ("I am not going to reproach or accuse anyone") and, on the other, more cryptic and indirect. The outright gesture of polemic is often replaced by the strategy of digression, a proliferation of the text that presents a thought not so much in conflict as something refracted in a multiplicity of splintered fragments. Nevertheless, it is quite possible to insist that even in the intellectual morass of Stalinism, the conflictual disposition of Eisenstein's thought does not disappear or essentially change. Perhaps unrecognizable at first sight and often allegorically transposed, it is still *polemos*—from Eisenstein's insistence on the "regressive" nature of art, which led to a short-lived desire to give up art completely, to the fateful diagnosis of Stalinism in his *Ivan the Terrible*—that provides the crucial orientation in the construction of Eisenstein's idea of cinema. Even when unrealized or when it is not carried all the way into the public, as was, for instance, the case with his intention to polemicize with Hanns Eisler and Theodor Adorno's *Composing for the Films,* it is still the polemical gesture that provides the initial spark and animates Eisenstein's thinking.[34]

The reflexive turns of Eisenstein's idea of cinema take place in relation to a polemical discursive field whose conflictual dynamism is essential to the idea's very existence. It is tempting to describe Eisenstein's theory of cinema as a "conflictual science," a term introduced by Louis Althusser in 1976 to describe the radical difference of Marxism and psychoanalysis from the knowledge produced and transmitted in the institutions of social and human sciences.[35] To practice a conflictual science means to forgo any recourse to some neutral position from which to grasp what one is attempting to theorize or to know. The very objectivity of theoretical discourse elaborated by a conflictual science depends, in other words, on the gesture of taking sides—taking the side of the proletariat and class struggle in the case of Marx, taking the side of the unconscious in the case of Freud, and taking the side of montage in the case of Eisenstein.

The essentially polemical character of the film-theoretical discourse goes hand in hand with the quest to establish cinema in the role of a historical form. De Baecque, for instance, observes an intimate relation between the two in the context of the French New Wave, which, in his description, was

> rife with filmographies, classifications, reassessments, devaluations of genres, the history of cinema was experienced as autonomous, weary of society and its representations, disdained as *films a thèse,* and endowed with a brand new touchstone—the auteur, now the principal reference, as well as a mode of writing, the polemic. Polemical writing fueled parochial rivalries, kindled clannish squabbles, and sharpened competing allegiances. Such and such lineage, and such and such family of *auteurs* versus another, *Cahiers du cinema* versus *Positif,* and so forth. This was how through collections of monographs, through edited volumes of critiques and interviews, through aligned or antagonistic journals, the history of cinema in the 1950s and 60s was written. A history that was

> lively, rigorous, erudite and written in the present tense of the new wave and its controversies, but that distrusted the academic world, which it considered scholastic and supercilious, even desiccating. The identification of cinema and history was so strong in this moment.[36]

Undoubtedly, it is a similar desire to identify his cinema with history, to turn cinema into a historical form that would give people access to the revolutionary sense of their time, that produces the combative and polemical spirit that pervades Eisenstein's theoretical writing.

Yet a polemical stance toward external positions is only half of the process described by Althusser's conception of "conflictual science." What, namely, characterizes the latter more crucially is also a certain shift from an external opposition to a moment of internal scission and transformation. A "conflictual science," according to Althusser, has a tendency to draw into itself the rivalry with what stands opposite it and thus to defend itself from attempts at its "annexation and revision" from outside by transforming internally. "The adversary always ends up by penetrating and producing a revisionism that provokes internal counterattacks and, finally, splits *(scissions).*"[37] The histories of Marxism and Freudian psychoanalysis are marked not merely by external opposition (to bourgeois economics, to psychology) but even more intensely by the violence of internal divisions and sectarian splits—to the extent that it becomes impossible to describe the unity of the Marxist or the Freudian field outside of its internecine struggles and fractional negations of unity.

The same mode of handling external oppositions informs the discursive strategy of Eisenstein's theoretical writing as well. The opposition is drawn in and for a brief moment held in balance, to then clear the ground by producing a new scission or cut in the discourse:

> Polemos, then, the declaration of thought, levels the ground; it is indeed "the father and king of all" not because it gathers everything together through a balancing of opposites but because it marks a reconfiguration of the very space of the debate in which previous oppositions are entirely disregarded. As a result, polemos is the introduction of something new beyond the debate and not simply the introduction of something new to the debate itself.[38]

When Eisenstein, for instance, polemicizes against Vertov and the constructivists of the Left Front of the Arts (LEF), he first recognizes their idea of the "nonplayed" cinema (documentary, anti-illusionist) as standing in opposition to the "played" cinema of the bourgeois West (fictive, illusionist), to which, according to Vertov and the constructivists, Eisenstein himself belonged. His subsequent strategy, however, does not consist simply of defending one of the terms *(played)* against the other *(nonplayed)* or of attempting some kind of compromise between them. Rather, his theoretical and critical gesture consists of assuming the perspective of the opposition itself, to draw it into his own discourse, so that he may be able to produce a new split, a new division, through which the initial opposition (played vs. nonplayed) itself becomes undermined and replaced by a new one: the true opposition, Eisenstein claims, is not between played and nonplayed but between the old opposition itself ("played" and "nonplayed" cinema) and what he calls the cinema of the "extra-played." The extra-played is a new orientation. It cannot simply be added to the debate over played and nonplayed cinema, because what it presupposes is the obsolescence of that very debate itself. The new term establishes an original conception of cinema through an act of division by separating itself polemically from a previous articulation of opposing terms.

If *Movement, Action, Image, Montage* seeks anything, it is not simply to add Eisenstein to the existing debate on cinema and its contemporary status but rather to see whether taking up the theoretical task of Eisenstein's idea of cinema may carry the polemical force to lead us beyond the limit and help us reconfigure the space of the debate itself. Any encounter with Eisenstein today should enable us to better measure the ways our own moment lags behind his thought, which is also our past, and which must therefore still be arrived at in the future.

ACKNOWLEDGMENTS

A book is a record of time as it is a record of encounters with people who populate the solitude of its writing. My first attempt to write about Eisenstein happened in graduate school in the Program in Literature at Duke University. I am grateful to Fredric Jameson, Jane Gaines, Roberto Dainotto, and Ken Surin for their encouraging responses to my dissertation. They gave me the confidence to expand into a book what in the dissertation was a single chapter dedicated to Eisenstein.

The most formative experiences during my graduate school days did not take place in the classroom but in conversations and study with my fellow graduate students, friends, and comrades, with whom I have shared what are still some of the most satisfying moments of my intellectual life. I am forever indebted to Nico Baumbach, Églantine Colon, Daniel Colucciello Barber, Amalle Dublon, Abe Geil, Keith Jones, Michelle Koerner, Russ Leo, Beatriz Llenin-Figueroa, Eric Owens, Lissette Rolon-Collazo, Alex Ruch, Britt Rusert, Corina Stan, and Jon Stapnes, as well as everyone else who participated in the project of Summer Study, where little bits of material included in this book were first presented.

I arrived at the University of Maryland in 2011 and consider myself very fortunate to have landed among an extraordinary group of colleagues in the film studies program and beyond. I am grateful to Jonathan Auerbach, Hester Baer, Peter Beicken, Marianne Conroy, Caroline Eades, Oliver Gaycken, Saverio Giovacchini, Fatemeh Keshavarz, Jason Kuo, Valérie Orlando, Gerard Passannante, and Orrin Wang for making the drab Maryland suburbs a welcoming place for thought and intellectual work. In particular, I thank Elizabeth A. Papazian. Her intellectual generosity and support for my work have been truly remarkable. She was one of this book's first readers and has helped me improve it significantly with her careful comments and expertise.

Mauro Resmini and Eric Zakim are my comrades in writing. Without them this book would not exist. Eric has been a mentor and a true friend. Our conversation is continuous, and I could not possibly count all the times he has helped me navigate through my professional and personal lives. Eric and his family, Yael Meroz, Jonah, and Dena, have helped make Washington, D.C., feel like home to me, for which I am deeply grateful.

I am grateful for Mauro's friendship and theoretical companionship. It was Deleuze who said in some place that friendship is a matter of perception, of being struck by someone's unhinged charm and recognizing suddenly that one shares with that person a kind of prelanguage, something groundless one grasps in common without which it is impossible to think. A just description! I have found pleasure and solace in all the time spent with Mauro and Viviana Maggioni, but especially in all the cigarettes we have shared in the past few years, standing on street corners, in front of buildings, and suspended aboveground on porches and balconies.

I wish to express gratitude to the Graduate School at the University of Maryland. The two Research and Scholarship Awards it granted in support of my project (summer 2012 and fall 2015) helped me research and made possible the timely completion of the book manuscript.

Throughout, the process of writing the book has benefited greatly from conversations with many people. They have offered the project their intellectual hospitality as well as material support. Thanks to Ada Ackerman, Deborah Auger, Nil Baskar, James Cahill, Timothy Corrigan, Gregory Flaxman, Marcel Gonnet Wainmayer, KINO!, Jela Krečič, Todd McGowan, Karla Oeler, Elena Petrovskaya, Valery Podoroga, Brian Price, Natalie Ryabchikova, Antonio Somaini, Meghan Sutherland, and Vanessa Teixeira de Oliveira. I am especially grateful to Naum Kleiman. People in the "Eisensteinian International" need no introduction to how singularly significant he is for our reception of Eisenstein's work. To say that his support decisively shaped the project of this book would be an understatement. From our conversations in the Eisenstein apartment in Moscow to his practical advice on finding sources or understanding this or that part of some text by Eisenstein, Naum has been and remains an essential guide and an inspiration.

My gratitude goes to my editor at the University of Minnesota Press, Danielle Kasprzak, for her guidance and her support for the project, and to her assistant, Anne Carter, for her expert advice in getting the book to print.

It is wishful thinking that one could ever properly acknowledge the influence of one's parents. What I can say is that my parents, Darij and Vida

Arsenjuk, have always made me feel that they have unconditional trust in me, which I have experienced as an immense gift of both freedom and responsibility. I hope the book makes them proud.

This book is for Lindsey Muniak, who has helped clarify so much of its language, and thus also its thought. She puts this materialist in the awkward and joyful spot of having to acknowledge that miracles exist: "I was wrong. / Love is not a symptom of time. / Time is just a symptom of love."

NOTES

INTRODUCTION

1. François Jost, "Á quoi sert Eisenstein?," in *Eisenstein: l'ancien et le nouveau,* ed. Dominique Chateau, François Jost, and Martin Lefebvre (Paris: Publications de la Sorbonne, 2001), 9.
2. Ibid., 10.
3. David Bordwell, *The Cinema of Eisenstein* (Cambridge, Mass.: Harvard University Press, 1993), 260–66.
4. V. V. Ivanov, *Ocherkii po istorii semiotiki v SSSR* (Moscow: Nauka, 1976).
5. Marie-Claire Ropars, *Le texte divisé: essai sur l'écriture filmique* (Paris: Puf, 1981), 33.
6. Gilles Deleuze, *Cinema 2: The Time-Image* (Minneapolis: University of Minnesota Press), 156–88.
7. Jean-Louis Schefer, *L'homme ordinaire du cinema* (Paris: Gallimard, 1980), 70–71.
8. Masha Salazkina, *In Excess: Sergei Eisenstein's Mexico* (Chicago: University of Chicago Press, 2009), 12.
9. See, e.g., Raymond Bellour, *Between-the-Images,* trans. Allyn Hardyck (Zurich: JRP/Ringier, 2012).
10. Sergei Eisenstein, *Notes for a General History of Cinema,* ed. Naum Kleiman and Antonio Somaini (Amsterdam: Amsterdam University Press, 2016).
11. Sergei Eisenstein, "The Author and His Theme," in *Selected Works,* ed. Richard Taylor, trans. William Powell, vol. 4, *Beyond the Stars: The Memoirs of Sergei Eisenstein* (London: British Film Institute, 1995), 792.
12. See the section "Cinematism, or the 'Synthesis of All Arts'" in the present introduction.
13. Sergei Eisenstein, "Pro domo sua," in *Metod,* vol. 2, *Tainy masterov,* ed. Naum Kleiman (Moscow: Muzei Kino and Eizenshtein tsentr, 2002), 583.
14. Sergei Eisenstein, "Chet-Nechet" [Even-odd], ibid., 174–75. And see, on a similar

theme, a remarkable text by Eisenstein titled "Razdvoenie edinogo" [The division of the one], ibid., 178–91.

15. The dialectical *doxa* would interpret the movement of the "three-point schema" presented by Eisenstein in the quoted passage in terms of the notorious dialectical triad. According to the triad, the initial moment of thesis finds itself surprised and subverted by its antithesis (the moment of division), yet the sense of this surprising division emerges only when canceled out in the moment of final synthesis, which raises up the discordant moment of division and reconciles it as re-membered in a higher unity offered by the result. The splitting of the intention would in this sense occur only as an instrument of testing and confirming the final unity of its aim. The discord of movement-in-recoil, which denies the direct reaching of the aimed-at object, would reveal itself merely as the tension of a spring that propels movement even more forcefully toward the attainment of its proper objective. And negativity would have to be seen in the final instance as something productive (i.e., not very negative, after all), its deployment leading ultimately to a positive, substantial outcome. Eisenstein himself often explicitly avowed this particular interpretation, which may be called the *dialectic of unity,* in his attempts to present the machinations of his own thought, assuming the latter as compatible with the "official" model of the dialectic that became codified in Stalin's doctrine of dialectical materialism.
16. Yuri Tsivian, *Ivan the Terrible* (London: British Film Institute, 2002), 29–34, emphasis added.
17. In *Savage Junctures: Sergei Eisenstein and the Shape of Thinking* (London: I. B. Tauris, 2003), Anne Nesbet has shown how Eisenstein's thought at its most elementary—what she calls his "figurative philosophy"—moves not by way of unity but rather through the medium of surprising, impossible, "savage junctures." "Eisenstein's approach to philosophy (and to political thought) was figurative: he mined Hegel, Engels, Lenin, Freud (and Stalin's speeches, too) for their figures, their images, which he then threw into sometimes blasphemous conjunction with images borrowed from literature, folklore, popular culture and myth" (2). Nesbet refers to the "Eisensteinian/Benjaminian project—philosophical thought that would 'emerge solely through the shock-like montage of the material'—as a 'surrealistic philosophy'" (11). Her book follows the route from the conceptual unity to the imagistic and figurative disunity. Eisenstein appears as a virtuoso practitioner of what Hegel called "picture-thinking"—an impure mode of thought that mixes the conceptual and the representational, the speculative and the figurative, the scientific and the mythical. In this descending movement from the concept to the image and figure, grotesque monsters are created—and Nesbet is interested as much in their shock as in their thought-value. Thought begins as (and must remain) an insult to good taste: a sudden bringing together of the high and the low, the sophisticated and the pornographic, Stalin and Disney, Hegel and Bororo Indian. In this sense, Nesbet's book shows to what remarkable extent Eisenstein's thinking depends not simply on synthesis or unity but on organizing disjunctions. Our own approach does not so much disagree with Nesbet's excellent study as it moves in the opposite direction: from Eisenstein's "picture-thinking" toward the elaboration of Eisensteinian concepts—from the imagistic and figurative richness of Eisenstein's thought toward the most elementary conceptual formulas of Eisenstein's idea of cinema.

18. Sergei Eisenstein, "Dickens, Griffith, and Ourselves," in *Selected Works,* vol. 3, *Writings, 1934–1947,* ed. Richard Taylor, trans. William Powell (London: I. B. Tauris, 2010), 223.
19. Ibid.
20. Ibid., 226.
21. Ibid., 225–26.
22. Sergei Eisenstein, "Dramaturgy of Film Form," in *Selected Works,* vol. 1, *Writings 1922–1934,* ed. and trans. Richard Taylor (London: I. B. Tauris, 2010), 161–62.
23. Sergei Eisenstein, "Speeches to the All-Union Creative Conference of Soviet Filmworkers," in *Selected Works,* 3:38.
24. For the most systematic and exhaustive account of Eisenstein's development of the fundamental problematic of art (what Eisenstein called the *Grundproblem* of art) during his studies in the 1930s and 1940s, see the remarkable work by Anna Bohn, *Film und Macht: zur Kunsttheorie Sergej M. Eisensteins, 1930–1948* (Munich: Diskurs Film Verlag Schaudig & Ledig, 2003).
25. For a useful discussion of the different meanings of "synthesis" in Eisenstein's work and the relationship of this term to his notion of cinema as the "synthesis of the arts," see Antonio Somaini, "Cinema as 'Dynamic Mummification,' History as Montage: Eisenstein's Media Archaeology," in Eisenstein, *Notes for a General History of Cinema,* 40–51.
26. Sergei Eisenstein, "Unity in the Image," in *Selected Works,* vol. 2, *Towards a Theory of Montage,* ed. Michael Glenny and Richard Taylor, trans. Michael Glenny (London: I. B. Tauris, 2010), 275.
27. Ibid., 276.
28. Sergei Eisenstein, "The Heir," in *Notes for a General History of Cinema,* 109.
29. Sergei Eisenstein, "Krupnym planom (vmesto predisloviia)" [On the close-up (in place of a foreword)], in *Metod,* vol. 1, *Grundproblem,* ed. Naum Kleiman (Moscow: Muzei kino and Eizenshtein tsentr, 2002), 38.
30. Sergei Eisenstein, "An Attack by Class Allies," in *Selected Works,* 1:264.
31. Sergei Eisenstein, "Laocoön," in *Selected Works,* 2:116.
32. Eisenstein, "An Attack by Class Allies," 264, emphasis added.
33. Sergei Eisenstein, "El' Greko i kino" [El Greco and cinema], in *Montazh,* ed. Naum Kleiman (Moscow: Muzei kino, 2000), 404–63.
34. The idea of "possibilization" comes from Robert Musil's *Man without Qualities.* Franco Moretti discusses it in relation to both Musil and James Joyce's *Ulysses* (an important influence on Eisenstein) in his *Modern Epic* (London: Verso, 1996), 145–49.
35. Ropars, *Le texte divisé,* 46.
36. Sergei Eisenstein, *Neravnodushnaia priroda,* vol. 2, *O stroenii veshchei,* ed. Naum Kleiman (Moscow: Muzei kino & Eizenshtein tsentr, 2006), 73–289.
37. Sergei Eisenstein, *"Monsieur, madame, et bébé,"* in *Selected Works,* 4:500.
38. Sergei Eisenstein, "Dvizhenie Myshleniia" [Movement of thought], in *Metod,* 1:88.
39. François Albera, introduction to *Cinématisme: peinture et cinéma,* by Sergei Eisenstein, ed. François Albera (Dijon, France: les Presses du réel, 2009), 11.
40. Bordwell, *Cinema of Eisenstein,* 112.
41. Sergei Eisenstein, "An Unexpected Juncture," in *Selected Works,* 1:115–22.
42. Bordwell, *Cinema of Eisenstein,* 137.
43. To name but a few instances: the close-up and parallel montage in Dickens (the

predecessor of D. W. Griffith); the relationship between imagicity *(obraznost)* and montage in Whitman or Shakespeare; the possibility of a montage that doesn't lead to an image but rather gives a sense of "indeterminate perception" and "vague feelings" in Mallarmé; *Ulysses* and Dreiser's *American Tragedy* as central for the conceptualization of montage as "interior monologue"; montage within the shot ("the 28mm effect") in Edgar Allan Poe; Pushkin and Tolstoy as "montageurs" of audiovisual counterpoint; Dostoyevsky's *The Idiot* as a lesson in mise-en-geste and mise-en-scène.

44. Ropars, *Le texte divisé,* 46.
45. Eisenstein, "Laocoön," 121.
46. Ibid., 178–79.
47. Mikhail Iampolski, "Theory as Quotation," *October* 88 (Spring 1999): 59.
48. Ibid., 68.
49. Ibid., 57.

1. THE FIGURE-IN-CRISIS

1. See especially the first section of chapter 7, "Thought and Cinema," in Deleuze, *Cinema 2*: "We will take the example of Eisenstein because the dialectical method allows him to decompose the nooshock into particularly well-determined moments (but the whole of analysis is valid for classical cinema, the cinema of movement-image, in general)" (157).
2. Jacques Aumont, *Montage Eisenstein* (Bloomington: Indiana University Press, 1987), 72.
3. "The strength of montage lies in the fact that it involves the spectator's emotions and reason. The spectator is forced to follow *the same creative path* that the author followed when creating the image. The spectator does not only see the depicted elements of the work; he also experiences the dynamic process of the emergence and formation of the image *in the same way* that the author experienced it." Sergei Eisenstein, "Montage 1938," in *Selected Works,* 2:309.
4. Aumont, *Montage Eisenstein,* 68.
5. Sergei Eisenstein, "Conspectus of Lectures on the Psychology of Art," in *The Eisenstein Collection,* ed. Richard Taylor (Calcutta: Seagull Books, 2006), 237.
6. Friedrich Engels, *Socialism: Utopian and Scientific,* https://www.marxists.org/archive/marx/works/1880/soc-utop/ch02.htm. Quoted by Eisenstein in "Speeches to the All-Union Creative Conference of Soviet Filmworkers," in *Selected Works,* 3:35.
7. This was, indeed, the aim of Engels's unfinished project in *Dialectics of Nature*: to provide a dialectical conception of nature as a dynamic totality compatible with the analytical project of modern natural sciences.
8. Eisenstein, "Speeches," 35.
9. We may pause here for a moment to remind ourselves that *sentence* comes from the Latin *sentire,* "to feel." The etymology of the word itself therefore suggests what Eisenstein attempts to demonstrate with his example: namely, that a new intuitive disposition will have to register its efficacy by appropriating for itself the form of the sentence as the elementary unit of discourse. The artistic intuition of movement must apply poetic pressure to and put into crisis the discursive form within which we make sense of our experience. We find a confirmation of this

intimate link between the intuition of movement and the problem of the sentence in Henri Bergson's *Creative Evolution* (New York: Cosimo, 2005), where the French philosopher of intuition relies on a similar overturning of the sentence—a "molding of language," he calls it—to demonstrate the difference between, on one hand, the intuitive grasp of reality as becoming and duration and, on the other, the commonsensical form of representing and perceiving reality: "When we say 'The child becomes a man,' let us take care not to fathom too deeply the literal meaning of the expression, or we shall find that, when we posit the subject 'child,' the attribute 'man' does not yet apply to it, and that, when we express the attribute 'man,' it applies no more to the subject 'child.' The reality which is the *transition* from childhood to manhood, has slipped between our fingers. We have only the imaginary stops 'child' and 'man,' and we are very near to saying that one of these stops *is* the other, just as the arrow of Zeno *is*, according to that philosopher, at all the points of the course. The truth is that if language here were molded on reality, we should not say 'The child becomes the man' [*l'enfant devient homme*] but 'There is becoming from the child to the man' [*il y a devenir de l'enfant à l'homme*]. . . . In the second proposition, 'becoming' is a subject. It comes to the front. It is the reality itself; childhood and manhood are then only possible stops, mere views of the mind; we now have to do with the objective movement itself" (339–40).

10. Eisenstein, "Speeches," 35–36.
11. Eisenstein, "Conspectus of Lectures," 239.
12. Sergei Eisenstein, *Disney*, ed. Oksana Bulgakowa and Dietmar Hochmuth, trans. Dustin Condren (Berlin: Potemkin Press, 2012), 15.
13. Gilles Deleuze, *Cinema 1: The Movement-Image* (Minneapolis: University of Minnesota Press, 1986), 5. It is worth noting that Eisenstein reads Disney as purely lyrical. He seems uninterested in how Disney's movement, once emancipated from the figure, might turn on the figure and become its torturer. Movement freed from the figure can compel and enslave the figure. This is the ambiguous nature of lyrically emancipated movement—escape and violence—which Disney thematizes in the films of the 1930s. The extraction of pure lyrical movement from figures is often represented as a way of organizing and disciplining them (military marches, torture, etc.). Eisenstein was certainly not unaware of this troubling dimension of liberated movement—a kind of lyrical nightmare. As we will try to show, it was crucial for him to present the figure as something that suffers movement, something that becomes impassioned and at times broken by the emancipated movement. Yet when it came to Disney, Eisenstein insisted on a more innocent type of lyricism.
14. We may evoke here Paul Klee's famous formula "not to render the visible, but to render visible."
15. We will be concerned here only with those of Eisenstein's drawings that do not seem to serve any purpose other than their own—with graphic work, in other words, that was not used for preparing scenic constructions in theater or for the development of character types, diagrams of action, and storyboards in Eisenstein's film work but that instead served the purpose of drawing alone, the purpose of the graphic line finding its autonomous use. The vast number of Eisenstein's drawings prevents us from presenting here a systemic and exhaustive account of his graphic work. Offered instead is something like a theoretical

sketch of Eisenstein's practice as a graphic artist, specifically as his drawing relates to the question of movement.

16. Sergei Eisenstein, "How I Learned to Draw (A Chapter about My Dancing Lessons)," in *Selected Works,* 4:578.
17. Ibid., 579.
18. Ibid., 576.
19. Ibid., 578.
20. Ibid., 585.
21. Ibid., 578.
22. Ibid., 586.
23. Ibid., 589.
24. Such a line, whose movement is individuated independently of the figure, appears most clearly in the ornament. The graphic line can, of course, provide us with a naturalistic depiction, or it might present us a phenomenon in the form of a generalized, "geometrical" schema. It can, in other words, be used to produce either a figure based on resemblance or one based on the operation of schematic reduction. But in its most elementary sense, the line is nothing other than rhythmic repetition, a pulse, which Eisenstein identifies with the ornamental. In Eisenstein's conception of drawing, the ornament moves into the center from the peripheral role it occupied in the classical conception of drawing. Eisenstein writes, for instance, that he considers it his crucial contribution to the understanding of the primordial form of drawing that he was able to separate *"geometrism from the ornament.* That is, this is not a *single* phenomenon, but rather, *two* distinct phenomena. I reduce repetitiveness in the ornament to . . . repeatability *as such* [in English], as an independent phenomenon, close to the organic, necessarily rhythmic, process." Sergei Eisenstein, "Zametki o linii i ornamente" [Notes on the line and the ornament], in *Metod,* 2:435.
25. The statements come from Eisenstein's diary, quoted in Bohn, *Film und Macht,* 246.
26. François Albera, "Eisenstein dans la ligne: Eisenstein et la question graphique," in *Eisenstein: l'ancien et le nouveau,* ed. Dominique Chateau, François Jost, and Martin Lefebvre (Paris: Publications de la Sorbonne, 2001), 83.
27. Eisenstein, quoted in Bohn, *Film und Macht,* 229.
28. Eisenstein, *Disney,* 17.
29. On fire as the element of figurability, see ibid., 15–28, and also the following passage in the same book: "There we are. *Fire is an image of formation, uncovering itself in the process. 'Absolute unrest'* apparently is the designation for the spirit of formation found in 'all-(omni)-possible phenomena and forms.' Ergo: there is nothing on earth as attractive as this" (63).
30. Sergei Eisenstein, "My Encounter with Magnasco," in *Selected Works,* 4:304.
31. Eisenstein likes to quote from the chapter on intricacy in William Hogarth's *The Analysis of Beauty* (Pittsfield, Mass.: Silver Lotus Shop, 1909), specifically the passage in which the English painter and caricaturist links the experience of the "waving" and "serpentine" line to the hunt. As in hunting, the attraction of drawing lies not in the entrapment of the object (the prey or the figure) but in the experience of the object's flight and the thrill of the pursuit. "Wherein would consist the joys of hunting, shooting, fishing, and many other favorite diversions, without the frequent turns and difficulties, and disappointments, that are daily

met with in the pursuit? How joyless does the sportsman return when the hare has not had fair play! How lively, and in spirits, even when an old cunning one has baffled, and out-run the dogs! The love of pursuit, merely as pursuit, is implanted in our natures, and designed, no doubt, for necessary and useful purposes" (49). The line is first a pursuit; only secondarily is it the capture of the figure. But as such, it also drives the figure's own fugitive movement. Even in the multilinear compositions of primary interest to Hogarth, the attraction of lines lies in the weaving and the unraveling of their intricacy rather than in their enclosure of the figure. "The eye has this sort of enjoyment in winding walks, and serpentine rivers, and all sorts of objects, whose forms, as we shall see hereafter, are composed principally of what, I call, the waving and serpentine lines. Intricacy in form, therefore, I shall define to be that peculiarity in the lines, which compose it, that *leads the eye on a wanton kind of chase,* and from the pleasure that gives the mind, intitles it to the name of beautiful" (50). Both passages are quoted by Eisenstein in *Nonindifferent Nature,* trans. Herbert Marshall (Cambridge: Cambridge University Press, 1987), 266.

32. Eisenstein, "My Encounter with Magnasco," 302.
33. Nicole Brenez, *De la figure en général et du corps en particulier: l'invention figurative au cinéma* (Paris: De Boeck Université, 1998), 144.
34. On the question of pathos and figure, see Vicente Sánchez-Biosca, "Eisenstein: une figuration, des corps pour le pathetique?," in Chateau et al., *Eisenstein,* 131–45.
35. Eisenstein, quoted in Bohn, *Film und Macht,* 246.
36. Brenez, *De la figure en général,* 149.
37. Sánchez-Biosca, "Eisenstein," 132.
38. Ibid., 139.
39. Brenez, *De la figure en général,* 144.
40. Eisenstein, "[Notes on Drawing]," in *Eisenstein Collection,* 194. Eisenstein develops the topology of this type of impossible space, a space "before" the divisions that create space, most notoriously in his writings on *Mutterleibsversenkung*—the drive for the return or the sinking into the mother's womb, which he adopts from the heretical Freudian psychoanalysts Otto Rank and Sándor Ferenczi as one of the fundamental drives at work in all forms of human expression. The maternal womb is imaginable for the subject, who is traumatically separated from it, only in the form of a fiction of an impossible place that makes indiscernible a series of binaries otherwise constitutive of our experience: birth *and* death, emergence *and* return, origin *and* end, temporal duration *and* absence of time, gravity *and* levitation/weightlessness, fullness or plenitude *and* negativity, nonbeing or not-yet-being. Though Eisenstein is certainly not always immune to psychologizing, it is crucial to note that the problem of the psychological drives, such as the one for the return to the maternal womb, is posed by him primarily in terms of formal questions. However fascinated by the psychological hypotheses Eisenstein might be, he is always interested in exploring how the psychological hypothesis interacts with and is mediated by the work of artistic form—how, for instance, a topology of an impossible place (womb) hypothesized by psychological research might be used to haunt and disorganize, unsettle and transform, the world of figures. For Eisenstein's writings on *Mutterleibversenkung,* see the section "MLB (Obraz materinskogo lona)" [MLB (the image of the maternal womb)], in *Metod,* 2:296–348. See also Sergei Eisenstein, "Pre-natal Experience," in *Selected Works,*

4:507–9. Eisenstein's fascination with the drive for a return to the womb is usefully discussed in Bohn, *Film und Macht,* 128–42.

41. Eisenstein, "How I Learned to Draw," 579.
42. Eisenstein produced the *Duncan* series in five sessions during June 1931 in Mexico. One may speculate that the drawings exhibit an awareness of the increasing clampdown on cultural and artistic production in the Soviet Union. They can be read as an attempt to figure a revolutionary act, insofar as for Eisenstein, parricide or the killing of the King or Leader represented a fundamental human urge (the oedipal counterpart to *Mutterleibversenkung*) and a necessary moment in the progressive becoming of a society of equals (the inspiration of Freud's *Totem and Tabu*). Yet if the drawings stage a revolutionary killing of a figure of authority, they also register—in the claustrophobic disposition of the pictorial space—the limits and the difficult consequences of such an act, as though the figures enlarged by their act were at the same time still trapped within a narrowly prescribed and empty space that may indeed cause them to suffocate. On parricide and the figure of the Father in Eisenstein, see Bohn, *Film und Macht,* 142–51. For Eisenstein's own account of his relationship to his father, and specifically how a rebellion against the Father relates intimately to the question of movement, see his memoirs. Eisenstein, "Wie sag ich's meinem Kinde?," in *Selected Works,* 4:424–53.
43. Albera, "Eisenstein dans la ligne," 81.
44. Eisenstein produced the drawings of *Nichts* by using fine lead pencil on paper. The figures appear faint and fragile, which prohibits a satisfactory reproduction of the drawings in the present volume. For images of the drawings from the series *Nichts,* see Naum Kleiman, *Eisenstein on Paper: Graphic Works by the Master of Film* (London: Thames and Hudson, 2017), 180.
45. Sergei Eisenstein, "Zametki k 'Grundproblem'" [Notes on the *Grundproblem*], in *Metod,* 2:381.
46. Yuri Tsivian, *Na podstupakh k karpalistike: Dvizhenie i zhest v literature, iskusstve i kino* (Moskva: Novoe literaturnoe obozrenie, 2010), 12.
47. Giorgio Agamben, "Notes on Gesture," in *Means without End: Notes on Politics,* trans. Vincenzo Binetti and Cesare Casarino (Minneapolis: University of Minnesota Press, 2001), 57. For Agamben, cinema is defined as the art that returns people to their gestures, to a form of expressivity that does not need to presuppose a domain of interiority as its condition.
48. Vilém Flusser, *Gestures,* trans. Nancy Ann Roth (Minneapolis: University of Minnesota Press, 2014), 2.
49. Eisenstein, "Conspectus of Lectures," 236.
50. The formulation seems apt because the word *dialectics* is etymologically related to the Old Greek *dia-legein,* "to speak through, thoroughly, across, apart from."
51. Brenez, *De la figure en général,* 376.
52. Eisenstein, "Dickens, Griffith, and Ourselves," 226.
53. Eisenstein, "El' Greko i kino," 426. Eisenstein began writing his remarkable essay on El Greco in the late 1930s. The essay was first intended as part of his essay *Montage* (1937). It was later reworked with the purpose of inclusion in the article "Vertical Montage" (1940) and later on in *Nonindifferent Nature* (1945–47). See the editor's note accompanying the French translation of the essay: Sergei

Eisenstein, "El Greco y el cine," in *Cinématisme*, ed. François Albera, 65–126 (Laussane: Les presses du reel, 2009).

54. André Gaudreault, *Film and Attraction*, trans. Timothy Barnard (Urbana: University of Illinois Press, 2001), 52.
55. André Gaudreault, "Les vues cinématographiques selon Eisenstein: que reste-t-il de l'ancien (le cinéma des premiers temps) dans le nouveau (le productions filmiques et scripturales d'Eisenstein)?," in Chateau et al., *Eisenstein*, 33.
56. Eisenstein, "El' Greko i kino," 426–27.
57. Eisenstein's organicism, the assertion of an "organic process of movement," here only clouds the fact that the mechanism he describes in the second part of the passage, the very logic of what he calls "another movement," has little in common with the recomposition and perception of kinematographic movement we saw him describe in the first part of the passage.
58. Gaudreault, *Film and Attraction*, 8.
59. It is, for instance, very clear that Eisenstein's descriptions of the basic kinematographic apparatus (the base) are most often derived from his idea of cinematic movement (the superstructure) rather than vice versa. Eisenstein—despite at times claiming to do so in his feverish desire to appear properly materialist—does not set up his idea of cinematic movement on the technical "base" of the kinematographic medium. In Eisenstein's case, it is rather the "superstructural" idea of cinematic movement, the "metaphysics" of gesture, that determines and gives meaning to the "physical" apparatus of kinematography. This is also the reason that his descriptions of the basic kinematographic apparatus and the mechanism of the perception of movement in cinema are at times inconsistent and sometimes simply empirically false: they are all motivated, colored, and modified by his idea of cinematic movement. The primacy of the idea does not necessarily make Eisenstein an idealist, for only a naive materialist would suppose that there is somehow more materiality in the technical medium of the basic kinematographic apparatus than there is in the thought of the form that determines its meaning and function.

2. THE FORM-PROBLEM

1. For documents connected to Eisenstein's experience in theater between 1918 and his shift to cinema in 1924–25 (gathered mostly from his correspondence), see Vladimir Zabrodin, *Eizenshtein: popytka teatra* (Moscow: Eizenshtein tsentr, 2005).
2. See, e.g., "Theatre and Cinema," in *Selected Works*, 3:2–15, and "How I Became a Director," ibid., 3:284–290.
3. For Eisenstein's statements on Meyerhold, gathered from his published articles, book and lecture notes, diaries, and letters, see Vladimir Zabrodin, *Eizenshtein o Meierkhol'de* (Moscow: Novoe izdatel'stvo, 2005).
4. Vsevolod Meyerhold, *Meyerhold on Theatre*, trans. Edward Braun (London: Methuen Drama, 1998), 119–42. For a very useful account of Meyerhold's development of his theatrical conception during this period, see the introductory text by Béatrice Picon-Vallin in Vsevolod Meyerhold, *Ecrits sur le théâtre*, vol. 1, *1891–1917*, trans. and ed. Béatrice Picon-Vallin (Lausanne: L'Age d'Homme, 1973).
5. Edward Braun, in his translation of Meyerhold's texts, translates *uslovnii teatr*

as "stylized theater" to stress Meyerhold's difference from "naturalist theater" (identified in the figure of the great Stanislavsky). Braun renders Meyerhold's explanatory note in a text from 1907, titled "The Theatre-Studio," in the following way: "With the word 'stylization' I do not imply the exact reproduction of a style of a certain period or of a certain phenomenon, such as a photographer might achieve. In my opinion the concept of 'stylization' is indivisibly tied up with the idea of convention, generalization and symbol. To 'stylize' a given period or phenomenon means to employ every possible means of expression in order to reveal the inner synthesis of that period or phenomenon, to bring out those hidden features which are to be found deeply embedded in the style of any work of art." Meyerhold, *Meyerhold on Theatre,* 43. The term *uslovnii teatr* suggests not only a theater that is consciously stylized or that plays with conventions but also the sense of a "conditional theater": a theater that brings to the surface and experiments with the very condition or the transcendental idea of theater as such. One could possibly translate the term *uslovnii teatr* also as a "provisional theater," which aptly suggests the constant transformation, the chameleonic nature, of Meyerhold's conception. The sense of the conditional and the provisional nature of theatricality point most clearly to the anti-institutional wager at stake in Meyerhold's work. The young Eisenstein is clearly under Meyerhold's influence when, in 1919, as he is undergoing a rapid self-education in theater during his time at the civil war–front, he notes in his theatrical diary, "We must not forget that, in all honesty, each play should not only have its own scene, but I would say even its own theatre (in its entirety: an auditorium and even a facade!), to say nothing of the very principle of staging. Each play should create its own 'theatre.'" Zabrodin, *Eizenshtein o Meierkhol'de,* 21.

6. Meyerhold, *Meyerhold on Theatre,* 119–21.
7. Alma Law and Mel Gordon, *Meyerhold, Eisenstein, and Biomechanics: Actor Training in Revolutionary Russia* (Jefferson, N.C.: McFarland, 1996). On the influence of pre-October theatricality on Meyerhold's reception of certain Taylorist ideas of movement, see Julia Vaingurt's account of biomechanics and its relationship to Soviet "Americanism" in *Wonderlands of the Avant-Garde: Technology and the Arts in Russia of the 1920s* (Evanston, Ill.: Northwestern University Press, 2013).
8. A passage from Eisenstein's memoirs might illustrate the extent to which, even at the height of constructivism in theater, it was by then an already anachronistic perception of Meyerhold that guided Eisenstein's thinking. He writes of his experience as a student in Meyerhold's workshop, "Overalls. Biomechanics. Industrialization of the theatre. Abolition of the theatre. . . . And it was all nothing more than a chance, newly-donned mask of that same Pierrot." "The Teacher," in *Selected Works,* 4:265. In his autobiographical narrative, there are two early experiences that Eisenstein presents as decisive events for sealing his relationship to art. "Two direct impressions, like two thunder claps, decided my fate in this direction." "How I Became a Director," 284. The two events illustrate the close association between Eisenstein's idea of art and the experience of theatricality in the milieu of prerevolutionary Russia. The first experience (in 1912, at the age of fourteen) was a staging of Gozzi's *Turandot* (directed by Fyodor Komissarzhevsky) at Nezlobin's theater in Riga. As Naum Kleiman notes, "in this production, Eisenstein not only saw for the first time a brilliant realization of the

Italian comedy of masks *(commedia dell'arte)*, which would crucially determine his future directorial conceptions, but he also experienced the shock of 'the play with the footlights' as the characters from time to time crossed the border between the stage and the auditorium, emphasizing the relativity of both stage and living reality." "Komentarii [Comments]," in Eisenstein, *Metod,* 1:448. It is such predilection for theatrical movement in which the very conventions of theater were experimented with that was then confirmed by the second "impression"—"overwhelming and definitive, which actually defined my unspoken intention . . . to 'give myself' to art" ("How I Became a Director," 284)—left on Eisenstein by the witnessing of Meyerhold's production of Lermontov's *Masquerade* in February 1917, two days before the abdication of Nicholas II and the collapse of the empire, which would eventually lead to the October Revolution.

9. Fredric Jameson, *The Ancients and the Postmoderns: On the Historicity of Forms* (London: Verso, 2015), 66–67.
10. Meyerhold, *Meyerhold on Theatre,* 134–35.
11. In Eisenstein's view, the Meyerholdian attempt to liberate movement from its subservience to naturalist verisimilitude, to set up theatrical mobility and action on its own independent ground, already made theater tend toward cinema. Late in his life, writing in the early 1940s, Eisenstein was able to reflect on the fulfillment of Meyerhold's theatrical revolution (the "most 'theatrical' of all theatres") in cinema—the fulfillment of Meyerhold in Eisenstein, so to speak. See "Peripetii krupnogo plana" [Peripeties of the close-up], in *Metod,* 2:92.
12. See Béatrice Picon-Vallin's introduction in Meyerhold, *Ecrits sur le théâtre,* 14.
13. Meyerhold, *Meyerhold on Theatre,* 56.
14. Ibid., 124.
15. In 1920, as he is developing a program for the "theatricalization" of physical culture, Meyerhold proclaims at one of the meetings, "Movement is the basis of theatrical spectacle. First movement, then emotion leading to the word, and then the word itself. And in the mass spectacle, first the enormous silent wave, the spreading of movement, a great accumulation of emotion and finally the great word." Law and Gordon, *Meyerhold, Eisenstein, and Biomechanics,* 31. "First movement"—a formula strikingly similar to Eisenstein's "first the movement, and then *what* moves" that we discussed in the previous chapter.
16. Meyerhold, *Meyerhold on Theatre,* 126.
17. Ibid., 123.
18. Ibid., 100.
19. "Banished from the contemporary theatre," Meyerhold writes, theatricality finds "a temporary refuge in the French cabarets, the German Überbrettl, the English music halls and the ubiquitous 'variétés.'" Ibid., 136.
20. Ibid., 127.
21. Ibid., 131.
22. Ibid.
23. See, e.g., the following statement recorded in Vladimir Nizhny, *Lessons with Eisenstein* (New York: Hill and Wang, 1962): "If an actor is hidden by a mask, what he has to do is to operate with movement and gesture. . . . Incidentally, the most active theatre from the viewpoint of gesture was the Masked Comedy [*commedia dell'arte*]. Thanks to the mask, the repertoire of movement and gesture was entirely reconstituted" (9).

24. Eisenstein, "Theatre and Cinema," 8–9.
25. Sergei Eisenstein, "On Disney," in *Eisenstein Collection,* 146–47.
26. Meyerhold, *Meyerhold on Theatre,* 129.
27. Ibid.
28. Perhaps this is what Meyerhold has in mind when he says that with his idea of theatricality, he wishes to purify the romantic of its sentimentality: to give us the impression of the sentimental action—and what could be more sentimental than weeping?—without the representation to which the sentimentality might attach itself. Or, as Eisenstein puts it in his theater diaries in response to Meyerhold's pre-October staging of *Don Juan* and *The Transfigured Prince,* the point is to move from the "'wild and uncultured' 'experience on the stage,' embellished with the naturalism of 'sorrow,' 'despair,' 'zealousness' (from the word 'jealousy'), and from the 'physiological' actor, . . . toward the refined musical rhythmic 'recitation' 'of the actor's grief'; attention will be paid not to the natural 'sniffling' with tears and so forth, but on the rhythmicality of the figures and their movements in unison with the beautiful spoken words." Diary entry from August 2, 1919, quoted in Zabrodin, *Eizenshtein o Meierkhol'de,* 25.
29. We are relying here on Vladimir Zabrodin's historical reconstruction of the relationship between Eisenstein's first theoretical writings on the concept of attractions and Meyerhold's idea of theatricality and grotesque. Zabrodin suggests that Eisenstein most likely borrowed the term "attractions" directly from Meyerhold. He also points out the influence of Meyerholdian terminology on Eisenstein's first published text, "The Eighth Art: On Expressionism, America and, of course, Chaplin," in *Selected Works,* 1:29–32—a text that Eisenstein cowrote with Sergei Yutkevich and that draws on some of Meyerhold's key terms, such as "naturalism," "illusionism," "stylization," and so on. See Vladimir Zabrodin, "Grotesk i attraktsion" [Grotesque and attraction], in *Eizenshtein,* 157–69.
30. Eisenstein, "Montage of Attractions," in *Selected Works,* 1:34.
31. Sergei Eisenstein, "The Montage of Film Attractions," ibid., 1:44.
32. Ibid., 46.
33. Ibid., 41.
34. Ibid.
35. On the significance of murder and the murder scene for film and film theory, see Karla Oeler, *A Grammar of Murder: Violent Scenes and Film Form* (Chicago: Chicago University Press, 2009). According to Oeler, who discusses the importance of murder scenes in relation to both montage and the poetics of classical genres, "the murder scene is a crucial site where cinema reflects upon itself" (19). What, namely, film shares with murder is a certain dialectic between the singular existence of objects or individuals and its negation: "Murder is such a foundational scene in the history of cinema because the obliteration of life that it revolves around dramatizes the way that cinematic representation . . . always is poised between conveying the reality of the object and registering the loss of reality, or disembodiment, intrinsic to representation itself" (4). Oeler points to the recurrence of murder in Eisenstein's films, unfinished projects *(American Tragedy),* his theoretical writings ("The Montage of Film Attractions," "Dramaturgy of Film Form"), and the course in film direction that he led at the State Institute of Cinematography (VGIK) in Moscow (Eisenstein, for instance, analyzes with his students the task of filming the murder scene in *Crime and Punishment*). The

question of working out the formal method of his cinematic work is, for Eisenstein, inseparably linked to murder and violence: "We shall naturally look for an example first and foremost among works of graphic art in which violent themes and bold ideas are forcibly expressed, for it is there that we find the phenomenon most fully and vividly presented. . . . The method is best discerned in the artistic treatment of aggression and violent action." Sergei Eisenstein, "Laocoön," in *Selected Works,* 2:126.

36. Eisenstein, "Montage of Film Attractions," 43.
37. Sergei Eisenstein, "Beyond the Shot," in *Selected Works,* 1:141.
38. Ibid., 1:142.
39. Sergei Eisenstein, "Dramaturgy of Film Form," in *Selected Works,* 1:163–64.
40. Marie-Claire Ropars, *Le texte divisé : essai sur l'écriture filmique* (Paris: Puf, 1981), 39–41.
41. Lev Kuleshov, "Volia. Uporstvo. Glaz" (1926), quoted in Anne Nesbet, *Savage Junctures: Sergei Eisenstein and the Shape of Thinking* (London: I. B. Tauris, 2003), 25.
42. Eisenstein describes Vertov's *Cine-Pravda* as a film in which the shortness of sequences, by which he must mean the speed and dynamism of Vertov's montage, merely conceals "the 'neutral' epic 'statement of facts.'" Despite his dynamism, Vertov fails to construct his film "dramatically" and takes "no account of attractions." Eisenstein, "Montage of Film Attractions," 41.
43. G. W. F. Hegel, *Aesthetics: Lectures on Fine Art,* vol. 2, trans. T. M. Knox (Oxford: Oxford University Press, 1975), 1063–64.
44. Jean-Pierre Dubost, "Erzählen/Beschreiben," in *Dictionary of Untranslatables: A Philosophical Lexicon,* ed. Barbara Cassin (Princeton, N.J.: Princeton University Press, 2014), 289.
45. Martin Heidegger, *Contributions to Philosophy (From Enowning),* trans. Parvis Emad and Kenneth Maly (Bloomington: Indiana University Press, 1999).
46. Eisenstein, "Montage of Film Attractions," 45.
47. Hegel, *Aesthetics,* 2:1089.
48. Aumont, *Montage Eisenstein,* 86.
49. Ibid., 106.
50. Sergei Eisenstein, "[The Grotesque]," in *Eisenstein Collection,* 325–26, emphases added.
51. The idea of the coexistence of different developmental stages encountered in *The General Line* became, for Eisenstein, one of the key themes and a central organizing principle of his next, tragically unfinished film, *Que Viva Mexico!* See Masha Salazkina, *In Excess: Sergei Eisenstein's Mexico* (Chicago: University of Chicago Press, 2009).
52. Sergei Eisenstein, "The Problems of the Soviet Historical Film," in *Selected Works,* 3:13.
53. Sergei Eisenstein, "Our *October*: Beyond the Played and the Non-played," in *Selected Works,* 1:101–2.
54. Adrian Piotrovsky, "*October* Must Be Re-edited!," in *Film Factory: Russian and Soviet Cinema in Documents 1896–1939,* ed. Richard Taylor and Ian Christie (London: Routledge, 1988), 216.
55. Yuri Tsivian, "Eisenstein and Russian Symbolist Culture: An Unknown Script of *October,*" in *Eisenstein Rediscovered,* ed. Ian Christie and Richard Taylor, 79–109 (London: Routledge, 1993).

56. Piotrovsky, "*October* Must Be Re-edited!," 216.
57. Ibid.
58. Ibid., 217.
59. Evgeny Dobrenko, *Stalinist Cinema and the Production of History: Museum of the Revolution* (New Haven, Conn.: Yale University Press, 2008).
60. "In the European-wide quest for national origins and identity of the early nineteenth century, heroic poetry held a special allure. It could embody a pure state of national feeling because its martial subject not only invokes the patriotic unity of a people at war but also provides the mythic memories that can mobilize them. . . . The Dark Ages, because they intervene between the periods of international commerce in European civilization, are thus the bedrock in which an original national spirit and culture can be located and mined. But this spirit and culture are already lost in the very darkness of the times." David Quint, *Epic and Empire: Politics and Generic Form from Virgil to Milton* (Princeton, N.J.: Princeton University Press, 1993), 353–54.
61. Ibid., 368.
62. Ibid., 361.
63. Ibid.
64. Ibid., 363.
65. Ibid., 364.
66. Ibid., 368.
67. Ibid.
68. In "The Tragic and Daily Life" (1896), in *Playwrights on Playwriting: From Ibsen to Ionesco,* ed. Toby Cole (New York: Hill and Wang, 1960), Maurice Maeterlinck writes, "Othello is admirably jealous. But is it not perhaps an ancient error to imagine that it is at the moments when this passion, or others of equal violence, possesses us, that we live our truest lives? I have grown to believe that an old man, seated in his armchair, waiting patiently, with his lamp beside him; giving unconscious ear to all the eternal laws that reign about his house, interpreting, without comprehending, the silence of doors and windows and the quivering voice of the light, submitting with bent head to the presence of his soul and his destiny—an old man, who conceives not that all the powers of this world, like so many heedful servants, are mingling and keeping vigil in his room, who suspects not that the very sun itself is supporting in space the little table against which he leans, or that every star in heaven and every fiber of the soul are directly concerned in the movement of an eyelid that closes, or a thought that springs to birth—I have grown to believe that he, motionless as he is, does yet live in reality a deeper, more human, and more universal life than the lover who strangles his mistress, the captain who conquers in battle, or 'the husband who avenges his honor'" (30–31).
69. Meyerhold, *Meyerhold on Theatre,* 63, emphases added.
70. Sergei Eisenstein, "Vertical Montage," in *Selected Works,* 3:327–399.
71. For the film's production history and its relationship to the historical context, see Joan Neuberger, *Ivan the Terrible* (London: I. B. Tauris, 2009).
72. Eisenstein, as quoted in Tsivian, *Ivan the Terrible,* 46.
73. On the question of Eisenstein's use of shadows in *Ivan,* Joan Neuberger writes, "The shadow is a natural metaphor for our ability to change shape. In almost every scene, shadows witness the action and offer a slightly altered version of

events occurring before them. . . . They seem to be both more powerful and, in important ways, freer than the people who cast them." Neuberger also links shadows and Eisenstein's fascination for Disney's "plasmatic" animated figures. "Eisenstein also believed that shape-shifting shadows, like animated figures of Walt Disney's early films, conveyed an escape from conventional identity." Neuberger, *Ivan the Terrible,* 110–11.

74. "Stalin, Molotov and Zhdanov on *Ivan the Terrible,* Part Two," in *Selected Works,* 3:302.
75. Quoted in Tsivian, *Ivan the Terrible,* 14.
76. Ibid., 17–18. Tsivian here follows in the wake of Kristin Thompson's analysis of the film, in which she writes of what she calls the visual "floating motifs" of *Ivan the Terrible,* which create redundancies, parallels, and "accumulate" sense in a manner distinct from the film's narrative meaning. See Thompson, *Eisenstein's Ivan the Terrible: A Neoformalist Analysis* (Princeton, N.J.: Princeton University Press, 1981), 158–72.
77. Tsivian, *Ivan the Terrible,* 18–22.
78. On the legitimizing function of the Stalinist historical epic, see Dobrenko, *Stalinist Cinema,* 18.
79. "Stalin, Molotov and Zhdanov on *Ivan the Terrible,* Part Two," 299.
80. Kevin Platt and David Brandenberger, "Terribly Romantic, Terribly Progressive, or Terribly Tragic," *The Russian Review* 58, no. 4 (1999): 635–54.
81. On eccentricity of heroic action with respect to power, see Maurice Blanchot, "The End of the Hero," in *The Infinite Conversation,* trans. Susan Hanson (Minneapolis: University of Minnesota Press, 1993), 370.
82. We rely here on Slavoj Žižek's discussion of *Ivan the Terrible* in his *Organs without Bodies: Deleuze and Consequences* (New York: Routledge, 2004). Writing about the famous color sequence of the dance of the *oprichina* in part 2 of the film, Žižek states, "Here we are at the obscene site where musical enjoyment meets political liquidation. And, taking into account the fact that the film was shot in 1944, does this not confirm the carnivalesque character of the Stalinist purges? We encounter a similar nocturnal orgy in the third part of *Ivan.* . . . Ivan and his Oprichniks perform their nightly drinking feast as a black mass. . . . Therein resides the true greatness of Eisenstein, namely, that he detected (and depicted) the fundamental shift in the status of political violence, from the 'Leninist' liberating outburst of destructive energy to the 'Stalinist' obscene underside of the Law" (185).
83. Hegel, *Aesthetics,* 2:1044.
84. The link between action and totality that takes the form of conquest ensures in the epic the production of an expansive sense of space. The epic must give us a sense that action has taken place everywhere, that somehow all the locations have been covered, strung one after another and included in the picture of the whole. Thus the action in *Strike,* for instance, maps out a remarkably differentiated territory that includes not only the factory (with its production hall, management offices, the lavatory, the yard, warehouses, the foundry, and the shipyard) but also the town (shopping streets, public transportation, the fairground, the state liquor store), the workers' quarters in the outskirts of the town (the place of nature and animal life, a would-be idyll of domesticity and the communal table), the headquarters of repressive apparatuses (military and the police), the capitalist

mansion, and that odd place that is somehow both a cemetery and a scrapyard, inhabited by the reserve army of lumpens or a zombie colony called on by power to provoke the striking workers into defeat—a space so unusual (we may say grotesque) that it is difficult to understand it in any other way than as a signifier of pure difference, an element that must be drawn into the series of places that makes up the space of the film's action if the series is to appear totalized.

85. Hegel, *Aesthetics*, 2:1048.
86. Ibid., 1040. See also Maurice Blanchot's version of the same claim in "The End of the Hero": "If there is heroism only through action, there are heroes only in and through speech. Song is the privileged abode. The hero is born when the singer comes forward in the great hall. He is told. He is not, he is merely sung" (371).
87. Mikhail Bakhtin, "Epic and Novel," in *Dialogic Imagination*, trans. Michael Holquist (Austin: University of Texas Press, 1981), 13.
88. Ibid., 14–17.
89. Ibid., 18.
90. Hegel, *Aesthetics*, 2:1069.
91. Ibid., 1070.
92. Charles Baudelaire, "On the Essence of Laughter," in *The Mirror of Art* (Garden City, N.Y.: Doubleday Anchor Books, 1956), 149–50 (translation modified).
93. Ibid., 144.
94. Wolfgang Goethe and Friedrich Schiller, "On Epic and Dramatic Poetry," http://www.schillerinstitute.org/transl/schil_epic_dram.html. The short text was, of course, the influence for Bertolt Brecht's famous distinction of his conception of epic theater from Aristotelian drama. It is also, consciously or unconsciously, echoed in Eisenstein's differentiation between "epic" and "dramatic" approaches to montage. The difference between the two revolutionary artists could perhaps be expressed in the following way: Brecht attempts to create in a "dramatic" situation the effect of "epic" distance (the estrangement effect), whereas Eisenstein seeks to produce the "dramatic" forms of action within the situation of the revolutionary "epic."

3. THE EVENT OF THE IMAGE

1. Wolfgang Eismann, "Zur Geschichte des Obraz-Begriffes in der russischen und sowjetischen Literaturwissenschaft," in Vyacheslav Ivanov, *Einfuhrung in allgemeine Probleme der Semiotik*, ed. Wolfgang Eismann (Tubingen: Gunter Narr, 1985), 3.
2. Ibid., 29.
3. Regine Robin, *Socialist Realism: An Impossible Aesthetic* (Stanford, CA: Stanford University Press, 1992), 149–54.
4. Bohn, *Film und Macht*, 312–18.
5. Sergei Eisenstein, "Béla Forgets the Scissors," in *Selected Works*, 1:80.
6. Sergei Eisenstein, "Perspectives," ibid., 154.
7. Sergei Eisenstein, *Selected Works*, vol. 2. Jacques Aumont, in his seminal study *Montage Eisenstein*, describes Eisenstein's writings between 1937 and 1940 as "one of the most powerful and concentrated stages of all of [Eisenstein's] thinking" (170). The discussion in the present chapter is indebted to Aumont's analysis of these texts. For a fuller reconstruction of Eisenstein's book on the theory of

montage, see the introduction and commentaries by Kleiman in *Montazh*, ed. Naum Kleiman (Moscow: Muzei kino, 2000).

8. The argument that toward the end of the 1920s and in the early 1930s there occurs a significant shift in Eisenstein's work, which allows us to speak of two Eisensteins, early and late, was first proposed by David Bordwell in his article "Eisenstein's Epistemological Shift," *Screen* 15, no. 4 (1974–75): 29–46. Most interpreters of Eisenstein, however, seem at this point to agree that the difference between the two Eisensteins is present throughout his works and must therefore be conceived as a tension between distinct aspects or tendencies that accompany his entire career. See, e.g., François Albera, "Eisenstein and the Theory of the Photogram," in Christie and Taylor, *Eisenstein Rediscovered*, 200–210.
9. Aumont, *Montage Eisenstein*, 176.
10. Sergei Eisenstein, "Montage 1937," in *Selected Works*, 2:11–58.
11. Aumont, *Montage Eisenstein*, 184.
12. Because the example of the barricade is the one in which the polarity between image and figurative representation is initially most strikingly explored, it in some sense grounds Eisenstein's analysis of cinematic composition or montage at all of its levels. It is therefore not a coincidence that the example of the drawing of the barricade reappears in Eisenstein's discussion of "Rhythm," where an integral composition of a scene on the barricade is discussed at all the three levels of cinematic composition: the single shot, shot sequence, and audiovisual (vertical) montage. See Sergei Eisenstein, "Rhythm," *Selected Works*, 2:241–42.
13. Eisenstein, "Montage 1937," 24.
14. Ibid., 25.
15. Ibid.
16. It is possible to think of the image in Eisenstein's conception as a kind of disaster that befalls an instance of representation. There is, for instance, no coincidence in the fact that Eisenstein found one of the most striking examples of imagicity—in this case, the imagicity of audiovisual composition—in Leonardo da Vinci's notes describing the depiction of "The Deluge." See Sergei Eisenstein, "Montage 1938," 305–9.
17. Eisenstein, "Montage 1937," 25. (Emphases of the cutting gestures in the quoted passage are Eisenstein's own.)
18. See, e.g., the role the term *dynamic* plays in "The Dramaturgy of Film Form," where Eisenstein writes, "I similarly regard the evolution of new concepts and attitudes in the conflict between normal conceptions and particular representations as a dynamic—a dynamization of the inertia of perception—a dynamization of the 'traditional view' into a new one" (162).
19. François Albera, *Eisenstein et le constructivisme russe* (Lausanne: L'Age d'Homme, 1990), 202.
20. Yuri Tynianov, "The Fundamentals of Cinema," trans. L. M. O'Toole, in *The Poetics of Cinema* (Oxford: RTP, 1992), 42–43.
21. Paul Klee, *Pedagogical Sketchbook*, trans. Sybil Moholy-Nagy (New York: Praeger, 1960), 16.
22. Ibid, 18.
23. Sergei Eisenstein, *Neravnodushnaia priroda*, 2:235–52.
24. Sergei Eisenstein, "Yermolova," in *Selected Works*, 2:97.
25. Eisenstein, "Rhythm," 227–48.

26. Aumont, *Montage Eisenstein,* 176–77.
27. Eisenstein, "Montage 1937," 25.
28. The dynamism and unmeasured rhythm of the graphic line in the second drawing of the barricade make appear what Mikhail Iampolski calls the phenomenon's "essential bone structure": "The line, for Eisenstein, has a special significance. In drawing a line, or even retracing it with our eyes, we miraculously gain access to the 'essence' of things, to their meaning. . . . Eisenstein arrives at a kind of pangraphism: the world, for all its diversity, is, under the phenomenal surface of things, governed by the semantically charged line. . . . This line or scheme Eisenstein calls the 'generalizing agent of meaning' *(obobshchaiushchii osmyslitel')."* Iampolski, *The Memory of Tiresias: Intertextuality and Film* (Berkeley: University of California Press, 1998), 226.
29. Eisenstein, "Montage 1937," 20.
30. Ibid., 26.
31. Ibid., 32–34.
32. Aumont, *Montage Eisenstein,* 177.
33. Ibid.
34. Eisenstein, "Montage 1937," 29.
35. Ibid., 32–33.
36. Ibid., 34.
37. Eisenstein, "Montage 1938," 303.
38. Guy de Maupassant, *Bel Ami,* quoted in Eisenstein, "Montage 1938," 303.
39. Ibid., 303–4.
40. Ibid., 304.
41. It does not matter for Eisenstein's example that Suzanne eventually does show up and that Duroy's plan ultimately works, setting up the final episode of this novel of success. The very fact that the fatefulness and decisiveness, the symbolic weight, that Eisenstein reads in this moment of *Bel Ami* can be so quickly dismissed by the narrative points perhaps to the larger claim of Maupassant's novel, which has to do with the collapse of the symbolic function in the social order of bourgeois capitalism of the Third Republic, of which the rapid rise of Duroy (a man with no great distinguishable abilities apart from his ambition) is itself a perfect example.
42. Walter Benjamin, *The Arcades Project,* trans. Howard Eiland and Kevin McLaughlin (Cambridge, Mass.: Belknap Press of Harvard University Press, 2002), 463 (convolute N, fragment 3,1).
43. Ibid.
44. Ibid., 462 (N2a,3).
45. Ibid., 462 (N3,1).
46. Ibid.
47. Ibid.
48. Georges Didi-Huberman, *Remontages du temps subi: l'oeil de l'histoire,* vol. 2 (Paris: Les editions de minuit, 2010), 16.
49. Sigmund Freud, "The Unconscious," *Standard Edition* 14 (1953): 187.
50. Georges Didi-Huberman, *L'image survivante: histoire de l'art et temps des fantomes selon Aby Warburg* (Paris: Les editions de minuit, 2002), 320.
51. Walter Benjamin, *Arcades Project,* 464 (N4,1).
52. Didi-Huberman, *L'image survivante,* 297.
53. Ibid.

54. On imprint, displacement, and reversal (antithesis), concepts Didi-Huberman draws from Charles Darwin's *The Expression of Emotion in Man and Animals* (1872), see *L'image survivante*, 231–46 and 295–98. A small portion of Didi-Huberman's book has been translated as Georges Didi-Huberman, "*Dialektik des Monstrums*: Aby Warburg and the Symptom Paradigm," *Art History* 24, no. 5 (2001): 621–45.
55. Didi-Huberman, *L'image survivante*, 296 ("*Dialektik des Monstrums*," 636).
56. Ibid., 304–5 ("*Dialektik des Monstrums*," 640).
57. Ibid., 305.
58. Ibid., 112.
59. Slavoj Žižek, "Hitchcockian *Sinthoms*," in *Everything You Always Wanted to Know about Lacan (but Were Afraid to Ask Hitchcock)*, ed. Slavoj Žižek (London: Verso, 1992), 126.
60. Jacques Lacan, *Le Séminaire XXIII: Le sinthome* (1975–76), text established by Jacques-Alain Miller, *Ornicar?*, published in issues 6–11 (1976–77).
61. Slavoj Žižek, *The Sublime Object of Ideology* (London: Verso, 1989), 75.
62. Benjamin, *Arcades Project*, 476 (N11,1).
63. Ibid., 464 (N4,1).
64. Roland Barthes, "Diderot, Brecht, Eisenstein," in *Image-Music-Text* (New York: Hill and Wang, 1977), 70–71.
65. Sergei Eisenstein, "Peripetii *pars pro toto*" [Peripeties of *pars pro toto*], in *Metod*, 2:99.
66. Žižek, *Sublime Object of Ideology*, 75.
67. On the difference between believing and identifying with the symptom, see Paul Verhaeghe and Frédéric Declercq, "Lacan's Analytic Goal: *Le sinthome* or the Feminine Way," in *Re-inventing the Symptom: Essays on the Final Lacan*, ed. Luke Thurston (New York: Other Press, 2002), 66–69.

4. MONTAGE OF FORMS

1. Sergei Eisenstein, *Izbrannye proizvedeniya v shesti tomakh*, vol. 1 (Moscow: Izdatel'stvo Isskustvo, 1964), 103.
2. See Jacques Aumont, *Montage* (Montreal: Caboose, 2013), 5–6.
3. In a diary entry from December 6, 1943, Eisenstein outlines the ex-centricity of his method in relation to the object of aesthetic inquiry in the following way: "If this [*Method*] is to be 'an aesthetics,' then it will be most dramatically opposed to the very concept of aesthetics. It will be a teaching of aesthetics *outside* of the concept of the *beautiful*. Not 'without,' not 'against,' but—*outside*. F. Th. Fischer calls his work: *Ästhetik oder Wissenschaft des Schönen* and in 'Einleitung, paragraph 1' writes: 'Die Ästhetik ist die Wissenschaft des Schönen . . .' Here, precisely *outside* of this, is where my *future work* must take place. And not in the form of a system, but as METHOD!" The entry is quoted by Naum Kleiman in "Problema Eizenshteina" [Eisenstein's problem], in Eisenstein, *Metod*, 1:5.
4. Aumont, *Montage Eisenstein*, viii.
5. Ibid., viii–ix.
6. Ibid., ix.
7. Ibid., 146.
8. A strikingly different position from the one offered by Aumont can be found in the characterization of Eisenstein's dialectical conception of montage in Gilles

Deleuze's *Cinema* books. Deleuze shares with Aumont the belief in Eisenstein's great philosophical value. Yet, if Aumont denies montage the status of a genuine concept, in *Cinema 1* Deleuze affirms the unity and the coherence of Eisenstein's concept of montage, which he describes with the term "organic–pathetic set": "Eisenstein substitutes a montage of opposition for Griffith's parallel montage, and a montage of qualitative leaps ('jumping montage') for convergent and concurrent montage. All kinds of new aspects of montage are brought together at this point. . . . We believe in the coherence of this organic–pathetic set" (37). We will return to "Deleuze's Eisenstein" in a more extensive fashion later.

9. Aumont, *Montage,* 16.
10. Theodor Adorno, *Aesthetic Theory* (Minneapolis: University of Minnesota Press, 1997), 152.
11. Ibid., 155.
12. Ibid., 156.
13. See Sergei Eisenstein, *Selected Works,* vol. 1.
14. Sergei Eisenstein, "Our *October,*" in *Selected Works,* 1:105.
15. Marie-Claire Ropars, "The Function of Metaphor in Eisenstein's *October,*" *Film Criticism* 2–3 (Winter–Spring 1978): 29–30.
16. Eisenstein, "Our *October,*" 104.
17. Ibid.
18. Ropars, "Function of Metaphor," 15.
19. Ibid., 16.
20. Ibid., 27.
21. Ibid., 17.
22. Ibid., 27.
23. For an example of the empiricist–associationist model in Eisenstein's thinking, see his discussion of the sequence of gods in relation to Ernst Kretschmer's *Medizinische Psychologie* (1922) in the chapter "'Dvizhenie' Myshelniia" [Movement of thought] in *Metod,* 1:82–85.
24. Ropars, "Function of Metaphor," 17.
25. Ibid.
26. Eisenstein, "'Dvizhenie' Myshelniia," 82.
27. Ropars, "Function of Metaphor," 25.
28. G. W. F. Hegel, *Science of Logic,* trans. A. V. Miller (New York: Humanity Books, 1969), 642.
29. Sigmund Freud, *Jokes and Their Relation to the Unconscious,* trans. and ed. James Stratchey (New York: W. W. Norton, 1960), 160.
30. Hegel, *Science of Logic,* 642.
31. Slavoj Žižek, *The Sublime Object of Ideology* (London: Verso, 1989), 207.
32. See also Mladen Dolar, "The Phrenology of Spirit," in *Supposing the Subject,* ed. Joan Copjec, 75–96 (London: Verso, 1994).
33. Sergei Eisenstein, *Nonindifferent Nature,* trans. Herbert Marshall (Cambridge: Cambridge University Press, 1987), 16.
34. Ibid., 18.
35. Ibid., 15.
36. Deleuze, *Cinema 1,* 33.
37. Ibid., 34.
38. Ibid.

39. Ibid.
40. Ibid., 35.
41. Ibid., 33.
42. Eisenstein, *Nonindifferent Nature,* 52.
43. Ibid., 53–57.
44. Deleuze, *Cinema 1,* 34.
45. Deleuze, *Cinema 2,* 157.
46. Deleuze, *Cinema 1,* 51.
47. Unlike German expressionist cinema, which delinks the sublime, spiritual construction of montage from organic nature, Eisenstein's dialectical–organic conception of montage appears in Deleuze's account as fundamentally tied to the vision of romanticism: "We can note, here, the considerable difference between Expressionism and Romanticism. For it is no longer the case, as in romanticism, of a reconciliation between Nature and Spirit, of Spirit as it is alienated in Nature, and of Spirit as it reconquers itself in itself. This conception was implied as the dialectical development of a totality which was still organic. Whilst Expressionism only conceives in principle the whole of a spiritual Universe engendering its own abstract forms, its creatures of light, its continuities which seem false to the eye of the sensible." Ibid., 54.
48. Eisenstein, *Nonindifferent Nature,* 16.
49. Ibid.
50. Ibid., 27.
51. Ibid., 179.
52. Ibid., 184.
53. Edouard Osmont, "Nothing to What I Once Saw!," illustrated by W. Heath Robinson, *Strand* 52 (July–December 1916): 466–69. In *Nonindifferent Nature,* Eisenstein wrongly lists the year 1914 as the date of the magazine issue.
54. A "Heath Robinson" or a "Heath Robinson contraption" is the British equivalent of a "Rube Goldberg machine."
55. Osmont, "Nothing to What I Once Saw!," 468–69.
56. Eisenstein, *Nonindifferent Nature,* 184.
57. Ibid., 185.
58. Ibid.
59. Ibid., 195.
60. Ibid., 196.
61. Sergei Eisenstein, "Komicheskoe" [The comic], in *Metod,* 1:424.
62. Ibid.
63. Ibid., 425.
64. Ibid., 426.
65. Sergei Eisenstein, "Zametki k *Grundproblem.* Komicheskoe" [Notes on the *Grundproblem*: The comic], in *Metod,* 2:390.
66. Ernst Bloch, *Heritage of Our Times,* trans. Neville and Stephen Plaice (Cambridge: Polity Press, 1991).
67. Ibid., 251.
68. Eisenstein, *Nonindifferent Nature,* 196.
69. Ibid., 196–98.
70. Ibid., 186.
71. Ibid.

72. Ibid., 187.
73. Ibid.
74. Ibid., 186.
75. Ibid.
76. See Gilles Deleuze, *Difference and Repetition* (New York: Columbia University Press, 1994).

CONCLUSION

1. Tom Gunning, "Moving Away from the Index: Cinema and the Impression of Reality," *differences* 18, no. 1 (2007): 29–52.
2. Deleuze, *Cinema 2*, 23.
3. See, e.g., Patricia Pisters, *The Neuro-Image: A Deleuzian Film Philosophy of Digital Screen Culture* (Stanford, Calif.: Stanford University Press, 2012).
4. Fredric Jameson, "Cognitive Mapping," in *Marxism and the Interpretation of Culture*, ed. Cary Nelson and Lawrence Grossberg, 347–60 (Urbana: University of Illinois Press, 1990). See also Fredric Jameson, *Postmodernism, or, the Cultural Logic of Late Capitalism* (Durham, N.C.: Duke University Press, 1991). For the application of the concept of cognitive mapping to cinema, see Fredric Jameson, *The Geopolitical Aesthetic* (London: British Film Institute, 1992), particularly the first, longer chapter on the 1970s genre of conspiracy thrillers ("Totality as Conspiracy"). For a more recent work that takes up the task of elaborating Jameson's idea of an aesthetics of cognitive mapping, see Alberto Toscano and Jeff Kinkle's book *Cartographies of the Absolute* (Washington, D.C.: Zero Books, 2015).
5. For the most extensive theoretical development of this position, see David Rodowick, *The Virtual Life of Film* (Cambridge, Mass.: Harvard University Press, 2007).
6. For a summary of this position and some useful reflections on the question of duration and the digital image, see André Gaudreault and Philippe Marion, *The End of Cinema? A Medium in Crisis in the Digital Age*, trans. Timothy Barnard (New York: Columbia University Press, 2015), 75–83.
7. Jacques Rancière, *The Future of the Image*, trans. Gregory Elliott (London: Verso, 2007), 1.
8. Ibid., 3.
9. Theodor Adorno, *Hegel: Three Studies*, trans. Shierry Weber Nicholsen (Cambridge, Mass.: MIT Press, 1993), 1.
10. Deleuze, *Cinema 2*, 210.
11. Rodowick, *Virtual Life of Film*, 91–93.
12. Ibid., 93.
13. Ibid., 143.
14. Gene Youngblood, *Expanded Cinema* (New York: Dutton, 1970).
15. Elena Biserna, Philippe Dubois, and Frédéric Monvoisin, eds., *Extended Cinema: Le cinema gagne du terrain* (Udine, Italy: Campanotto, 2010).
16. Francesco Casetti, *The Lumière Galaxy: Seven Key Words for the Cinema to Come* (New York: Columbia University Press, 2015).
17. Jonathan Beller, *The Cinematic Mode of Production: Attention Economy and the Society of the Spectacle* (Hanover: Dartmouth College Press, 2006).
18. Gabriele Pedulla, *In Broad Daylight: Movies and Spectators after the Cinema* (London: Verso, 2012), 2.

19. "Rather than saying that he put the young art of cinema at the service of communism, it would be more accurate to say that he put communism through the test of cinema, through the test of the idea of art and modernity that Eisenstein saw incarnated in cinema." Jacques Rancière, "Eisenstein's Madness," in *Film Fables* (Oxford: Berg, 2006), 31.
20. Antoine de Baecque, *Camera Historica* (New York: Columbia University Press, 2012), 21.
21. Ibid., 321.
22. Sergei Eisenstein, "Perspectives," in *Selected Works,* 1:155.
23. Sergei Eisenstein, "Magiia iskusstva" [The magic of art], in *Metod,* 1:47.
24. Eisenstein, "Montage of Attractions," 35.
25. Eisenstein, "Perspectives," 154.
26. Sergei Eisenstein, "The Principles of the New Russian Cinema," in *Selected Works,* 1:202. The text of a lecture held at the Sorbonne in February 1930.
27. Sergei Eisenstein, "The Problem of the Materialist Approach to Form," in *Selected Works,* 1:59–64.
28. Sergei Eisenstein, "Dramaturgy of Film Form," in *Selected Works,* 1:163.
29. Sergei Eisenstein, Vsevolod Pudovkin, and Grigori Alexandrov, "Statement on Sound," in *Selected Works,* 1:114.
30. Sergei Eisenstein, "Help Yourself," in *Selected Works,* 1:219–237.
31. Eisenstein, "Principles."
32. Sergei Eisenstein, "Speeches to the All-Union Creative Conference of Soviet Filmworkers," in *Selected Works,* 3:16–46.
33. Sergei Eisenstein, "The Mistakes of *Bezhin Meadow,*" in *Selected Works,* 3:100.
34. Naum Kleiman, "Pafos Eizenshteina" [Eisenstein's pathos], in Sergei Eizenshtein, *Neravnodushnaia priroda,* vol. 1, *Chuvstvo kino,* ed. Naum Kleiman (Moscow: Muzei kino & Eizenshtein-tsentr, 2004), 18. See also Lea Jacobs, "Composing for the Films," in *Reading with Eisenstein,* ed. Ada Ackerman and Luka Arsenjuk (Montreal: Caboose, forthcoming).
35. Louis Althusser, "On Marx and Freud," *Rethinking Marxism* 4, no. 1 (1991): 17–30.
36. De Baecque, *Camera Historica,* 7.
37. Althusser, "On Marx and Freud," 19.
38. Joan Copjec et al., "The First Rule of Polemos," *Umbr(a),* 2001, 5.

INDEX

Luka Arsenjuk is associate professor of film studies and core faculty member in comparative literature at the University of Maryland, College Park.